Criminal
Justice
Research
Methods

Theory and Practice

Second Edition

Criminal Justice Research Methods

Theory and Practice

Second Edition

Gerald J. Bayens
Cliff Roberson

CRC Press
Taylor & Francis Group
Boca Raton London New York

CRC Press is an imprint of the
Taylor & Francis Group, an **informa** business

CRC Press
Taylor & Francis Group
6000 Broken Sound Parkway NW, Suite 300
Boca Raton, FL 33487-2742

© 2011 by Taylor and Francis Group, LLC
CRC Press is an imprint of Taylor & Francis Group, an Informa business

No claim to original U.S. Government works

Printed in the United States of America on acid-free paper
10 9 8 7 6 5 4 3 2 1

International Standard Book Number: 978-1-4398-3696-5 (Paperback)

Library of Congress Cataloging-in-Publication Data

Bayens, Gerald J.
    Criminal justice research methods : theory and practice / Gerald J. Bayens, Cliff Roberson. -- 2nd ed.
       p. cm.
    Includes bibliographical references and index.
    ISBN 978-1-4398-3696-5 (pbk. : alk. paper)
    1. Criminal justice, Administration of--Research--Methodology. I. Roberson, Cliff, 1937- II. Title.

HV7419.5.B39 2011
364.072--dc22   2010037027

Visit the Taylor & Francis Web site at
http://www.taylorandfrancis.com

and the CRC Press Web site at
http://www.crcpress.com

contents

preface

Before writing the first edition of this text, we identified several key issues that greatly influenced what materials would be covered on the subject of research. First, we noted that most college students who are studying research for the first time do so during a single semester and usually while taking several other academic courses. In the second edition, we have updated the examples, reworked the exercises, added additional discussion points, and updated the research-in-action sections.

Trying to learn a vast amount of information about the subject of research in a 14- to 16-week time frame can be problematic, if not impossible. This is especially true if a very complex and technical textbook is adopted for the course. Second, experience in the classroom tells us that some students are intimidated by research textbooks. Complicated research terminology, mathematical formulas, and the lack of practical examples can cause the best of students to become perplexed and dread the study of research. Third, there are all types of research documents available to students in the 21st century. Thousands of research books, periodicals, and electronic print documents covering specific types of research, research designs, methodologies, analyses, and other subjects are currently available to enable students to become more educated in certain aspects or areas of research. Finally, and probably most important, we firmly believe that the art of learning research occurs in only one place— the field. It is not until the student actually conducts research under the watchful eyes and direction of a veteran researcher that real research knowledge is set in place.

Having considered each of these matters, we ambitiously have written an introduction to this criminal justice research textbook that is, foremost, easy to understand. In this book, you will not find undue complicated research language, and the complexities often associated with research have been kept to a minimum. Also, we adopted a straightforward approach and cover a sufficient amount of material to allow first-time research students to get "comfortable" with the study of research. Moreover, parameters were established with regard to the length of the textbook, so that the subject matter can easily be covered within a single academic semester.

This text provides a clear approach to the study of research, enabling students who are experiencing their initial exposure to this subject to be fundamentally prepared to go out into the real world and become proficient researchers in criminal justice and criminology.

Gerald J. Bayens
Cliff Roberson

the authors

Gerald J. Bayens, PhD, is a professor and chair of the Criminal Justice and Legal Studies Department at Washburn University. He also provides direct services and technical assistance to criminal justice agencies, focusing on strategic planning and policy development.

Dr. Bayens teaches courses in law enforcement and correctional management, criminal justice policy, and research methods. He earned an interdisciplinary doctorate in criminal justice, political science, and research methods from the Union Institute and University, a master's in criminal justice from the University of Alabama, and a BA in criminal justice from Washburn University.

Dr. Bayens worked in the criminal justice field for 22 years. He is a former special agent of the Kansas Bureau of Investigations, director of Juvenile Corrections, and director of Intensive Supervised Probation. He served as a military policeman in the U.S. Marine Corps from 1974 through 1978.

He is the author of more than 20 research articles and government technical reports, including "Defining Law Enforcement's Role in Protecting American Agriculture from Agroterrorism," "Campus Crime Data: The Need to Collect Simple Assault Statistics," "The Impact of the New Penology on ISP," and, most recently, "Best Practices in the Prevention of Agroterrorism: A Descriptive Study of the Readiness of Nine Beef-Producing States." He has delivered more than 50 lectures, conference papers, and presentations in the United States and abroad. He is also a co-author of *Criminal Justice Research Methods: Theory and Practice* (2000, Wadsworth Publishing, Belmont, California) and *Community-Based Corrections* (forthcoming 2011, McGraw-Hill Publishing, New York).

Dr. Bayens is a member of the Academy of Criminal Justice Sciences and serves on the Academic Review and Certification Committee. He is the recipient of the 1993 Washburn Fellow Award. In 1992 and 1993, he served as president and past-president of the Kansas Correctional Association.

Cliff Roberson, LLM, PhD, is the editor-in-chief of the *Professional Issues in Criminal Justice Journal* and is academic chair for the Master of Science in Criminal Justice Program of Kaplan University. He is also an emeritus professor of criminal justice at Washburn University, Topeka, Kansas.

In 2009, a research study conducted by a group of professors from Sam Houston State University determined that Cliff Roberson was the leading criminal justice author in the United States based on his publications and their relevance to the profession (see *Southwest Journal of Criminal Justice*, Vol. 6, Issue 1, 2009). He has authored or co-authored over 50 books and texts on legal subjects. His books include *Procedures in the Justice System*, 9th ed. (with Harvey Wallace and Gilbert Stuckey), Pearson, Upper Saddle River, New Jersey, 2009; *Constitutional Law and Criminal Justice*, Taylor & Francis, Boca Raton, Florida, 2009; *Principles of Criminal Law*, 4th ed. (with Harvey Wallace), Allyn & Bacon, Boston, 2008; *Police Field Operations: Theory Meets Practice* (with Michael Birzer), Pearson, 2008; *An Introduction to Comparative Legal Models of Criminal Justice* (with Dilip Das), Taylor & Francis, 2008; *Ethics and Criminal Justice* (with Scott Mire), Taylor & Francis, 2010; and *Family Violence* (with Harvey Wallace), Pearson, 2010.

Dr. Roberson also served as associate vice president for academic affairs at Arkansas Tech University; dean of arts and sciences, University of Houston, Victoria; director of programs, National College of District Attorneys; professor of criminology and director of Justice Center, California State University, Fresno; and assistant professor of criminal justice, St. Edwards University. Dr. Roberson's nonacademic experience includes U.S. Marine Corps service as an infantry officer, trial and defense counsel and marine judge advocate, and director of the Military Law Branch, U.S. Marine Corps. Other legal employment experiences include assignment as trial supervisor, Office of State Counsel for Offenders, Texas Board of Criminal Justice and judge pro tem in the California courts. Dr. Roberson is admitted to practice before the U.S. Supreme Court, U.S. Court of Military Appeals, U.S. Tax Court, federal courts in California and Texas, and the Supreme Courts of Texas and California.

He earned a PhD in human behavior from U.S. International University, an LLM in criminal law, criminology, and psychiatry from George Washington University, a JD from American University, a BA in political science from University of Missouri, and pursued a year of postgraduate study at the University of Virginia School of Law.

introduction to research

nature of criminal justice research

The subject of research can be anxiety-provoking for many criminal justice students. One reason for this distress is the belief that research is synonymous with statistics, which in turn equates to mathematics. After a hearty dose of curriculum that is typically immersed in the social sciences, it is understandable that many students are intimidated by a course that is more closely aligned with pure science and requires analytical skills. Another reason that students shy away from the study of research is the misconception that research is solely an academic enterprise that will likely never be required of the practitioner.

There are various conceptions of what constitutes research. If you ask three research workers from different academic fields what the process of research involves, you may receive three different responses. However, a principal component is likely to be that research implies finding solutions to problems. This comprehension of research is particularly important to criminal justice practitioners who actively work in the field. Both law enforcement and corrections personnel are often quick to explain that much of what they do is research. For example, police detectives are often dispatched to crime scenes because they possess the knowledge of investigative techniques necessary to solve crimes. A typical investigation might include personal observation and recording of the events, interviewing witnesses and suspects, searching computer files for occurrences of similar crimes, and other exploratory tasks. Likewise, correctional personnel working in institutions are routinely required to observe prisoner behavior, document the effects of treatment programs, solve problems relating to prisoner supervision, and perform other related duties.

Criminal justice professionals know the tribulations of on-the-job problem solving by means of trial and error. With patience and enough guesses, this process will often lead to successful results. However, this form of experimentation lacks uniformity in its procedure, can be very time consuming, and usually limits what knowledge is gained by the individual who is trying to resolve the problem. As a matter of normal practice, this subjective approach of inquiry may prove useful as a means of piecing together loosely related bits of information but lacks the important disciplines that define credible research.

However, if a problem-solving process such as trial and error is not all there is to research, what is? This chapter addresses this question by discussing several preliminary matters relating to scientific inquiry. Our aim is to help students establish a framework for thinking about and understanding the nature of research. We start with a definition of research and continue with a discussion of the research process. Next, we consider the purpose of research by comparing pure and applied research, leading us into an analysis of the scientific method. Finally, we conclude the chapter by examining theories, hypotheses, and variables.

what is research?

Several definitions have been given for the term. **Research** is typically defined as:

- A systematic investigation of phenomena, behaviors, or processes that relies on empirical data and logical study and analysis[1]
- A systematic and planned study of a phenomenon using explicit, carefully documented procedures and processes subject to review by one's research peers[2]
- A systematic, controlled, empirical, and critical investigation of natural phenomena guided by theory and hypotheses about the presumed relations among such phenomena[3]

For the purposes of our discussion, we define *research* as a systematic method of inquiry into a phenomenon. While we attempt to keep this definition simple, several descriptive characteristics and concepts involved in research require elaboration. First, research is systematic. This means that the researcher deliberately conforms to a planned sequence of steps in order to study a **phenomenon**. Every natural event (phenomenon) is assumed to have a cause that is preceded by a number of conditions that are responsible for it. Consequently, if these causal factors can be distinguished and reinstituted, the event may be duplicated. This assumption in scientific research—known as **determinism**—presumes that a certain level of predictability can be achieved regarding the occurrences of natural events.

Another concept important to research is that it is always subject to analytical review by others. Peer review is essentially a system of checks and balances to ensure the integrity of research methodology as well as the purported significance of research findings.

research processes

Five basic stages of research are typical for any research study:

- Conceptualizing a research question or problem
- Designing the study
- Collecting the data
- Analyzing and interpreting the results of the data
- Publishing findings

Within each stage a number of activities take place. During the conceptualization stage, the basic task is to generate an idea for a research study. At this initial stage, the originality of the research should be considered. Is the idea original or do previous studies exist? In many cases, this question can be answered by reviewing the literature, which in turn helps refine an idea into a research problem. Likewise, researchers often obtain original ideas for investigation by reading journal articles, theses, and dissertations written by other researchers. Becoming totally familiar with a subject by means of a thorough review of the literature is a superb way of noting gaps that exist in the information presented about the topic.

For example, studies assessing the need for prison programs may not focus on juvenile prisoners who are incarcerated as a result of judicial waivers. If a researcher has an interest in judicial waivers or the treatment of juveniles in adult institutions, a project could be developed to address this gap in the literature. Often such gaps are explicitly mentioned in the discussion sections of prior studies. Implications for future research are integral parts of many published journal articles, theses, and dissertations. In most cases, these implications are easily identified; authors commonly state that "additional study is needed..." or "future research should address..." or "further inquiry...." Occasionally, an article is written about the need for research on a particular subject. Consider the following excerpt from an article written by Linda Zupan and titled "The Need for Research on Direct Inmate supervision." Note that the author suggests that several study gaps exist regarding direct supervision jails. She further explains that more scientific research is needed to substantiate the claims about direct supervision.

> Despite the enthusiasm among practitioners, the academic community has been almost apathetic toward direct supervision. Only a meager amount of research has been conducted on the innovation as indicated by the quantity of scholarly research articles and books. Research articles appearing in the academic journals number fewer than 10 and only one book has been published on direct supervision. This lack of scholarly research appears incredibly neglectful, particularly considering that direct supervision is no longer a recent phenomenon or merely a passing fad.
>
> ...The effectiveness of direct supervision has yet to be either proved or disproved. Consequently, the claims are still merely suppositions and hypotheses. To test the validity of these claims requires a thorough, rigorous, and scientific investigation. Such an investigation must address the claims that direct supervision jails are more cost-effective than traditional jails ... research must also assess the quality of employees' work life ... [and] the study must address organizational efficiency and effectiveness. In sum, there remain a vast number of questions concerning the effectiveness of direct supervision that have not yet been subjected to the rigor of scientific inquiry.[4]

Ideas for research come from other sources as well. A criminal justice student working in a police or corrections agency may determine the need for a research project simply by considering existing problems in the agency that require immediate attention. A project may be generated from a researcher's knowledge of the workplace and familiarity with its day-to-day problems. During the process of conceptualizing a research idea, one of the most important factors to consider in selecting a topic is to determine the purpose of the research. In the next section, we identify two different purposes that help define the focus of the research effort.

pure versus applied research

Understanding the difference between pure and applied research is not an easy task. It has been suggested that **pure research** is firmly designed and oriented to answering intellectual questions and **applied research** is often considered to be non-scholarly. In summary, the aim of pure research is to get to the "big picture" while applied science is a more "hands-on" activity. In terms of purposes then, research varies along a continuum that ranges from theory to practice. The different purposes affect other considerations as well: the original research concept, the formulation of research questions, the research design approach, data collection strategies, the type of data analysis, the implications of the findings, and the nature of the research publication.

The basic tenet of pure research is knowledge for the sake of knowledge. Researchers engage in pure research because they are attracted to investigating phenomena to understand why events occur as they do and are essentially interested in understanding and explaining the world's realities. For example, a penologist studying reformation may determine that the process of prisonization inhibits prisoners from ever benefiting from treatment programs while they are imprisoned. The results of such a study may provide knowledge in relation to existing theories of rehabilitation and also help estimate the success of future attempts at treatment programs in other correctional environments such as jails, work-release centers, and boot camps.

Criminal justice researchers endeavor to contribute to the knowledge bases established in the disciplines of criminology and criminal justice. They attempt to augment answers to fundamental questions pertaining to crime causation, criminal behavior, and other phenomena related to the fields. The most distinguishing contribution usually occurs when a researcher develops a theory that explains a phenomenon under investigation. Therefore, an objective of pure criminal justice research is to generate new theories or test existing ones. The knowledge of a discipline is best acquired by understanding its theories.

The findings of pure research are published in scholarly journals. The criminal justice discipline has its own standards for deciding what constitutes valid research. Some publications require a central focus for research. For example, the *Journal of Research in Crime and Delinquency*, published in cooperation with the National Council on Crime and Delinquency, is devoted to reports of original research in crime and delinquency, new theories, and the critical analysis of theories and concepts especially pertinent to research development in this field. *Crime, Law and Social Change* is a journal that seeks essays and reviews dealing with the political economy of organized crime at the international, national, regional, and local levels. On the other hand, *Justice Quarterly*, a publication of the Academy of Criminal Justice Sciences (ACJS), is more broad-based and serves as a clearinghouse for all criminal justice research. According to its statement of purpose included in each publication:

> The purposes of the Academy of Criminal Justice Sciences are to foster excellence in education and research in the field of criminal justice in institutions of higher education; to encourage understanding and cooperation among those engaged in teaching and research in criminal justice; and to build cooperation between criminal justice programs in higher education and operational criminal justice agencies and related fields. Moreover, it is the academy's intent to provide a forum for the exchange of information among persons involved in education and research in the criminal justice field; to serve as a clearinghouse for the collection and dissemination of information related to or produced by criminal justice educational or research programs; and to foster the highest ethical and personal standards in criminal justice educational programs as well as in operational agencies and allied fields.[5]

Applied research is concerned with problems affecting people in the here and now. Sometimes referred to as "practical" research, its purpose is to identify the rationales for and underlying root causes of problems. Applied research is most powerful when it contributes knowledge that is useful in generating solutions to human and societal problems. Practitioners looking for immediate answers to real-life problems often favor applied research. A fundamental premise of applied research is to recognize the results of pure research and apply them to real-life problems. Therefore, the intent of applied research is to identify knowledge gained from pure research and use it to construct and apply solutions to practical problems.

Applied research is closely aligned with program evaluation and policy analysis. The usual focus of this type of inquiry is to create an information base of known facts that have direct relevance to an organization's operations. That knowledge is then used in the decision-making process to choose a course of action in an attempt to remedy a problem situation. A major difference between applied and pure research is that applied researchers attempt to understand how best to confront a problem that requires an immediate response while pure researchers attempt to understand and explain the basic nature of a phenomenon.

The findings of applied research are published in journals that specialize in that area within the traditions of a problem area or particular discipline. For example, *Federal Probation* is a journal of correctional philosophy and practice published by the Administrative Office of the United States Courts in Washington, DC. According to its statement of purpose:

> *Federal Probation* is dedicated to informing its readers about current thought, research, and practice in corrections and criminal justice. The journal welcomes the contributions of persons who work with or study juvenile and adult offenders and invites authors to submit articles describing experience or significant findings regarding the prevention and control of delinquency and crime.[6]

Pure Research	Applied Research
• Academic search for knowledge • Presupposition that world realities are determined • Contribution to theory	• Seeks to understand human and social problems • Tries to solve problems • Assumes societal problems can be solved with right knowledge

Although the academic interests of applied research may tend to be secondary to its quest for practical application, many criminal justice scholars argue that a major objective of criminal justice research should be to make its results more applied and practice-relevant. Joan Petersilia argues that criminologists and criminal justice researchers have a duty to use scientific knowledge to inform and influence public policy and practice. She believes that research is a critical source of information to:

- Generate new ideas and stimulate new thinking about policy issues
- Identify and draw attention to future policy problems and issues
- Provide a basis for selecting policy options from an array of possible choices
- Provide analytic support for implementing policy choices
- Defend or promote policy recommendations adopted for political, bureaucratic, or other reasons[7]

A criticism of criminological research is that many of the empirical studies in the discipline are deficient in scientific rigor. If a research study fails to meet the standards of scientific inquiry, it may be flawed and of little use to policy decision makers. Because this is a potential pitfall in research, it is important that we briefly explore what constitutes meaningful scientific inquiry.

scientific inquiry

Researchers use a standard approach to scientific inquiry that is most often referred to as the scientific method. The **scientific method** serves as a tool for developing scientific knowledge and skills. The general structure of the method—viewed as necessary for any scientific study or experiment—involves the following elements:

- Gathering a set of observations or measurements from natural phenomena or experiments
- Formulating a hypothesis to explain the observations or data
- Making some prediction, then conceiving and executing an experiment to test the hypothesis
- Analyzing test results and stating conclusions
- Generalizing the hypothesis into a theory if experimental results confirm the hypothesis

Note that two terms consistently appear within the general structure of the scientific method: theory and hypothesis. In common usage, a **theory** is merely a vague set of facts. However, to a scientific researcher, a theory is a conceptual framework that explains existing facts and predicts new ones. For example, we can observe a ball tossed into the air fall to the ground. Theorizing that any object tossed into the air will drop to the ground seems plausible because it happens so often that we accept it as true. The scientific researcher though, understands that this fact is best explained by Isaac Newton's theory of gravitation. Knowing this theory helps explain other facts such as the motion of the entire solar system. It also allows for accurate predictions about what will happen tomorrow. And finally, it inspires future experimentation, thus paving the way for new knowledge about the world around us. Consider how common it is to launch today's satellites into space. Likewise, think about the stunning achievements of our space probes that have landed on Mars and flown past Uranus and Neptune. Both of these aerospace conquests owe their success to Newton's insight, which was originally postulated in the late 1600s.

assessing goodness of theory

Under the canons of scientific inquiry, it is important that theory be explicitly stated. Theories accomplish this principle by containing statements that establish a relationship between two or more phenomena. In addition, certain other tests are generally recognized and articulated as elements of "good theory" that, by definition, allows for a plausible explanation of why events occur.

Empiricism

The first element, **empiricism**, requires that the events under study be observed directly. *Observe* is a very appropriate term in science, where attention to the various aspects and features of an event is required. Although *observation* usually refers to a visual (or at least partly visual) event, empiricism requires understanding the world through the use of all senses. Knowledge streams into us through hearing, sight, smell, taste, and touch, and to avoid introducing error we remain passively observant and receptive to the experience.[8]

The element of empiricism in theory also means that scientists self-impose limits to problems and issues that can be resolved by making observations of some kind. Theory then must be testable and therefore have the ability to identify the observable events it predicts and the observable conditions under which it applies.

Objectivity

The notion of **objectivity** is a powerful element in scientific research. When research is conducted, standardized procedures should be identified and followed to ensure that each step of the scientific method is free from emotion, conjecture, or personal bias on the part of the scientist testing the theory. Objectivity in scientific research requires a researcher to explicitly describe a research problem, outline the methods of observation, disclose the reasoning behind the type of data analysis, and communicate the findings. The research should then be so objective that arbitrary acceptance of the findings is not based upon a researcher's reputation.

Skepticism and Replication

The value of theory is that it inspires further observations. As skeptics, researchers should raise questions about every aspect of a research project. Generally, this attitude toward research leads to replication—a way of assuring the reliability of results. This process of re-examination is intrinsic to verifying a set of findings. The observations will be known to occur because they will have been identified under comparable, if not identical, conditions by independent observers. **Skepticism** and **replication** then are identified as distinguishing elements of assessing good theory because of their abilities to legitimize.

Falsifiability

Similarly, the criterion of falsifiability serves as an important element in the verification of theory. Any assertion qualifying as a scientific assertion must, at least in principle, be able to specify the conditions under which it may be falsified.[9] Falsifying a theory means asking, "What observations would disprove the theory?" Or put another way, "What could we observe that would reveal a particular theory to be incorrect?"

Dynamic Nature of Theory

The **dynamic nature of theory** means it does not have to make precisely accurate predictions to be judged as scientifically useful. Rather, whenever an idea emerges, it is still a scientific theory, provided that it predicts results that may conceivably confirm or disprove it. Theory is never totally complete, nor is it stagnant. Rather, theories are working models of reality that continue to grow as a result of additions made by continued research.

Ethics

In order for criminal justice researchers to convince others that the discipline is worthy of independence and prestige, it is essential that they subscribe to a code of ethics. Considering that the scientific research process begins with formulating a theory from a set of concepts, it makes sense that ethical demands should be imposed at this initial stage. Consequently, an individual researcher testing a theory must be aware of potential conflicts that may occur, such as when research involves involuntary participation, intentional deception, or invasion of privacy. Also, where physical, social, or psychological danger to subjects is a clear possibility, a researcher must take special care to inform the subjects of the risks involved before beginning the research.

The element of ethics is extremely important, not only when assessing goodness of theory, but also in every aspect of scientific research. Consequently, we dedicate an entire chapter of this textbook to the subject of ethics in criminal justice research.

constructing scientific theories

Theories are constructed to provide a general framework for investigating the nature of all relationships. Moreover, theories are formulated to help a researcher understand cause-and-effect relationships. Science systemically constructs theories and conceptual schemes, uses them, and submits them to repeated tests. Theories are constructed from ideas. Sometimes these ideas are based on presumption or speculation. A researcher who operates in this fashion generally applies theory loosely and not systemically. What does it mean when we say that someone has a theory? Let us consider what happens when someone (e.g., Scarlett) constructs theory T.

Scarlett believes that T is true or that it is plausible to think it is true because it just makes sense. She is able to argue that certain realities exist that seemingly support her theory, but in actuality Scarlett does not know that T is true. We agree with her claim that she has a theory because we understand that Scarlett at present does not possess the knowledge to demonstrate the truth of the theory. If Scarlett later comes to know that T is in fact true, then it is no longer appropriate to say that she has a theory, T.

The simple point is that theory construction sometimes begins as a search for unknown facts. In our example, Scarlett begins with a theory and will now conduct research to test her theory. This process is known as **deduction** and involves moving from theory to a specific hypothesis. Conversely, known facts are useful when they generate new ideas and allow the construction of new theories. Sometimes researchers observe in a very broad sense, and then later develop theory. When this occurs, the process of reasoning is called **induction** and requires making inferences about a whole group on the basis of known facts about one or more cases.

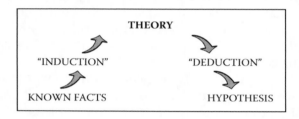

Before we leave our discussion of theory, it is important to note that researchers typically work for many years developing a partic-ular theory. They may continue to revise a theory over a lifetime, knowing that others may challenge its principles and applications. In a sense, a theorist's personal reputation is always at stake. We take this opportunity to recognize a few of the great theorists for their contributions to research in the disciplines of criminology and crimi-nal justice. Figure 1.1 provides a few examples of some of the better known theorists and their works. This list is only a representative snapshot of the innumerable theories relating to crime causation, criminal behavior, justice, and punishment. It is offered as an intro-ductory list for students to begin exploring some of the more familiar theories in related disciplines.

research hypotheses

Scientific inquiry requires that theoretical assumptions be expressed in hypothesis form. A **hypothesis** is a general statement or predic-tion about the relationship of two or more variables. It is an idea of

Classical and Rational Choice Theories: Crime as Choice
Based on works of Cesare Becarria and Jeremy Bentham
Lawrence Cohen and Marcus Felsons's Routine Activities Theory

Biological Theories: The Physiology of Criminals
Founded on Cesare Lombroso's work on the "born criminal"
William Sheldon's "somatotyping"

Psychological Theories: The Criminal Mind
Based on works of Sigmund Freud, Alfred Adler, Jean Piaget, and others
Samuel Yochelson and Clifford Samenow's Criminal Personality Theory
Albert Bandura's Modeling Theory

Social Conflict Theory
Based on writings of Karl Marx and Friedrich Engels
Applied to criminology by Willem Bonger, Ralf Dahrendorf, and George Vold
Richard Quinney's Social Reality of Crime Theory

Sociological Theories: Crime and Social Structure
Emile Durkheim's Anomie Theory
Clifford Shaw and Henry McKay's Chicago Area Study
Walter Miller's Focal Concern Theory

Sociological Theories: Crime and Social Process
Edwin Lemert's Primary and Secondary Deviance Theory
Edwin Sutherland's Differential Association Theory
Travis Hirschi's Social Bond Theory

Theories in Criminal Justice
Robert Martinson's work on Rehabilitation and Recidivism
Philip Zimbardo's Deindividuation Theory
Michel Foucault's work on Punishment and Discipline
Donald Clemmer's Prisonization Theory
David Fogel's Justice Model for Corrections
James Q. Wilson's work on Law Enforcement and Crime Causation
Alfred Blumstein's Stability of Punishment Theory
Arthur Neiderhoffer's Police Anomie Theory
Edwin Schur's Radical Non-Intervention Theory
John Braithwaite's Reintegrative Shaming Theory
Donald Black's Theory of Law
Michael Gottfredson's General Theory of Crime

Fig. 1.1 Theories in criminology.

or guess about how the researcher thinks the results will appear. Creating a hypothesis involves three requisites. It must be:

- Well constructed and plausible
- Grounded on theory
- Empirically testable

The first item requires that a hypothesis statement is reasonable and conveys a definite meaning about a relationship. The statement of the hypothesis should also be articulated in the language of research and seem believable. Next, theoretical grounding suggests that the hypothesis is based on known truths in the discipline. If entirely original, it must be consistent with the bulk of previous scientific knowledge. In the final requirement, the empirical approach emphasizes knowledge that comes through factual investigation. Recall our earlier discussion regarding empiricism. Facts are discovered through sources external to the researcher and involve direct experience or objective observation through the senses. Consider the following hypothesis applicable to academic failure and delinquency.

$$Ha = \text{Adolescent males with low IQs are at risk of becoming delinquent}$$

The hypothesis clearly states what relationship is to be explained and appears compatible with the bulk of knowledge. We know indeed that a child's inability to learn can stimulate acting-out behaviors that may escalate into delinquent behavior. As to being empirically testable, Ha clearly satisfies this requisite because a variation in IQ would, according to the hypothesis, make a difference in the at-risk-to-become-delinquent frequency.

A research hypothesis is one that a researcher believes to be true. As with the hypothesis above, a single research hypothesis describes the results in positive terms. In effect, it predicts that data will support a relationship of variables.

Occasionally, a research hypothesis is not stated as a direct relationship. Rather, it is stated in terms indicating that the effect is a function of the cause. Consequently, there is another way of stating the Ha hypothesis relating to low IQ and delinquency.

$$Ha = \text{Delinquency is a function of low IQ in adolescent males}$$

**RESEARCH IN ACTION 1: RELATIONSHIP OF
LOWER GRADES AND DELINQUENCY**

In 1980, Josefina Figueira-McDonough conducted research to explore the usefulness of Robert Merton's Anomie Theory in explaining delinquent behavior among high school students. Using data from self-administered surveys of 1,735 tenth grade students, the findings suggested that all types of delinquency increased inversely with grade average; the lower the grades of the students, the more their involvement in delinquent behavior. In sum, the results of this study support the hypothesis that failing students are under high strain. A conclusion is drawn that more attention should be paid to the strain of failing students as a motive force for delinquency. (*Source:* On the usefulness of Merton's Anomie Theory: academic failure and deviance among high school students. *Youth and Society*, 14(3): 259–279, 1983.)

Becoming Acquainted with Hypotheses

A good way for research students to become familiar with hypotheses is to turn to the journals for examples of the uses of hypotheses by practicing researchers. For the most part, a formal hypothesis is evident in a published research report. Other resources for studying how hypotheses are written are theses and dissertations. Remember that scientific research does not always involve a study of a single hypothesis. Sometimes a particular research study may cover a number of related hypotheses. Using our previous single hypothesis, it is clear that a number of related hypotheses may exist. When this occurs, the hypotheses are listed and numbered, for example:

It is hypothesized that adolescent males with low IQs are at risk:

1. To become truants
2. To use controlled substances
3. To become runaways
4. To become involved in vandalism

The researcher's contention in this example is that a relationship exists between low IQ and each of the four outcomes. The researcher asserts that data collected as part of this study will support each of the hypotheses. Put another way, the research study attempts to show that low IQ is a cause that puts an adolescent male at risk for truancy, drug use, runaway status, and involvement in vandalism.

Null Hypothesis

Another type is the **null hypothesis** represented by the Ho symbol. A null hypothesis predicts no effect. A review of the following null hypotheses should help clarify this point.

Ho = Delinquency is not a function of low IQ

Ho = Adolescent males with low IQs are not at risk
of delinquent behavior

In scientific research, the null hypothesis is tested statistically and may be rejected for an alternative hypothesis. If the null hypothesis is rejected, we accept the alternative hypothesis and conclude that there is an effect; that is, the independent variable affected the dependent variable.

Concepts and Variables

Variables are **concepts** that have been subjected to **operationalization**; that is, the concepts held about some phenomenon will be defined and translated into values that can be measured. Variables can be thought of as categories that contain two or more values. For example, demographic variables such as race, gender, and age are categories in which two or more values exist. We often refer to values that make up variables as attributes. For instance, the "race" variable has several attributes: American Indian, Asian, black, Hispanic, and white. Gender, on the other hand, has only two attributes: male and female. After variables have been identified, data can be collected and analyzed to measure them.

Another example will help you to understand how concepts are cultivated into variables. Assume that you hypothesize that aggressive behavior among teenagers is linked to TV violence; that is, continued exposure to acts of violence on television programs causes the development of aggressive behavior. Your assumption is that the more persistent the exposure to violent TV programming, the more likely that an adolescent will exhibit aggressive behavior. We could formulate the following research hypothesis:

Ha = A relationship exists between television violence and
aggression among teenagers

The null hypothesis would be stated:

Ho = No relationship exists between television violence and
aggression among teenagers

Two ideas are at work in our hypotheses: television violence and aggressive behavior among teenagers. Our first task is to refine these ideas into variables. We could operationalize television violence to mean television shows that display physical or verbal acts intended to cause injury to others. We then could describe aggression as criminal behavior such as robbery or battery. Finally, our teenage population could consist of high school students. Now that our concepts have been converted into variables, we can develop data collection strategies and measure the relationships of the variables.

There are several types of variables, but for the purposes of our preliminary discussion of the nature of criminal justice research, we choose to introduce three: independent, dependent, and extraneous variables. **Independent variables** explain the dependent variables. They are the predictors and are identified by a capital X. Treatment variables and demographic variables are always independent. **Dependent variables** are the outcomes that result from the influence of the independent variable. A capital Y identifies dependent variables. To illustrate the relationship between independent variables and dependent variables, consider the following hypothetical statement.

Ha = There is a direct relationship between alcohol consumption
and reckless driving

In this example, the independent variable X is alcohol consumption and the dependent variable Y is reckless driving. The researcher expects to find higher incidences of reckless driving among those who exhibit higher levels of alcohol consumption and lower incidences of reckless driving among those who consume less alcohol. Note that we could change the word "direct" to "positive" in the Ha hypothesis without changing its meaning.

TABLE 1.1: FIVE ASSERTIONS AND RELATIONAL PROPOSITIONS

Proposition Type	Assertion
Existence of relationship; a relationship merely exists	Relationship exists between X and Y variables
Direction of relationship; asserts a direct (positive) or inverse (negative) relationship	Positive relationship exists between X and Y if increase in one is followed by increase in the other; or negative relationship exists
Probabilistic nature of relationship; refers to degree of certainty of occurrence	If X, then always Y; if X, then always Y if no conditions interfere
Strength of relationship; identifies intensity of relationship between two variables	A weak (or moderate or strong) relationship exists between X and Y
Symmetry of relationship; identifies continuity of relationship in two ways: symmetrical (reciprocal) or asymmetrical (irreversible)	Symmetrical: if X, then Y and if Y, then X. Asymmetrical: if X, then Y; if no X, no conclusion can be drawn about Y

The hypothesis therefore provides a clear indication of the aim of the research. More specifically, that aim is to demonstrate the existence of a relationship between X and Y. Table 1.1 lists five types of assertions and relational propositions. We also recognize that **spurious relationships** or false relationships exist. Close associations between the X and Y variables may actually result from their linking to a common source or extraneous Z variable; Z can be related to X and Y in either of the following ways:

$$X \to Z \to Y, \; Y \to Z \to X, \; \text{or} \; Z \nearrow^X_{\searrow Y}$$

In most cases, this variable intervenes between the independent and dependent variables. In our hypothesis, another Z factor that indicates velocity of travel may mediate between alcohol consumption and reckless driving.

Sometimes **extraneous variables** are categorized into control variables. In research, the control variables are held constant or prevented from varying during the course of observation in order to limit the focus of the research. For example, suppose that a researcher wanted to explain variations between adolescent levels of aggression. If he or she controlled for gender by studying only male teenagers, then the gender variable could not account for any of the observed variation in aggression. Holding variables constant is a method of ruling out variables that are not of immediate interest but may otherwise explain part of the phenomenon that the researcher wishes to understand.

---

summary

Research is defined as a systematic method of inquiry into a phenomenon. The process of research was outlined and the five basic stages of any research study were identified. When a research idea is developed, an important factor to consider is whether to conduct pure or applied research. Pure research seeks knowledge for the sake of knowledge. Applied research is concerned with finding solutions to problems. Academic scholars have suggested that a major objective of criminal justice research should be to make its results more applied and relevant.

A theory is a broad statement that attempts to explain why things occur as they do. When assessing theory, it is essential to determine what qualities make a theory good. Several qualities were discussed, including empiricism, objectivity, skepticism and replication, falsifiability, dynamic nature, and ethics. Theory construction was illustrated as a deductive or inductive process. A hypothesis was defined as a specific statement regarding the relationship of variables. Three requisites for creating a hypothesis are that it must be (1) well constructed and plausible, (2) grounded on theory, and (3) empirically tested. Variables may be independent (denoted by X, also known as the predictor variable), dependent (denoted by Y, also known as the outcome variable), or extraneous (denoted by Z, also known as the intervening variable).

---

terminology

Research

Phenomenon

Determinism

Pure Research

Applied Research

Scientific Method

Theory

Empiricism

Objectivity

Skepticism

Replication

Falsifiability

Dynamic nature of theory

Ethics

Deduction

Induction

Hypothesis

Null hypothesis

Concepts

Variables

Operationalization

Independent variables

Dependent variables

Extraneous variables

Spurious relationships

discussion points

Describe the five basic stages that occur in any research study.

What is the difference between applied and pure research? Give an example of each type.

Identify several values of criminal justice research cited by Joan Petersilia.

Explore several articles from criminal justice journals to identify theories, hypotheses, and variables.

endnotes

1. J. D. Senese. *Applied Research Methods in Criminal Justice.* Chicago: Nelson-Hall, 1997.

2. M. Q. Patton. *Utilization-Focused Evaluation: The New Century Text*, 3rd ed. Newbury Park, CA: Sage, 1996.

3. F. N. Kerlinger. *Foundations of Behavioral Research*, 3rd ed. New York: Holt, Rinehart & Winston, 1986.

4. L. Zupan. The need for research on direct inmate supervision, *American Jails* 12(1): 21–22, 1993.

5. Academy of Criminal Justice Science. Statement of Purpose. Further information may be obtained from ACJS Secretariat, 1500 North Beauregard Street, Suite 101, Alexandria, VA 22311.

6. *Federal Probation.* Statement of Purpose. Further information may be obtained from Superintendent of Documents, Administrative Office of U.S. Courts, Washington, DC.

7. J. Petersilia. Defending the practical value of criminological research, *Journal of Research in Crime & Delinquency* 30(4): 497–505, 1993.

8. R. A. Singleton, Jr., B. C. Straits, and M. M. Straits. *Approaches to Social Research*, 2nd ed. New York: Oxford University Press, 1993.

9. T. J. Bernard and R. R. Ritti. The role of theory in scientific research. In *Measurement Issues in Criminology*, K. L. Kempf, Ed. New York: Springer, 1990.

2

research design

what is research design?

Research design is a crucial aspect of the total research process. It is the strategic plan that will guide the remainder of the research study. Within this plan, the researcher decides the purpose of the research, the method of investigation, and the measuring principle to be utilized. As used in this chapter, **research design** refers to the processes of planning and carrying out a research study after the research question or problem has been conceptualized.

The administrative role of the researcher cannot be overemphasized because he or she is responsible for making decisions at every step of the process and must vigorously embrace this important role. This obligation is perhaps analogous to an architect who designs award-winning buildings for a living. Consider the following definition of design and style provided by Catherine Hakim:

> Design deals primarily with aims, purposes, intentions, and plans within the practical constraints of location, time, money, and availability of staff. It is also very much about style, the architect's own preferences and ideas (whether innovative or solidly traditional) and the stylistic preferences of those who pay for the work and have to live with the finished result.[1]

This statement speaks of the designer's freedom to interject his or her own ideas while still maintaining sensitivity to design issues

23

for a successful project. In applying this concept to criminal justice research, we recognize that the researcher must be flexible and sensible. The researcher adopts a design that allows for creativity but also adheres to the general rules of scientific method. The researcher who understands this relationship maximizes the potential for a successful research project. Let us consider the following illustration of this juxtaposition.

Kiel, a young soccer player with many years of playing experience, obeys the rules of the game. As an aspiring athlete, he understands if he makes it to the professional ranks, he will be held to the highest standards of athletic competition. However, beyond an understanding of the rules, and perhaps more importantly, the way that Kiel plays the game within the rules that determines whether he is a skilled professional or an amateur. To play well, Kiel must possess skill based on athleticism, good practice habits, the ability to capitalize on opportunities during the game, and the inventiveness to create ways to help his team win soccer matches.

Now that a definition of research design has been provided and the administrative responsibility of the research designer has been introduced, we turn our attention to other matters relating to the design process. In the next section, we look at various types of research designs in the broad categories of quantitative, qualitative, and evaluation designs. Moreover, we'll connect these designs with the subject of research intent by offering an in-depth discussion of the purposes of exploratory, descriptive, and explanatory research. Next, we seek to sensitize you to the issues involved in choosing a research strategy. An overview of experimental, quasi-experimental, survey, and case study strategies is provided. The concluding portion of this chapter relates to levels of measurement followed by a brief introduction to validity and reliability.

types of research designs

Various designs are available to carry out criminal justice research. Some designs allow direct causal inferences to be made, while others provide less indisputable evidence of causation. Still other designs are not concerned with causal inferences; rather, these designs focus merely on classifying relations among measures, discovering characteristics or describing events in terms of a set of characteristics.

Quantitative Research

Research design is characterized by three divergent approaches: quantitative, qualitative, and evaluative. In **quantitative research**, the researcher tends to gather data in the form of numbers. Using the methods of quantitative research, the researcher can employ various statistics to explore the relationships of selected variables. For example, a researcher may be interested in studying the relationship between the number of traffic citations administered by police and attitudes of citizens toward police. He or she may hypothesize that an increase in the number of traffic citations decreases citizens' positive attitudes toward police. The hypothesis lends itself to using numbers to measure the relationship. Therefore, we now consider a statistical technique to test the hypothesis.

The two broad categories of statistical techniques are descriptive statistics and inferential statistics. **Descriptive statistics** includes frequency distributions such as rates, proportions, and percentages, as well as graphic representations of data such as pie charts, bar graphs, and frequency polygons (line charts). Descriptive statistics also includes measures of central tendency such as mean and median and measures of dispersion such as range and standard deviation. Whatever the combination, statistical data allow a researcher to understand the nature of a relationship by summarizing or describing the data.

Inferential statistics, on the other hand, attempts to make inference from a sample of people compared to some larger population. The aim of inferential statistics is to generalize and assess the probability of certain findings. A comprehensive discussion of both categories of statistical measures is provided in Chapter 3.

Qualitative Research

A second approach to research design is **qualitative research**. With this method, a researcher tends to gather data in the form of words. In our previous example, the researcher may be interested in the comments of citizens rather than numbers. Consequently, he or she will likely design the research study to include interviews of citizens to gather narrative information about their opinions, beliefs, and knowledge about the police in the community.

The aim of qualitative research is to capture the dynamics of a phenomenon. A researcher chooses methods that allow in-depth inquiries in the hopes that they will reveal the breadth of the problem under study. Sociologist Max Weber described this process as a **verstehen** (meaning *empathy* in German) in which the researcher immerses himself or herself in the subject matter with the desire of developing a sympathetic understanding and explanation of reality.[2]

In qualitative research, the researcher relies on such data-collecting techniques as observation, videotaping, collecting personal documents (letters, memoirs, etc.), and developing questionnaires, with the idea of studying human activity in its natural setting. In Chapter 7, we provide a thorough discussion of the two qualitative strategies of participant observation and case studies.

Before proceeding, we offer a comparison of both quantitative and qualitative approaches to research by providing a segment of an article written by Bruce DiCristina. In these portions of the essay, the author addresses the actual and potential contributions of quantitative and qualitative research.

> It has never been demonstrated that the application of quantitative methods in criminal justice research produces a kind of knowledge logically superior to that produced by qualitative methods, and there seems little reason to believe that such a demonstration will be made soon. In the natural sciences, arguments suggesting that a single research orientation is logically superior to all others have been unconvincing. If the goal of criminal justice research is to discover the truth about crime and criminal justice processes, it would be reckless to assume that quantitative methods are the most plausible means of doing so.[3]

Quantitative and qualitative methods perhaps are best viewed as complementary approaches, each at least partially compensating for the shortcomings of the other.

Evaluative Research

A third design approach is referred to as **evaluative research**; the researcher is interested in the evaluation of social action programs. The objective is to define social relevance or social worth and may apply to people, objects, and actions. The researcher tends to measure the degree to which a social action program possesses certain valued characteristics. The evaluative research design is intended to resolve some immediate policy concerns. For example, a research study of the organizational behavior at a county jail may involve identifying organizational problems and conflicts in an effort to resolve issues, assist the organization to accomplish its objectives, and help make the facility a better place to work.

research purposes

While the eventual **purpose of research** is to produce reliable and valid information, not all research is conducted for the immediate purpose of testing relationships. Moreover, a research design may include more than one specific purpose. Three of the more common goals of research are:

- Exploratory
- Descriptive
- Explanatory

Exploratory Research

The **exploratory research** designation suggests that little is known about a subject and therefore the task is to "do some digging," "delve into," or "investigate." In a criminal justice research context, we consider a study for exploratory purposes when we want to:

- Determine what is occurring
- Gain new insights
- Assess phenomena in a new light

The process of exploration begins when a researcher develops a general description of a phenomenon. Because variables are typically not well defined at this stage, the central concept or idea to be explored should be clearly understood. This central concept may be a single idea or represent several sub-ideas.

Exploratory research may be utilized to gauge how other jurisdictions handle certain problems within their criminal justice agencies. For example, a local jail facility may unexpectedly experience overcrowding and need to determine how other adult jails have handled a similar problem. The jail administrator would be interested in exploring all possible solutions to overcrowding. What will it cost to add additional jail space? How do you develop a prisoner population management plan? Will it work? Is it feasible to contract with other jails to house overflow prisoners? Are alternative placements in community corrections programs available?

Exploratory research also enables a researcher to learn more about a specific phenomenon with the desired result of applying what is learned to larger issues of policy and practice. For example, Henry Hamilton and John Smykla conducted an exploratory study of guidelines governing undercover tactics of law enforcement agencies in 100 of the largest cities in the United States. The objectives of this research were (1) to learn more about police undercover guidelines and (2) shed some light on the larger debate about the control of police. The study explored five questions:

- How many police departments conduct undercover investigations?
- What types of crimes are investigated by undercover operations?
- Of the departments that conduct undercover operations, how many have guidelines?
- Why do departments that conduct undercover investigations have guidelines?
- Why do departments that conduct undercover investigations not have guidelines?[4]

Descriptive Research

As its name implies, **descriptive research** provides a description of some phenomenon and is the most commonly utilized research in the field of criminal justice. While its purpose is similar to that of exploratory research (fact finding), the nature of the research differs considerably. In descriptive research, the goal is to capture the essence of some event by gathering precise measurements from a set of carefully selected cases and then generalize the findings to a larger population. Descriptive research is very useful to estimate future events. Accordingly, in criminal justice research we consider a study for descriptive purposes when we want to:

- Portray an accurate profile of an event or situation
- Estimate the proportion of people in a specified population
- Provide a quality description that is representative of a larger group

An example of descriptive research is a recent study by one of the authors of this text. In an assessment of the impact of judicial waiver laws in Kansas, a population study was conducted to describe juvenile prisoners who were incarcerated in adult correctional institutions in the state. One objective of this research was to provide descriptive profiles of prisoners below 18 years old who were incarcerated during the 3 years from 1995 to 1997. The demographic characteristics of gender, race and/or ethnicity, age, and offense were used to describe these juveniles. Descriptive statistics were then used to convey information about this specific prisoner population.[5]

Explanatory Research

The third common purpose is referred to as **explanatory research.** In explanatory studies, a researcher attempts to go beyond the level of description and explain a phenomenon by testing relationships among variables of the hypotheses. This type of research requires the researcher to carefully develop a plan to control all influences except the influence under study. In other words, after the study is completed, the researcher will want to attribute the results to the treatment. In order to accomplish this with confidence, all other possible explanations must be eliminated or their probability minimized. In criminal justice research, we consider a study to be for explanatory purposes when we want to:

- Find explanations to problems
- Test the probability that certain relationships of variables exist
- Understand the relationships of variables

To illustrate the explanatory purpose of research, we cite a study of police behavior in a Midwestern city. Richard Lundman examined legal and extralegal variables to explain factors that influenced police disposition of drunk driving encounters. Impolite demeanor of a driver was found to increase the probability of arrest over other extralegal variables such as sex, race, and class. Among legal variables, the degree of intoxication was found to explain the probability of arrest more accurately than whether the driver was involved in an automobile accident.[6]

choice of research design

After the purpose of a research study has been established, the researcher then chooses a research design. This involves selecting a method of investigation. As an introduction to design issues, we have chosen four design methods to overview: experimental, quasi-experimental, survey, and case study. A complete discussion of each of these methodological designs is provided in subsequent chapters.

Experimental Method

An **experimental design** measures the effects of manipulating one variable on another variable. The researcher deliberately introduces change (treatment) into the research environment and observes the effects of the change. Therefore, experimental designs are adopted when a researcher is attempting to discover a cause-and-effect relationship between independent and dependent variables.

When conducting experimental research, a researcher decides which subjects will be assigned to the **experimental group** and to the **control group**. This is usually accomplished through randomization: all persons in each group must be equally likely candidates and the persons who participate in the experiment should be drawn randomly from all persons who could conceivably be candidates. Drawing from the total population of all possible candidates is called **random selection**. After a pool of participants is randomly selected, they are randomly assigned to the experimental and control groups. The experimental group receives the experimental treatment. The control group does not receive the treatment. Figure 2.1 illustrates this process.

Example: Suppose that you want to test the effectiveness of recreational exercise in reducing negative behavior at a juvenile detention center. You hypothesize that when the residents increase their exercise, the number of rule infractions will decrease. The following specifications apply to the design:

- The population consists of all juveniles to whom this treatment may be applied. If 100 residents are housed in the juvenile detention center, then the population is 100.
- RS indicates a random selection of the sample. If we want a sample size of 50% (half of the juvenile population), then

Fig. 2.1 Random selection of experimental and control groups.

our sample will include 50 juveniles who will be randomly selected.

- The arrows and RA indicate that the sample of 50 juveniles will be randomly assigned to either an experimental group (25 residents) or a control group (25 residents).

- The top row (O, E, and another O) designates the experimental group. The first O represents an initial observation (measurement). The E represents the experimental treatment group, and the other O represents a second measurement of the effect of the treatment. The 25 juveniles included in the experimental group will receive increased recreation and exercise activities. If the initial measurement indicated that an average of 10 rule infractions occurred each day, we would expect, according to our hypothesis that this number would decrease in the experimental group (second O classification.

- In the bottom row the C represents the control group that receives no treatment and therefore the amount of recreational exercise does not increase. We would expect, according to our hypothesis, that the number of rule infractions would not decrease in the control group.

In our examination of the effectiveness of recreational exercise in reducing negative behavior at a juvenile detention center, we used what is known as the **classical experimental design**. The central features of this design are independent and dependent variables, identifying the total population, random selection of a sample size, random assignment into experimental and control groups, pre-testing of both groups, treatment of the experimental group only, and post-testing of both groups.

There are many variations of the experimental research design. Some designs do not include pre-testing and others emphasize several treatments rather than the simple effect of one independent variable. Each of these experimental designs will be discussed in Chapter 5. For our purposes of introducing design issues we next consider the quasi-experimental research design.

Quasi-Experimental Method

The **quasi-experimental design** attempts to emulate the classical experimental design with two exceptions. First, a quasi-experimental design is adopted when the treatment and comparison groups cannot be assigned by randomization. Second, this research design is more appropriate if the experimental design is deemed too intrusive upon the subjects or not practical because of established legal or ethical rules governing the treatment of subjects. For example, let's consider our study of the effectiveness of recreational exercise in reducing negative behavior at a juvenile detention center. It may be difficult, if not impossible, to randomly assign juveniles to the experimental and control groups. Regulatory standards governing the operations of a detention center typically mandate that all juveniles receive fair and equal treatment. All juvenile residents must thus be afforded the same opportunities for increased recreational exercise. In this case, the researcher would likely choose to measure the effects of the treatment on the entire juvenile population over a long period. This is referred to as a **time series design** and is one of several quasi-experimental designs that will be explained later.

The quasi-experimental design approach is very attractive to a researcher trying to maintain a basic experimental scheme while conducting research outside a controlled environment. Also, an advantage of these types of experiments is that they are often cheaper and more feasible than randomized experiments. In determining feasibility, the researcher assesses the level of control over the subjects. If a high degree of control is present, then the true experimental design may be feasible. If not, the researcher may consider a quasi-experimental design or even decide to choose a survey or case study design.

Survey Method

Another design method that a researcher may choose as a method of investigation is **survey research**. As previously mentioned, survey research methods will be described in detail in Chapter 6, but in this section we attempt to familiarize you with what is considered the most common research strategy chosen by criminal justice researchers.

As with experimental and quasi-experimental research, several choices of survey research designs are available; the major design options are in-person interviews, telephone interviews, and self-report questionnaires. The focus of survey research is quite different. Survey research focuses not on the testing of a hypothesis by tight control of the environment and adherence to strict rules of experimentation. Rather, the emphasis is on measuring variables by asking questions and then examining the relationships among the measures. The three general features of survey research design are:

- A large number of respondents are chosen through probability sampling procedures to represent the population of interest.
- Systematic questionnaire or interview procedures are used to ask prescribed questions of respondents and record their answers.
- Answers are numerically coded and analyzed with the aid of statistical software.[7]

Survey research involves several modes of inquiry. One such mode is the face-to-face interview that requires the researcher to conduct direct interviews with the sample population. A second technique is the telephone interview whereby the researcher contacts respondents via the telephone and asks them questions. A final mode of survey research is the self-administered survey. Typically, self-administered surveys are either hand-delivered or mailed to the respondents by the researcher.

As you no doubt have noticed, with each discussion of the various designs available to the researcher, we drift farther away from the classical experimental design; that is, we lean toward research designs that are more conducive to field work than to experiments in a laboratory and that by nature do not necessarily follow experimental procedures. This is not to say that experimentation can't take place in the field. A work setting, for instance, may very well be used as a laboratory for the purposes of conducting experiments. For example, in a research study focused on the counseling behaviors of jailers, the researcher could essentially turn the jail facility into a laboratory and develop a research strategy based on the classical experimental design. For our purposes then, the **field work** term infers research that takes place in a natural setting. It also suggests that some form of observation on the part of the researcher will occur.

Case Study

The final research design to consider in this introduction to design issues is the case study. A **case study** involves developing detailed, intensive knowledge about a single case (or a small number of related cases) of a situation, individual, or group of interest to the researcher. There are several reasons for choosing a case study design. First, very little may be known about a problem under study. Therefore, the researcher focuses on one or two representative cases in order to understand the intensity and magnitude of the concern. Another reason for choosing a case study design is to examine certain cases that epitomize success or failure. If, for example, we wanted to study the relationship between public attitude and successful community corrections programs, we could identify and study programs that have gained positive public support. The idea is to engage in an in-depth review of these programs to identify conditions that effect success.

The final reason for conducting case studies is simply researcher preference. Many criminal justice researchers view the case study as a better way of gathering explicit and revealing information as compared to other data collection strategies.

levels of measurement

By now, it should be apparent that the process of planning a research study requires consideration of several factors before an appropriate design can be chosen. Thus far in this chapter, we have noted that a researcher must determine both the purpose of the study and the type of design that will be most feasible. These two decisions are crucial to the strategic planning process. Another matter of equal importance is measurement. This simply means that the researcher must have a basic understanding of how the variables will be measured in the study and that different variables may represent different levels of measurement.

When a researcher is faced with the task of selecting what to measure, the focus of the measurement is on the dependent variable. In other words, the treatment is identified as the independent variable while the dependent variable is the issue being measured in the experiment. Let's consider an example mentioned earlier in this chapter regarding a study of the effectiveness of recreational exercise in reducing negative behavior at a juvenile detention center. In this example, the researcher is not measuring exercise; he or she is studying exercise as an independent variable. What is being measured will somehow have to do with effectiveness. The immediate task for the researcher is to determine how the effectiveness may be measured. You will recall that we hypothesized that when resident exercise increases the number of rule infractions decreases. The number of rule infractions becomes our gauge of effectiveness. Therefore, in our example, the number of rule infractions would be measured.

Measurement involves counting to assess the impact of the treatment. Singleton, Straits, and Straits provide a clear definition of measurement: "The assignment of numbers or labels to units of analysis to represent variable categories."[8] Knowing the **level of measurement** helps a researcher decide how to interpret the data from variables. Typically, variables are measured on four levels:

- Nominal
- Ordinal
- Interval
- Ratio

Nominal Variables

The simplest level of measurement involves nominal variables. A **nominal variable** contains attributes (recall our discussion of attributes in Chapter 1) that offer simple labels. Demographic variables such as gender, race, and religion are nominal variables. For example, within the variable gender, male and female are just "named" attributes.

In nominal measurement, a researcher may choose to attach numerical values to the attributes. Doing this allows him or her to make distinctions among several values. Numerical attachments serve as a convenient way of identifying data when it is collected and analyzed, but they do not convey statistical significance in regard to relationships. For example, the numbers on soccer uniforms are measures at the nominal level. Tara, a player with the uniform 12 is not necessarily better skilled at soccer than Jessica who wears a lower 10. Nor is Tara twice as capable a player as Samantha, a teammate who wears uniform 6. Finally, not one of the three girls is more skilled than the goalie whose uniform bears no number at all. The practical purpose of having numbers on soccer uniforms is to provide coaches and fans a way to distinguish the players. The uniform numbers do not display a relationship between players and their levels of skill.

Ordinal Variables

The next level of measurement involves **ordinal variables**. The attributes or ordinal measurements can be rank-ordered. However, distances between attributes have no significance. For example, you might code educational attainment on a survey as 0 = elementary school; 1 = some high school; 2 = high school diploma; 3 = some college; 4 = college degree; and 5 = post-college. In this measure, higher numbers mean more education. However, is the distance between 0 and 1 the same as the distance between 3 and 4? Of course the distances are not the same because the intervals between values are not interpretable. Moreover, even though we understand that a college degree represents more education than some college, the difference is not exact. We simply cannot determine how much more education has been attained.

Interval Variables

The third level of measurement involves **interval variables** that are rank-ordered and maintain equal distances (intervals) between attributes. A classic example of interval measurement is the Fahrenheit temperature scale. When we measure temperature, the distance between 40 and 50 degrees is the same as the distance between 70 and 80 degrees. Both distances equal 10 degrees. Similarly, the difference between 60 and 61 degrees is the same as that between 20 and 21 degrees (exactly 1 degree). The interval between values is interpretable. The Fahrenheit temperature scale is considered an interval measurement because the zero point is arbitrary. In other words, a temperature reading of 0 degrees does not mean the absence of temperature. It means only that the 0 temperature is colder than a reading at 10, 20, or 30 degrees and warmer than readings below 0.

In interval measurement, the distances between numbers must be equal. In the above example, we used the measurement unit (metric) of degrees. Likewise, if we were measuring time, our measurement unit could be seconds.

Ratio Variables

The final level, the **ratio variable**, includes the characteristics of ordinal level measurement plus an absolute zero point. This means that a meaningful fraction (ratio) can be constructed that shows how many times greater one value is than another. Weight, age, and number of children are examples of ratio variables.

In criminal justice research most "count" variables are ratios. Let's consider the number of probation clients over the past 6 months. This is a ratio variable because we could have zero clients. Likewise, it is substantive to say, "We had twice as many clients in the past 6 months as we did in the previous 6 months." It is important to recognize that a hierarchical system is at work with regard

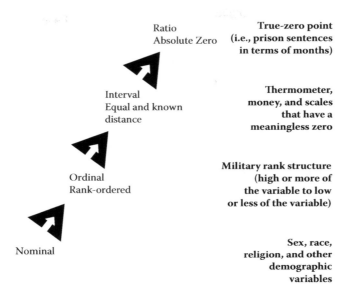

Fig. 2.2 Levels of measurement.

to the four levels of measurement. At each level up the hierarchy, the current level includes all the qualities of the one below it and adds something new. In general, it is desirable to have a higher level of measurement (interval or ratio) rather than a lower one (nominal or ordinal).

When criminal justice researchers construct and evaluate measurements, two key properties must be taken into account because they exert a direct influence on the design measurement procedures that will be chosen for collecting data on the variables of interest. These properties are validity and reliability. We provide abbreviated definitions above as a means of introduction (see Figure 2.2). A more comprehensive discussion of validity and reliability strategies is provided in Chapter 4.

validity and reliability

Validity is a property of empirical measurement that assures that we are measuring what we think we are measuring. The two types of validity are internal and external. Internal validity simply means that the experimental treatment, and only the experimental treatment, was responsible for the outcome. A researcher makes a more convincing case that measurement and assessment procedures are

A Question of Validity
How can we be sure that: • We are measuring what we think we are? • That which we are measuring is not being confounded or contaminated by something else? • Our findings can be generalized to a larger population?

Fig. 2.3 A question of validity.

valid if they accurately measure the variables. External validity indicates the degree to which the findings may be applicable in everyday use outside the experimental context. See Figure 2.3.

Reliability constitutes the consistency and stability of a measurement. If a study were duplicated, would the instrument yield the same answer to the same question on second testing? If so, the results are considered stable. Consistency indicates whether a measurement may be applied universally.

Both validity and reliability are important characteristics of measurement. Moreover, reliability is a necessary but not sufficient condition for validity (i.e., you can have reliability without validity, but in order to achieve validity you must have reliability). A comprehensive discussion of validity and reliability is provided in Chapter 4.

summary

- A research design is a well thought-out strategic plan that guides a study. The planning process occurs after the question or problem has been conceptualized.
- Various research designs are available to a criminal justice researcher. Typically, they fall into the categories of quantitative, qualitative, and evaluative research.
- In quantitative research, the researcher is concerned with measuring variables with numbers. This approach infers that variables will be analyzed with statistical procedures in order to determine the predictive generalization of the theory.
- Quantitative research is affiliated with experimentation and the focus is on understanding a social or human problem by using words rather than numbers. It may involve describing observations that occur in their natural settings, interviewing and reporting detailed views of people, or providing

chronological accounts of the life stories of people or historical events.

- The third approach is evaluative research and typically involves the analysis of policy-related problems. A feature of evaluative research is that the researcher is often tasked to provide potential solutions to immediate problems.

- While a research study may involve multiple purposes, the primary focus tends to be for exploratory, descriptive, or explanatory reasons.

- Exploratory research occurs when little is known about a subject. The researcher wants to gain a basic understanding of an event.

- In descriptive research, the aim is to describe what is occurring.

- Explanatory research involves attempts to explain what is occurring.

- After the purpose of the research has been established, the researcher chooses a design. The best design is not always immediately apparent because he or she has many designs from which to choose.

- The experimental methods of data collection require random assignment of subjects to experimental and control groups. Illustration of this design by means of a visual diagram and an associated example provides an introduction to this design.

- When the classical experimental design is not practical, a criminal justice researcher chooses another option. Three such methods of data collection include the quasi-experimental design, survey research, and case study. Each option has its own unique way of gathering data that the researcher uses to measure the variables under study.

- The level of measurement refers to assumptions about relationships of the data. These assumptions can be differentiated when the researcher assigns numerals to the various attributes found in the variables.

- The four common levels of measurement (from weakest to strongest) are nominal, ordinal, interval, and ratio.

- In nominal measurement, the purpose of numbers is to simply provide a name as well as distinguish between differences of kind.

- In ordinal measures, different numbers indicate a rank.
- In interval measurement the numbers imply the existence of a known and countable distance between attributes.
- Ratio measurement contains an absolute zero, making it possible to form ratios of the numbers assigned to attributes.
- A valid measure assures that we are measuring what we think we are measuring. The two types of validity measurements are internal and external. Reliability refers to the stability or consistency of the measurement.
- An important issue that a researcher must consider when choosing a design is the environment in which the research will occur. Sometimes it is not possible to utilize a certain design (no matter how strongly he or she feels about the "best empirical" method) because the environment is not able to accommodate the study.

terminology

Research design

Quantitative research

Descriptive statistics

Inferential statistics

Qualitative research

Verstehen

Evaluative research

Purpose of research

Exploratory research

Descriptive research

Explanatory research

Experimental design

Experimental group

Control group

Random selection

Classical experimental design

Quasi-experimental design

Time series design

Survey research

Field work

Case study

Level of measurement

Nominal variable

Ordinal variable

Interval variable

Ratio variable

Validity

Reliability

discussion points

What are the distinguishing features of quantitative and qualitative research?

What potential benefits for criminal justice agencies can be derived from evaluation research?

Compare and contrast exploratory, descriptive, and explanatory purposes of research.

What two distinguishing features can be noted between quasi-experimental and true experimental designs? Which of these two designs do you think are used more often in studies of correctional settings? Why?

What is the primary focus of survey research?

Can you think of a research idea that might use the case study method to collect data? Name and explain why.

Why is level of measurement an important consideration when choosing a research design?

How are validity and reliability different?

endnotes

1. C. Hakim. *Research Design: Strategies and Choices in the Design of Social Research.* London: Allen & Unwin, 1987.

2. M. Weber. *The Methodology of Social Sciences.* Translated by Edward A. Shils and Henry A. Finch. New York: Free Press, 1949.

3. B. DiCristina. The quantitative emphasis in criminal justice education. *Journal of Criminal Justice Education* 8(2): 181–199, 1997.

4. H. Hamilton and J. O. Smykla. Guidelines for police undercover work: new questions about accreditation and the emphasis of procedure over authorization. *Justice Quarterly* 11(1): 135–151, 1994.

5. G. J. Bayens. Characteristics of juveniles confined in Kansas adult jails and prisons, 1995–1997. *American Jails* 12(6): 59–68, 1999.

6. R. Lundman. City police and drunk driving: baseline data. *Justice Quarterly* 15(3): 525–546, 1998.

7. R. Singleton, B. Straits, and M. Straits. *Approaches to Social Research*, 2nd ed. New York: Oxford University Press, 1993.

8. Ibid., p. 110.

statistics in research

introduction

Statistics relates to the methods of designing and conducting research studies by describing the data collected and serving as the foundations of decisions based on that data. In one sense, statistics is a descriptive language. Statistics is a branch of applied mathematics that we use to plan research, gather, organize, and analyze data; present data in research papers; and make inferences about data. Psychologists, for example, use statistics to support or refute various predictions concerning the behaviors of humans and animals.[1]

In another sense, statistics is an inferential language. An understanding of statistics is essential before undertaking even the most elementary types of research. Many people are intimidated by empirical research because they lack an understanding of statistics. In addition, statistics is associated with mathematics and any type of math scares them. Mathematics is merely a convenient and efficient language for accomplishing logical operations inherent in good data analysis.[2]

role of statistics

Statistics is a research tool for answering questions. It is also used by the researcher to calculate the relative accuracies of measurements they use. Generally, statistics is used in one of four basic roles to aid in:

- Locating the center of a mass of data. In this role, it assists a researcher in determining the best prediction.
- Indicating the diversification of the data. In this role, it indicates the likelihood or smaller likelihood of an expected outcome and serves as an aid in determining how closely related data elements are within a group or groups of data.
- Determining the probability that the event in question may have occurred by chance or may have been influenced by other events.

The two basic types of statistics are descriptive and inferential. **Descriptive statistics** is a method for presenting quantitative descriptions in a manageable form and is used to describe data in a form that allows readers to readily understand it. For example, a research study conducted in Travis County, Texas, revealed that 1,884 of the 4,485 persons booked in the county jail were released within 4 hours of booking. The researcher used the descriptive statistic that 42% of all persons booked in the county jail were released within 4 hours of booking—the 42% is easier to understand than 1,884 out of 4,485.

Inferential statistics is the process of inferring characteristics about a population from the data variables observed in a sample. Researchers rarely, if ever, study samples simply to describe the samples per se. In most cases, their purpose is to make assertions about the larger population from which the sample has been selected. Suppose that in a random sample of 300 college students 30 students (10%) had been arrested for crimes within the past 2 years. From this sample, a researcher could infer that 10% of all college students have been arrested for crimes within the past 2 years. If all college students were examined and a determination was made that 10% of them had been arrested in the past 2 years, the statistic would no longer be an inference because the researcher measured all the students. The statistic would now be descriptive, not inferential. Figure 3.1 compares types of statistics.

Descriptive Statistics	Inferential Statistics
Measures of central tendency	Hypothesis testing
Measures of dispersion or variability	z-tests and t-tests

Fig. 3.1 Comparison of types of statistics.

basic principles and conventions

Statistical reasoning is based on certain basic principles.[3] The first is that in developing statistics, *one should seek to reduce the level of error as much as possible.* The goal of research is to answer questions. In order to answer them correctly, a researcher must be as accurate as possible. The best statistic provides the most accurate statement about a study. Accordingly, in defining a statistic or choosing which statistic to use, a researcher must consider the level of error that each statistic presents. While it is almost impossible to develop an error-free description of every fact or event, we should choose the approach that will generally produce the fewest mistakes and thus reduce the level of error. The second basic principle is that *the best statistics utilize the maximum amount of information and are generally preferred over those based on less information.* This principle is common to most forms of information gathering. Good decisions are based on good information. Accordingly, the more information available, the better a researcher can weigh his or her options and make an educated decision.

The third basic principle is that *outliers may present a problem in choosing and interpreting statistics.* **Outliers** are situations or events that are very different from all others measured in the study. For example, in a case study involving career criminals, one criminal may have committed thousands of thefts and the next most active criminal committed only a few hundred. While cases that are very different from all the others (outliers) are components of a study, they can result in significant changes in choice of statistics and presentation of results. In some cases, the outliers may be overlooked if a researcher is preoccupied with other relevant statistical concerns.

A fourth principle is that *whatever method of research is used, the researcher must strive to systematize the procedures used in data collection.* As noted by Albert J. Reiss, Jr., observations and recordings must follow explicit procedures that permit replication and also follow the rules that will permit the use of scientific inference.[4]

Common Terms

Statistics is a language and contains certain common terms that have special meanings with reference to statistical concepts. The more common terms are described below.

Population	Sample
Entire group that is subject of research	Subset of population
N = population size	n = sample size
μ = population mean	$\bar{X}$ = sample mean
Population characteristics are parameters	Sample characteristics are statistics

Fig. 3.2 Relationships of populations and samples.

Population refers to an entire or total data set under consideration. A **sample** is a subset of a population. Samples are normally used when working with inferential statistics. Generalizations from a sample are made about the population as a whole. For example, if the student body of a university is the population under consideration and you wish to determine what percentage have been arrested within the past 2 years, you could examine the entire student body or select a random sample (smaller group), then use the random sample to make an inference about the entire population. Figure 3.2 illustrates relationships between populations and samples.

Descriptive statistics are used to summarize information that is already known about a population. Inferential statistics are used to arrive at broader generalizations or inferences from sample data and apply them to populations. **Multivariate statistics** allows researchers to examine a series of variables at one time. It allows us to solve a different type of problem in research by isolating one factor while taking into consideration a host of others.

Data are the numbers or elements used to describe some fact about a population or a sample. **Raw data** are data elements that have not been processed. **Discrete data** elements exist independently of other data elements. For example, students or books are considered discrete elements. **Continuous data** elements exist in a continuum. Examples are colors, degrees of temperature, and measurements of length.

An **assumption** is a statement that a researcher takes to be true at the outset of a statistical test. Assumptions are the foundations upon which the rest of the tests are built. **Correlation** is the measure of a relationship between two variables. **Independence** indicates that two events are unrelated—that the occurrence of one does not impact the occurrence of the other.

A **bivariate table** displays joint frequency distributions of two variables. A **univariate table** displays only one variable in a population. If more than two variables are displayed, a table is multivariate. A table that displays the number of cases in each category is a frequency distribution. A **non-parametric test** is one in which no assumptions are made regarding the distribution or shape of the population tested.

Terms for measures of central tendency

- The **median** is the score that occupies the middle position in a spread of scores.
- The **mode** is calculated by identifying the score or category that occurs most frequently.
- The **deviation from mean** is the extent to which each individual score differs from the mean of all the scores.
- The **least squares property** is a characteristic of the mean whereby the sum of all the squared deviations from the mean is a minimum. It is lower than the sum of the squared deviations from any other fixed point.
- The mean is calculated by dividing the sum of the scores by the number of cases. It is the arithmetic average of the scores.
- Outliers are exceptional cases that substantially deviate from the general pattern of scores.
- **Skewed distribution** describes a spread of scores that is clearly weighted to one side.
- **Variable** is a trait, characteristic, or attribute than can be measured at least at the nominal level.

Terms for measures of dispersion

- The **coefficient of relative variation** is a measure of dispersion calculated by dividing the standard deviation by the mean.
- The **index of qualitative variation** is calculated by dividing the sum of the possible pairs of observed scores by the sum of the possible pairs of scores expected when cases are equally distributed across categories.
- The **mean deviation** is calculated by adding the absolute deviations of each score from the mean and then dividing the sum by the number of cases.
- The **range** is calculated by subtracting the smallest score from the largest score and adding 1.
- **Standard deviation** is calculated by taking the square root of the variance.

- **Variance** is calculated by adding the squared deviation of each score from the mean and then dividing the sum by the number of cases.
- The **variation ratio** is calculated by subtracting the proportion of the cases in the modal category from 1.

Terms for frequency distributions

- The **frequency distribution** is the arrangement of scores from the lowest to the highest that shows the number of times each score occurs.
- A **histogram** is a bar graph used to represent a frequency distribution.
- A **normal curve** is the representation of a normal frequency distribution on a graph by use of a continuous line.
- A **standard deviation unit** is a unit of measurement used to describe the deviation of a specific score or value from the mean in a z-score distribution.
- A **standard normal distribution** is a normal frequency distribution with a mean of 0 and a standard deviation of 1. Normal frequency distribution can be converted into the standard normal distribution by using a z formula.

Conventions Used in Statistics

Certain common conventions are observed to assist researchers in interpreting statistical methods and results. Greek letters denote the characteristics of population parameters, Roman letters are generally used to demonstrate those characteristics associated with samples. A bar above a letter X indicates an arithmetic mean of a group of data. The letters x, y, and z are used to denote variables or observations of individual cases. The Greek upper-case sigma (Σ) is used to indicate summation. When used in a formula, it indicates a direction to add the sums of all totals expressed immediately following the sign. An independent variable is normally indicated by X, and a dependent variable by Y.

descriptive statistics

The two types of descriptive statistics generally encountered are measures of central tendency and measures of dispersion. Measures of **central tendency** determine typicality. They help describe an average case; for example, the average salary of police officers is a measure of central tendency. If we were considering law enforcement as a career, the average salary of a law enforcement officer would be important. We would also want to know whether the salary range is very large. A salary range presented in a descriptive statistic is a **measure of dispersion.**

Because the primary purpose of descriptive statistics is to describe the data in question, the process of data reduction is used to present the data in a format that is easy for a reader to understand. In the earlier example regarding bookings in a county jail, the 42% figure represents a form of data reduction for the 1,884 out of 4,485 statistic. While measures of central tendency allow researchers to describe a typical case, measures of dispersion allow a researcher also to describe to what degree other cases in the study are different or similar to the typical case.

Measures of Central Tendency

The three basic measures of central tendency are the mode, the median, and the mean. Using these three basic measures, a researcher can determine and describe the central tendencies of data.

Mode

The mode is a number or measurement that occurs with the greatest frequency. For example, in a sample of 100 criminal cases, the defendants were defended by privately retained attorneys in 32 cases, by public defenders in 60 cases, and by court-appointed attorneys in 8 cases. The measurement scale would be at the nominal level because the only assumption is that the categories are different. The mode would be public defenders, as it is the category with the largest number. It may also be referred to as the most popular measure.

When one category is defined as the **modal category**, the researcher may then provide a summary view of the type of case that is typical to the sample or population. Using the above example, the researcher could assume that in a typical criminal case a defendant is defended by a public defender. An advantage of using the mode is that it is relatively easy to determine. It can also be used with all scales of measurement. Unlike the median and the mean, many cases may involve two or more modes. If two modes occur, the data is described as bimodal. It is possible that some distributions will not exhibit a mode, for example, with a sample size of 100 items evenly distributed into 5 categories of 20 items each, there is no mode.

Median

The median may be defined as the middle score in a distribution. For ordinal scales, the median is the category in which the middle score lies. If on a recent criminal justice examination the scores were 95, 91, 90, 89, 83, 78, and 60, the median score would be 89. If the above scores were grouped by tens (90s, 80s, 70s, and 60s), the median group would be where the middle score lies, the 80s. The median in an even number of scores lies midway between the two middle numbers; for example, in a group consisting of 40, 36, 32, and 30, the median is 34.

The median assumes that the data is rank ordered in some manner. Therefore, the nominal scale cannot be used with the median. The median may be used with the ordinal, interval, and ratio scales of measurement. An advantage of the median is that it is relatively easy to determine: one half the scores are above it and one half are below it. In most cases, the median is a good representative of the central measure of tendency.

Mean

The **mean** is the arithmetic average of a group of data. It is calculated by multiplying each measurement by the number of times it occurs, adding the totals and dividing the sum by the number of items measured. The mathematical formula for the mean is:

$$M = \frac{\text{sum of X}}{N} \tag{3.1}$$

where M = mean, X = amount or quantity of each measurement, and N = total number of measurements. One of the major problems with using the mean is that it is affected by the presence of extreme scores. If extreme scores are present, the researcher may need to reconsider whether to use the mean as a measure of central tendency. For example, if examination grades were 94, 92, 88, 84, 83, and 0, the mean (73.5) would not provide a good measure of central tendency. The median (86) would be a better measure of central tendency.

Deciding which measure of central tendency to use should depend on the scales of measurement available, the shape of the distribution, and the stability of the measurement. Although the mode may be used with any of the scales of measurement, its use is normally considered with the nominal scale. The mean is an arithmetic average and applying it to data measured by the use of nominal or ordinal scales would be meaningless. The mean is normally used only with the ratio or interval scales of measurement.

Measures of Dispersion

While measures of central tendency provide descriptions of the typical, measures of dispersion tell us how typical the typical case is. Stated as a question, to what degree are the cases concentrated in the modal category? Measures of dispersion indicate the spread of the data in contrast to the measures of central tendency that indicate groupings of data. The general measures of dispersion include proportion, percentage, variation ratio, index of qualitative variation, range, variance, and standard deviation.

Proportion

Proportion is the most straightforward way to describe the proportion of cases that fall in the modal category. The modal category is the most frequent occurrence. The equation for determining proportion is

$$\text{Proportion} = \text{Ncat} \div \text{Ntot} \tag{3.2}$$

We take the number of cases in a category (Ncat) and divide it by the total number of cases (Ntot). The largest proportion in any project is 1.0, meaning that all the data are grouped in only one category. To determine proportion assume in a sample of 60 cases involving criminal defendants, 45 were defended by public defenders. What proportion of cases in the sample were defended by public defenders? The answer would be 45 divided by 60 or 0.75.

Percentage

Many times researchers will transform a proportion to a percentage because people are accustomed to dealing with percentages. The equation for determining percentage is:

$$(\text{Ncat} \div \text{Ntot})\ 100$$

Variation ratio

The variation ratio is based on the same logic as the proportion. It examines the extent to which cases are dispersed outside the modal category. The variation ratio is obtained by subtracting the proportion from 1. In the proportion example above, the answer was 0.75. The variation ratio is thus 1.00 – 0.75 = 0.25.

The proportion and variation ratio are primarily used for describing dispersion in nominal scale measurements. They may also be used for describing ordinal scale categories. The problem with using the proportion and variation ratio with ordinal scale measurements is that proportion and variation ratio are based on the mode, which does not take into account the positions of scores in a measure and thus may provide a misleading view of the data.

Index of qualitative variation

The **index of qualitative variation (IQV)** is one measure of dispersion that is not based on the mode, and can be used for both nominal and ordinal scales. The index is a comparison of the amount of variation in a sample to the total amount of variation that is possible based on the number of cases and categories in the study. Because the IQV is a standardized measure, the number of cases or categories can vary only between 0 and 100. An IQV of 0 means that all the cases are in one category. An IQV of 100 means that the cases are evenly dispersed across all the categories. The following equation is used to compute IQV:

$$\text{IQV} = \frac{\sum Nobs_i \ Nobs_j}{\sum N\exp_i \ N\exp_j} \times 100 \qquad (3.3)$$

Nobs represents the number of cases within a category. *Nexp* represents the number of cases that would be expected in a category if the measure were equally distributed across the categories. The summation symbol (Σ) indicates that the summing should be across products of distinct categories, not across cases. The subscripted *i* and *j* are examples of a shorthand method to indicate that we should multiply all the potential pairs of categories.

The example below illustrates how the equation works. In a sample of 20 defendants, 3 had no prior arrests, 4 had one prior arrest, 6 had two prior arrests, and 7 had three or more arrests. Because there are four categories of defendants, each expected category (*Nexp*) is 20 ÷ 4 or 5.

$$IQV = \frac{[(3 \times 4) + (3 \times 6) + (3 \times 7) + (4 \times 6) + (4 \times 7) + (6 \times 7)]}{[(5 \times 5) + (5 \times 5) + (5 \times 5) + (5 \times 5) + (5 \times 5) + (5 \times 5)]} \times 100$$

$$IQV = \frac{[(145)]}{[(150)]} \times 100 \tag{3.4}$$

$$IQV = 96.6667$$

The maximum IQV is 1.0. The IQV of 96.6667 in the above sample indicates that the cases in the sample are very dispersed among the categories in the measure.

Range

A common method for describing the spread of scores in interval or higher scales of measurement is the range between the highest and lowest scores. The range is the easiest measure of dispersion to compute; it is simply the distance between the highest and lowest scores. A problem with using a range is that a single score will greatly affect the range. The formula is: Range = high score − low score + 1. For example, if the scores on an examination are 90, 90, 89, 88, 87, 86, 84, 83, 78, 77, 71, and 0, the range would be the highest score (90) minus the lowest score (0) +1 or 91. The range is 91 (not 90) to include both the high and low scores.

To reduce the effect of extreme scores, the **interquartile range (IQR)** may be used. The IQR represents the range of the middle 50% of the scores or the distance between the highest 25% and the lowest 25%. Using the above examination scores, the range of the middle 50% (IQR) would be 88 − 78 = 10. The major advantage of the IQR is that it is less affected by a few extreme scores. The major disadvantage is that it is a narrow measure of dispersion, and thus may not give a representative presentation of dispersion of the data.

Variance

The variance is a measure of dispersion that examines how much the average score differs from the mean. The variance is calculated by adding the squared deviations of all scores from the mean and then

Sector	Number of Crime Calls	Deviation from Mean	Deviation Squared
1	21	21 – 30 = –9	81
2	19	19 – 30 = –11	121
3	34	34 – 30 = 4	16
4	1	1 – 30 = –29	841
5	71	71 – 30 = 41	1,681
6	31	31 – 30 = 1	1
7	31	31 – 30 = 1	1
8	31	31 – 30 = 1	1
		Total = 0 Σ = 2,743	
Variance = 2,743 ÷ N (number of sectors or 8) = 342.875			

Fig. 3.3 Analysis of crime calls for eight city sectors.

dividing the sum by the number of cases. This measure is used to reduce the instability of the range caused by extreme scores.

$$\text{Variance} = \frac{\sum (X_i - \bar{X})^2}{N} \tag{3.5}$$

To understand the above equation, let us use an example. A small city is divided into eight sectors. Figure 3.3 shows an analysis of the numbers of crime calls from each sector. To calculate variance:

Step 1: Determine the mean of the above data. X = 30.

Step 2: Subtract each score from the mean to get the deviation for each category.

Step 3: Square each deviation.

Step 4: Find the sums of the deviations squared.

Step 5: Divide the total by the number of categories.

After determining the variance, we have a statistic based on the deviations from the mean. Note that had we merely added the sums of the differences from the mean, the number would always be 0. To eliminate this problem, the differences were squared. Notice that the square of –9 becomes +81. The squaring solves one problem and creates another. The numbers obtained for the variance are generally larger than the actual units in the distributions examined. To solve this problem, the standard deviation is used.

Standard deviation

The standard deviation is a measure of dispersion based on the variance. It is calculated as the square root of the variance. Accordingly, it reduces the estimate of dispersion using methods similar to those employed to solve the problem of positive and negative differences from the mean. In our example from Figure 3.3, the variance was 342.875. Accordingly, the standard deviation is the square root of 342.875 or 18.52.

Mean deviation

The mean deviation also allows us to measure the dispersion in the interval scale by taking into account the deviation from the mean of each score, but using only the absolute value, i.e., ignoring the positive or negative signs. For example, in the earlier example involving crime calls, the deviation in Sector 1 would be considered 9 instead of –9. Adding the absolute numbers in column 3 (deviations from means) equals 98. Dividing 98 by the number of sectors (8) yields a mean deviation of 12.25.

data grouping

Although measures of the central tendency and dispersion describe the basic character of a variable, to present the array of data in an easily understood manner, it is necessary to group the variables. To accomplish this, we will consider ranked distribution, frequency distribution, cumulative frequency, and graphing techniques.

Ranked Distribution

A ranked distribution is created by simply rearranging or listing the data so that the highest number is at the top of the list and the lowest number at the bottom. After scores are ranked, it is easy to identify the highest and lowest numbers and the range. A glance at the ranking makes it easy to see that certain scores appear more often than others. In ranking a large number of scores, however, distribution is difficult to understand and interpret. To make the data arrangement of large numbers of scores more meaningful, we use frequency distribution to array the data.

Frequency Distribution

A frequency distribution shows the number of times each observation occurs when the values of a variable are arranged according to their magnitudes. To illustrate the grouping of data in a frequency distribution, consider a sample of 20 defendants and the numbers of their previous arrests. The prior arrests per defendant are listed in the order in which the records were examined: 4, 6, 3, 0, 2, 7, 2, 3, 6, 1, 4, 1, 2, 1, 3, 0, 5, 4, 3, and 8. Figure 3.4 shows a frequency distribution grouping of the data. Grouping data in a frequency distribution is normally the first step in presenting an array of data. For the most part, the grouping will be performed automatically by a computer.

In grouped frequency distribution, the raw data are combined into equal sized groups known as class intervals. To determine the appropriate number of class intervals needed to display data, compute the range: high score – low score + 1. The 1 must be added because both the high and low scores must be included in the range. For example, for a range of scores from 919 to 400, the range would be 919 – 400 + 1 = 520. The upper limit of this distribution is 919 and the lower limit is 400. If we need 10 intervals to display the data, we would then

Number of Prior Arrests	Frequency
0	2
1	4
2	3
3	4
4	3
5	1
6	2
7	1
8	1
Total (Σ)	20

Fig. 3.4 Prior arrests and frequencies.

divide the range (520) by the number of intervals (10). This would leave us with a class interval of 52. If the interval size is an odd number such as 25.8, it may be rounded off to the nearest whole number in most cases. We determined that the class interval should be 52. Each interval actually extends from 0.5 units below the lower apparent limit to 0.5 units above the upper apparent limit. For example, if one class interval is 520 to 572, the apparent upper and lower limits would be 520 and 572. The true upper and real lower limits would be 519.5 and 572.5.

The exact center of an interval is called its **midpoint**, usually designated as X. The midpoint is calculated by adding the lower limit and the upper limit and dividing by 2.

Cumulative Frequency

The frequency is the total number of scores that fall within a class interval. The **cumulative frequency** is the total number of scores that fall below the true upper limit of an interval. For example, expressing your examination score as a cumulative frequency of 91% means that 91% of the test scores were below your score.

Graphing Techniques

Frequency distributions are often displayed as graphs—pictorial presentations of relationships of variables. Graphs are excellent tools for displaying data. The types include histograms, pie charts, scatter plots, frequency polygons, and frequency and normal curves.

Histogram and bar graph

A **histogram** utilizes bars to indicate the frequency of occurrence of observations. A histogram is a bar graph that displays a frequency distribution of data (see Figure 3.5). It may be used with interval- or ratio-scaled variables. When used with an interval scale, the zero point is arbitrary. When used with a ratio scale, a true zero point is present. The scores and values may be presented in a pictorial form. In Figure 3.5, the bars represent each value. The heights of the bars indicate the number of attributes in each category; for example, the frequency distributions of prior arrests discussed earlier.

Pie chart

A **pie chart** has a circular shape and contains wedges indicating categories (Figure 3.6). The sizes of the wedges should be proportionate

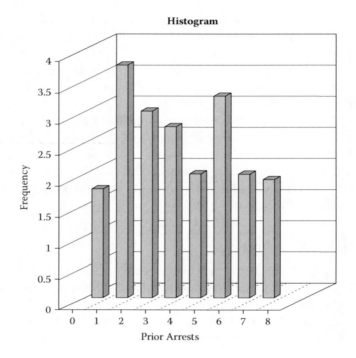

Fig. 3.5 Histogram.

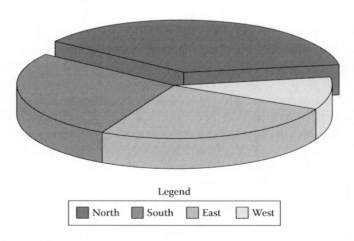

Fig. 3.6 Pie chart.

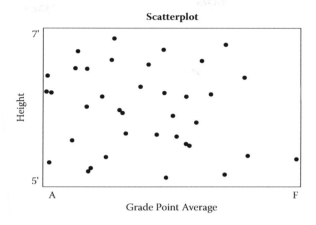

Fig. 3.7 Scatter plot.

to the sizes of the categories. To construct a pie chart, each category must be converted into a percentage. After a circle (the pie) is drawn on paper, it is divided into segments (wedges) representing the percentages of all the segments. Each segment should be clearly labeled.

Scatter plot

A **scatter plot** is a graph whose two axes are defined by two variables, and upon which a point is plotted for each subject in a sample according to its score on the two variables (Figure 3.7). A scatter plot is often used to demonstrate the correlation coefficient.

Frequency polygon

A **frequency polygon** consists of points on a graph connected by lines. The lines form a geometric polygon. The frequency polygon uses a single point rather than a bar to represent an interval on a graph. If you wish to compare two or more frequency distributions and the sizes of the distributions are the same, each distribution may be plotted on the same graph with a relative frequency polygon. The plotting of a relative frequency polygon is the same as plotting a frequency polygon, except that instead of using the frequencies, you use the relative frequencies and plot them as the midpoints of the intervals.

To convert a frequency to **relative frequency**—the proportion of scores from the distribution that fall within the limits of an interval—divide the frequency in the interval by the total number of scores in the distribution (N). For example, if an interval has 15 scores and the entire distribution totals 100 scores, the relative frequency for that interval is:

$$= \frac{\text{frequency}}{N} = \frac{15}{100} = 0.15 \qquad (3.6)$$

Frequency curve

The **frequency curve** is a form of graph in which the frequency distribution is arrayed in the form of a continuous line that traces a histogram (Figure 3.8). The most common types of frequency curves are the cumulative frequency curve, the normal curve, and the skewed curve. A **cumulative frequency curve** consists of a continuous line that traces a histogram in which bars in all the lower classes are stacked up in the adjacent higher class; it normally has a positive slope. The **normal curve** is bell-shaped. A skewed curve departs from symmetry and tails off at one end.

Normal curve

A normal curve is frequently used to describe the distribution of data. Abraham de Moivre, an eighteenth-century mathematician, developed the formula that permits a normal curve to be displayed as a bell-shaped curve. The normal curve is a theoretical model of a frequency polygon that is symmetrical and smooth. Generally, most data sets do not fit the perfectly symmetrical and smooth theoretical model of a normal curve, but most are close enough to allow use of the model as a descriptive device. The concept of the normal curve is also used in inferential statistics, as will be discussed later in this chapter. A curve that is not symmetrical but has one side stretched out longer than the other side is considered skewed. If its right side is longer than its left side, it is considered to be positively skewed. If the left side is longer, the curve is considered to be negatively skewed.

The common measure of dispersion used with the normal curve is the standard deviation. The symbol for the standard deviation of a population is the Greek lower case sigma (σ); a lower case a indicates a sample. As noted earlier, the standard deviation is the square root of the variance. Under the principles of the normal curve, approximately 68.26% of all scores will be located within 1 a (plus or minus) of the mean. Approximately 95.46% of all scores will be within 2 a of the mean. For example, if the average score on an exam is 80 and a = 8, 68% of the scores fell between 72 and 88 (1 a). In addition, 95% of the scores should be between 52 and 96 (2 σ).

When dealing with a normal curve, approximately 50% of the scores will be below the mean and 50% above it. Accordingly, when

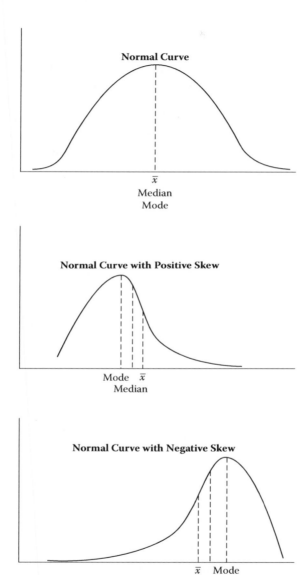

Fig. 3.8 Frequency curve.

it is stated that 68% of all scores will be within 1 σ of the mean, it is assumed that half (34%) will be above the mean and half (34%) below it. Another way of stating this is that approximately 34% of the scores will be within a + 1 σ and 34% will be within a − 1 σ of the mean. Notice that we used the qualifying words *about* and *approximately* because if the mean is vastly different from the median, the midpoint assumptions will be off to some degree.

The σ values below the mean are plotted to the left of the mean on the curve and are considered negative. Those above the mean are plotted to the right and are considered positive. The most useful characteristic of a normal curve is that it always includes a set number of cases between the mean and the points measured from the mean.

Not all scores will exhibit symmetrical distribution and normal shape. By using a simple equation, we can convert all normal distributions, regardless of their means or standard deviations, to a single standard normal distribution that may be used to find the exact location of any score. This is accomplished by converting actual scores to z-scores. A **z-score** represents the standard deviation units for the standard normal distribution. The standard normal distribution has a mean of 0 and a standard deviation of 1. The equation for determining the z-score of a sample is:

$$Z = \frac{X_i - X}{S} \tag{3.7}$$

The equation for converting a score in a population to a z-score is similar.

$$Z = \frac{X_i - \mu}{\sigma} \tag{3.8}$$

In the above equation, X represents the mean of a sample or the mean of a population; S represents the standard deviation of a sample; σ represents the standard deviation of a population; and X_i represents the score of interest, which, in this case, is the deviation from the mean. Here is the method for determining the z-score of an examination score. Suppose you score 86 on an examination. Assume that the standard deviation for the examination is 6 and the mean is 78. To determine the z-score for that sector, take the following steps:

Step 1: Subtract the score of interest (the score on which we are calculating the z-score) from the mean of the distribution. 86 – 78 = 8.

Step 2: Divide that score (8) by the standard deviation of the distribution (6) to determine the z-score. The result is a z-score of 1.33.

Step 3: Use a standardized table to identify the location of the z-score. Our z-score is equivalent to 0.4082. Because our score is a positive, we must add 0.50 to 0.4082, yielding a score of 0.9082, rounded to 0.91. This means that approximately 91% of the students made lower scores on the exam.

Correlation coefficient

The **correlation coefficient** is used to measure the degree and direction of a relationship between variables. It is a measure of the extent variables vary together. A perfect correlation is 1.0. This means that as one variable varies, the other is directly varied to the same degree. A scatter plot is used frequently to demonstrate the correlation coefficient of two variables. The vertical axis of the scatter plot reflects one variable and the horizontal axis reflects the other variable. A series of dots are then placed on the graph at the intersection of each location of the variable. The end result will show a scattering of dots. If there is a correlation, the dots will form an elongated pattern. The tighter the pattern, the greater the correlation.

inferential statistics

Descriptive statistics is concerned primarily with the display of data. A researcher uses inferential statistics to make inferences or predictions about a population based on information obtained from a sample. In inferential statistics, we are concerned primarily with the estimation and the testing of statistically based hypotheses. Tests of significance are used primarily as bases for inferences made about a population.

Probability Theory

Probability theory is based on the concept that events may be expected to move in the most probable direction. Using this concept, predictions about events are made and types of risks can be calculated. Professional gamblers utilize theories of probability. For example, in the blackjack card game, a player decides whether to take another card based on the chances that the extra card will benefit or hurt his hand.

A **binomial distribution** means that a probability distribution has only two possible outcomes; for example, a toss of a two-sided coin. A binomial formula is used to determine the probability that a given set of binomial events will occur in all possible arrangements. We refer to the events as independent when the occurrence of one event does not impact the occurrence of the other. For example, you toss the coin in the air and it lands on its head and then you toss it a second time. The first toss has no effect on the outcome of the second toss because there is still a 50–50 chance that the coin will land on its head. Accordingly, the two events are independent of each other. The arrangements are the different ways or specific ordering of events that result in a single outcome.

There is only one arrangement whereby you can toss a coin five times and it will land on heads all five times. If you are seeking to have the coin land on heads four out of five tries, five different arrangements can yield this result. The possibility of a two-sided coin landing on its head is one out of two. Accordingly, if the coin is tossed in the air 50 times, it should land on its head approximately 50% or 25 times. The laws of probability tell us that if the coin is tossed in the air 50 times, there is only one chance in 2,500 that it will land on heads all 50 times.

Where used in inferential statistics, **statistical significance** means that a test statistic is deemed statistically significant if it falls within the rejection region defined by the researcher. When this result is obtained, the difference studied is considered to have statistical significance. Statistical significance is not the same as substantive significance. Statistical significance means that certain sample differences would not normally occur frequently by chance if there were no differences in the populations. The concept of statistical significance will be discussed later in this chapter.

Often researchers place heavy emphasis on trends established by statistical concepts and assume causal relationships that may not exist. For example, the results of a Superbowl football game probably have no effect on the stock market. However, during the 20 years from 1966 to 1987, each year that a team from the original National Football League won the Superbowl, the New York Stock Exchange index rose for that year. Each year that a team from the original American Football League won, the index declined for that year. The single exception was 1984 when the Los Angeles Raiders from the AFL won, but the index rose only 1.3%.

The **confidence interval** is the interval of numbers within which the actual element or number is believed to lie. For example, a researcher predicts that candidate A will receive 53% of the votes cast in the next election with a confidence interval of 4%. This means that the researcher believes that candidate A will receive 49 to 57% of the vote. Normally the width of the confidence interval decreases as the sample size increases.

Multiplication Rule

The multiplication rule allows us to determine the probability that a certain event will occur during a series of events. If you toss the coin discussed earlier, it will land on its head or its tail. Accordingly, the probability that it will land on its head if 0.5 or 50%. What is the possibility that it will land on heads two consecutive times when fairly tossed? There are two events: two tosses. The odds that the coin will land on heads both times are the odds for each event multiplied by each other. Thus, the odds that it will land on heads twice in a row are 0.5 × 0.5 = 0.25 or 25%. The odds may also be expressed as 1/2 × 1/2 = 1/4.

What are the odds that the coin will land on heads three times in a row? The answer is 1/2 × 1/2 × 1/2 = 1/8. The use of the multiplication rule in the coin tossing examples assumed that each coin toss is independent of the next.

In a standard deck of 52 cards, what are your chances of drawing an ace of clubs on the first draw? One in 52. You draw a card that is not the ace of clubs, so you throw the card in a wastebasket. What are your chances of drawing an ace of clubs on the next draw? One in 51. The odds are lowered because the two drawings are not completely independent of each other (you did not return the first card to the deck). Had you returned it and shuffled the cards, your odds would again be 1 in 52. What are the odds of drawing two aces of any suit in your first two draws?

A normal deck of 52 cards contains 4 aces, so chances of drawing an ace on the first draw will be 4 in 52 or 1 in 13. If the first draw is an ace, what are the chances that your second draw will be an ace? The deck now contains only 51 cards, More importantly, only 3 aces remain, so your chances of drawing an ace drop to 3 in 51. To return to the original question, what are your chances of drawing two aces in a row? By multiplying the number of aces in a normal deck (4/52) by the number of aces remaining after one is removed (3/51), the calculation is: $4/52 \times 3/51 = 12/2652$ or $1/221$.

Logic of Statistical Inference Testing

The first step in statistical testing is to set up or develop a research question. To answer the research question, a researcher establishes a research hypothesis or proposed answer to the research question. The hypothesis should be formulated in such a manner that it can be directly examined by conducting research. Hypotheses are also statements suggesting relationships that researchers believe will help explain a certain phenomenon. Statistical testing in inferential statistics involves the testing of hypotheses.

The testing permits researchers to decide whether the observed differences between variables are so large that the differences justify the conclusions that the populations from which samples are taken are different. Frequently, researchers will construct a research hypothesis and also a null hypothesis that is the opposite of the research hypothesis. After a research hypothesis is formulated, the researcher normally makes the necessary assumptions, develops a null hypothesis, selects a sampling distribution and level of confidence, computes the test statistic, and then makes decisions based on the test.

Generally, the null hypothesis rather than the research hypothesis is actually tested. For example, if the research hypothesis states that a distinct difference exists between two populations, the null hypothesis states that there is no difference between the two sets of data. If testing rejects the null hypothesis, the researcher may conclude that a difference exists and thus establish the research hypothesis. Suppose he or she seeks to determine whether former boy scouts are less likely to be arrested than individuals who were never boy scouts. The research hypothesis may be that former boy scouts are less likely to be arrested for drug abuse than individuals who have never belonged to the boy scouts. The null hypothesis would be that there is no difference between the two populations.

The null hypothesis would be tested. Suppose it is rejected after being tested. Then the hypothesis that there is a difference would be accepted as true. If the differences are considered statistically significant, the researcher could conclude that the difference did not appear because of chance and that there is a difference in the two populations.

Statistical Significance

As noted earlier, statistical significance has a special meaning. It states the degree of probability that any association observed by research may have occurred by chance. When conducting tests, a researcher sets a level of confidence (alpha level) that he or she is willing to accept. If the researcher is willing to accept a probability not more than 1 out of 20 (0.05) that an association detected in the sample occurred by chance, the confidence (or alpha) level is 0.05.

The decision as to the level of significance that will be accepted has a bearing on the results of the research. There are no rules to follow. The decision is usually based on the degree of risk a researcher is willing to assume for a project. The level most generally used is 0.05. With large samples, many researchers use 0.01. In cases with fewer than 30 samples, some researchers use the 0.10 level. If similar research studies exist, the same levels may be used to achieve better comparisons of the results.

In testing a null hypothesis, there is always the possibility of rejecting a true null hypothesis; i.e., no difference. For example, a researcher is willing to accept the possibility of an error of 1 in 20 (0.05 level) by incorrectly rejecting the null hypothesis that there is no difference between two data elements. This is known as a Type I error. In this case, the possibility of a Type I error is 0.05 or 5%. In some cases, the alpha level is set at 0.01; this means that the researcher is taking the chance of wrongly rejecting a null hypothesis of no difference only 1 in 100 times (1%). In this situation, the possibility of a Type I error is also 0.01, or 1%.

A Type II error is inversely related to a Type I error. A Type II error is from failing to reject a false null hypothesis. For example, there is a difference in two data sets, but the researcher fails to reject the null "that there is no difference." If you decrease the possibility of making a Type I error, you increase the possibility of making a Type II error.

The major limitations of hypothesis testing are that the tests represent a function of four independent factors. Of these factors, only the first is beyond the control of the researcher. The four factors are:

- Size of observed differences
- Established alpha level
- Whether a one-tail or two-tail test is used
- Sample size

Determining Statistical Significance

Tests used to determine the statistical significance of associations between data collected include the chi-square test, the t-test, the normal curve, the Mann-Whitney U test, the runs test, z-scores, and the analysis of variance (ANOVA) test.

Chi-square test

One of the most popular and useful tests of association is the chi-square test. It can be used with parametric data that has been modified to discrete and non-parametric data. One advantage is that the chi-square test requires no assumptions regarding the shape of the distribution. It is a test for independence of two variables that have been organized in a bivariate table. A disadvantage is that the test may yield an erroneous assumption that there is no association with the data when the sample sizes are large.

The test is based on the concept that if two populations are similar, their samples will be similar. This concept is tested using a null hypothesis that there is no difference between the two populations. The test is conducted by first using the scores from one sample of one population and then making a prediction regarding the expected scores of the other sample. If the observed scores of the second sample are not similar to the expected scores, then the null hypothesis that there is no difference between the two will be rejected and it is stated that there is a significant difference between the two populations. The following assumptions are used:

- The data variables are or can be converted to non-parametric and discrete.
- The samples from each of the populations are representative of the populations.
- The proportions can be expressed in percentages and compared. The expressed data numbers are stated in the positive.
- A null hypothesis can be that there is no difference between the two populations. Accordingly, if there is no relationship between the two populations, then independence exists.
- The null hypothesis will be rejected if the calculated value is equal to or greater than the critical score determined from a chi-square table.
- The sample size must be large enough to ensure that 80% of the cells have values in excess of 5. Cells are individual classes of variables.

- The degree of freedom (df) used is the number of rows minus one multiplied by the number of columns minus one [df = (R − 1)(C − 1)].

For example, 99 murders occurred in a Midwestern city in one year. The city was divided into Sectors A, B, and C. Sector A is an area with no neighborhood social organizations, Sector B has a moderate number of neighborhood organizations, and Sector C has many neighborhood organizations. The research hypothesis is that there are differences in the murder rates for the sectors. The null hypothesis is that there are no differences. A look at the 99 murders shows that 45 occurred in Sector A, 34 in Sector B, and only 20 in Sector C. To determine the chi-square, we would use Equation 3.9. Because the null is that there is no difference, the expected frequency for each sector would be 33. Equation 3.9 shows the calculation:

$$\chi^2 = \sum \frac{(f_0 - f_e)^2}{fe} \tag{3.9}$$

where χ^2 represents chi-square, f_o represents observed frequency, and f_e represents the expected frequency. Thus,

$$\chi^2 = \frac{12^2}{33} + \frac{1^2}{33} + \frac{-13^2}{33} = 9.515$$

There are two degrees of freedom (three cells times one row minus one). We next take the 9.515 score to the Table for Critical Values of χ^2 (Appendix B) (www.itl.nist.gov/div898/handbook/eda/selection3/eda3674.htm) and check for the critical score at the 0.05 level. The critical value is 5.991. Since the chi-square score is greater than 5.991, we can reject the null that there are no differences in murder rates in the three sectors. Accordingly, the research hypothesis (there is a difference) is accepted.

t-test

In tests in which the researcher has samples from two different populations and is interested in determining whether the two populations differ on a specific variable, he or she may use the t-test, also known as the two-sample test. For example, a researcher wishes to know whether the percentage of murders involving the use of firearms differs in Houston and Chicago. The t-test will allow a comparison of the two populations. It assumes that the populations from which the samples were taken are normally distributed.

Using normal curve

The principles involving the normal curve discussed in the section on descriptive statistics may also be used to estimate probabilities. This is accomplished by assuming that the theoretical normal curve can also be a distribution of probabilities. In using this process, first a sample of the population is used to construct the curve and determine the standard deviation for the sample. The next step is using the curve and the standard deviation to determine the probabilities that the scores of the population will fall within certain ranges. Accordingly, using the probabilities of the curve, descriptive statements can be made about the data of the population.

Runs test

The runs test, like the Mann-Whitney U test (see next section), involves the pooling and ranking of scores from two samples. The runs test does not assume any shape or distribution of the populations. After samples are taken from each population, the samples are pooled and an overall ranking is established. Next, the number of runs (sequences of scores from one population) are counted. For example, if rankings 1, 2, 3, 7, 9, and 11 are from sample A and rankings 4, 5, 6, 8,10, and 12 are from sample B, there are eight runs (1–3, 4–6, 7, 8, 9, 10, 11, and 12) from 12 data elements. The fewer the runs, the greater the probability that the samples are different. In the above example, it appears that the samples are very similar.

Mann-Whitney U test

Most tests for the significance of differences assume that the population distribution is similar to the theoretical (bell-shaped) curve. The Mann-Whitney U test is a non-parametric or distribution-free test and does not make any assumptions about the shape or distribution of the population. It does not require that the interval ratio scales of measurement be used, as do most other tests.

The test is based on the ranking of the scores in the samples combined. All scores in both samples are pooled and ranked from highest to lowest. Next, the rankings of each sample are totaled and compared. If the two samples are similar, the totals of each should be about the same. The larger the difference, the more likely that the null of no difference will be rejected.

z-scores

The scores located in the critical area of an array are called **z-scores**. The critical region is the area under a sampling distribution, where it is unlikely that the differences between the two or more elements compared occurred by chance. Accordingly, when a z-score falls into the critical region, the null hypothesis that there is no difference between the two or more data elements compared is rejected, with the conclusion that the populations are different.

In many cases, the researcher may be interested only in whether the samples are different in only one direction. In these cases, the researcher uses a one-tail test and considers only that part of the theoretical curve in the direction of the test. For example, if you wanted to know whether managers with college degrees perform better than individuals without college degrees, a one-tail (one direction) test would be used. If, however, you wanted to know whether there is a difference between managers who are college graduates and those who are not, a two-tail test would be used. In the latter case, you are not trying to determine whether one group is better than the other, but whether the two groups are different positively or negatively (in two directions).

ANOVA

The analysis of variance (ANOVA) test is used to determine whether the means of three or more populations are equal to each other. It is accomplished by testing the null hypothesis that there are no differences in the means of the three or more populations. This test is an extension of the test for the significance of the difference in the sample means.

---

summary

- Statistics involves the methods for designing and conducting research studies, describing the data collected, and making decisions based on that data. In one sense, statistics is a descriptive language.

- Statistics is used to analyze and describe the data collected. Its role is to clarify and not to confuse. It is a research tool to answer questions. Statistics is also used to calculate the relative accuracy of measurements used. The two basic types of statistics are descriptive and inferential.

- Descriptive statistics is a method for presenting quantitative descriptions in a manageable form. It is used to describe data so that readers can readily understand it.
- Inferential statistics is the process of inferring characteristics about a population from the data variables observed in a sample.
- In dealing with descriptive statistics, we are generally concerned with two types of statistics: measures of central tendency and measures of dispersion. Measures of central tendency are measures of typicality. They describe the average case.
- The three basic measures of central tendency are the mode, the median, and the mean. Using three basic measures, a researcher can determine and describe the central tendencies of data.
- Although measures of central tendency provide a description of the typical, measures of dispersion show how typical a typical case is. Measures of dispersion indicate the spread of data, in contrast to the measures of central tendency that indicate groupings of data.
- With inferential statistics, the researcher attempts to make inferences or predictions about a population based on information obtained from a sample. Tests of significance are used primarily as bases for inferences about a population.

terminology

Descriptive statistics

Inferential statistics

Outliers

Population

Sample

Multivariate statistics

Raw data

Discrete data

Continuous data

Assumption

Correlation

Independence

Bivariate table

Univariate table

Non-parametric test

Median

Range

Mode

Deviation from mean

Least squares property

Skewed distribution

Variable

Coefficient of relative variation

Index of qualitative variation

Mean deviation

Standard deviation

Variance

Variation ratio

Frequency distribution

Histogram

Mean

Normal curve

Standard deviation unit

Standard normative distribution

Central tendency

Modal category

Proportion

Index of qualitative variance (IQV)

Interquartile range (IQR)

Midpoint

Cumulative frequency

Bar graph

Pie chart

Scatter plot

Relative frequency

Frequency curve

Correlation coefficient

Binomial distribution

Statistical significance

Confidence interval

z-score

t-test

Chi-square

analysis of variance (ANOVA)

discussion points

1. Why does a researcher need to use statistics?
2. Differentiate between inferential and descriptive statistics.
3. Why is it necessary in inferential statistics to use an unbiased sample?
4. What are the measures of the central tendency of data?
5. What are the measures of dispersion of data?
6. What is meant by the statement that the data curve is skewed to the left?
7. Why are z-scores important in inferential statistics?
8. If an average score on an exam is 75 and the standard deviation is 4, what percentage of the scores falls within the range of 71 to 79? What percent falls above 79?

endnotes

1. M. W. Vernoy and J. A. Vernoy. *Behavioral Statistics in Action.* Belmont, CA: Wadsworth, 1992, p. 3.
2. E. Babble. *The Practice of Social Research*, 6th ed. Belmont, CA: Wadsworth, 1992, p. 430.
3. D. Weisburd. *Statistics in Criminal Justice.* St. Paul, MN: West Publishing, 1997, p. 8.

4. A. J. Reiss, Jr. A systematic social observation of social phenomena. In *Sociological Methodology*, H. Costner, Ed. San Francisco:
Jossey Bass, 1971, p. 3.

measures, validity, and reliability

introduction

Measurement is a tool of research. An old adage states, "If it exists, it is measurable." Validity asks, "Does the study really say what I think it says?" The reliability question is, "Will the study yield the same results each time the study is repeated?"

measurement

Measurement is the process of limiting data of any phenomenon so that the data may be examined mathematically according to an acceptable qualitative or quantitative standard. The word *measure* originally meant "to restrain or limit in quantity." The concept of setting a limit or restraining the data is present in all ideas of measurement. Measurement erects a barrier between data. For example, we observe that the distance from one goal line on a football field to the other goal line is a long way. Suppose we measure the distance in yards and discover that the distance between the 2 goal lines is 100 yards. Each yard is a set distance and is governed by a numerical restraint. The statement that the ball is located on the 48-yard line from the visitor's goal sets a limitation or restraint on the location of the ball. The statement that the total distance is 100 yards also sets limitations or restraints on the distance.

What can we measure? Researchers will tell you that if an object exists, it can be measured; and the statement includes intangibles. For a test of this proposition, ask one of your colleagues to name a phenomenon that cannot be measured. Then conceptualize how that phenomenon may be measured. During this exercise, you will note that although everything can be measured, some things can be measured with more precision than others. For example, the length of the football field can be measured with more precision than the degree of prejudice in your community. As a general rule, precise measurements, if attainable, are superior to imprecise ones.

Often, however, students confuse precision with accuracy. Describing someone as 42 years old is more precise than saying he is in his 40s. Suppose, however, that the person is 49 years old. Describing him as being in his 40s is more accurate than the more precise statement that he is 42 years old. Measurements start with distinguishing one phenomenon from another. The distinguishing process is called **classification**, and it implies that we can place objects or people in clearly defined categories. Scientific measurements require systematic criteria for determining what each category represents and also determining its boundaries.

To compare data to other data, they must first be measured at some level or scale. Levels or scales of measurements are sets of assumptions about the relationship of data to other data. The four most common scales of measurements are **nominal**, **ordinal**, **interval**, and **ratio**. The nominal scale is the weakest level and nominal scale measures simply differentiate one phenomenon from another. There is no assumption that the elements are greater or lesser than other elements. For example, each basketball player wears a number on his jersey. One player wears an 18 on his jersey and another wears a 25. This does not indicate that 18 is a better or worse player than 25; it only indicates that they are different players. Nominal scale measures are common in criminal justice research. For example, we attempt to determine whether individuals are offenders or non-offenders. Nominal measures provide us with limited knowledge about the phenomenon under study and are thus considered the lowest scale or level of measurement.

While the nominal scale assumes that categories are different, the ordinal scale assumes that the categories have a clear order. The assumption that categories are clearly ordered allows researchers to rank events in order of seriousness—and not simply categorize them as different. At the ordinal level, the data are rank-ordered according to some quality or quantity. For example, with an ordinal scale, a researcher could rank crimes by the amount of damage or personal harm involved. A researcher using the ordinal scale could ask respondents whether they were afraid to go outside their homes at night because of crime, then ask, "Are you very concerned, quite concerned, mildly concerned, a little concerned, or not at all concerned?"

The **interval scale** of measurement assumes that the categories are different and can be rank-ordered and also that the distance from one category or number to another has some meaning. For example, Offender A has one prior arrest and Offender B has three prior arrests. With the interval scale, we can that B has a more serious arrest history than A and also that his history is three times more serious. This additional information provides a whole range of new possibilities for describing and analyzing research findings.

The **ratio scale** is the highest scale of measurement. To express a measurement at the ratio level, not only must the categories be different and capable of being rank-ordered, but the distance between the categories must have meaning and the categories must also be capable of being compared to other categories via a ratio. For example, if an individual is speeding in a school zone at 40 miles per hour and another speeder is going 80 miles per hour, the latter driver is going twice as fast as the former.

Although ratio scales represent the highest level of measurement, in criminal justice research most statistical presentations will not require more than the interval level scale. However, if a statistic is appropriate for an interval scale, you may generally assume that it is also appropriate for a ratio scale. In analysis and reporting of research results, the ratio and interval level scales are generally preferred over the lower levels of measurement because they take into account more information.

variables

Variables are continuous or discrete. **Continuous variables** have infinite values, such as measurements of tire tracks. If the intervals of measurement are made smaller, an indefinite number of measurements becomes possible. If the interval spaces are larger, the number of measurements will be smaller. Continuous variables include age, height, weight, and time. For example, you can measure time in seconds or in years. **Discrete variables** have only a definite number of values. For example, gender is a discrete variable: a student is a female or a male. Figure 4.1 illustrates measurement scales and variables.

Continuous Measurement	*Ratio:* Continuous measurement scale with equal-appearing intervals and presence of absolute zero point *Interval:* Continuous measurement scale with equal-appearing intervals
Discrete Measurement	*Ordinal:* Measurement with implied rank order from one category to next *Nominal:* Categories of measurements that are different

Fig. 4.1 Comparison of measurement scales.

indexes and scales

Indexes and scales are data reduction devices used for data analysis. They are based on the concept of simultaneously considering all the particular responses in a situation and summarizing the responses.

Indexes

An **index** is a composite measure that summarizes several specific observations. It is constructed through the assignment of scores to individual attributes. An index may also be defined as a measure of the number of attributes an item or person possesses that can be counted as part of the same variable. To construct an index, you select items on the basis of their face validity. Thus, if it looks good, you use it. An index does not rate how important the items are relative to each other and no partial credit is given. For example, serious crimes reported in the Uniform Crime Report (UCR) are indexed or assigned to one of eight categories. There is no indication that one index is more important than any other and a crime must fit in one of the categories, not partially in one and partially in another.

Scales

Scales and indexes are ordinal measures of variables. They both attempt to rank-order units of analysis in terms of specific variables such as prejudice and socioeconomic status. Scales and indexes are composite measures of variables; i.e., measurements based on more than one data item. A **scale** differs from an index by taking advantage of any intensity structure that may exist among the individual items. For example, a scale, unlike an index, allows a person

Index	Scale

Check all states that you have visited:
California
Texas
Virginia
Ohio
New York
[etc.]
	Do you feel that California is a good
	  state to live in?
	[Enter your score based on 1 to 5
	  scale below.]
	5 = highly agree
	4 = agree
	3 = no opinion
	2 = dislike
	1 = greatly dislike

Fig. 4.2 Relationship of indexes and scales.

to indicate the strength of his choice; e.g., he may strongly agree or strongly disagree. As noted earlier, indexes are constructed through simple accumulation of scores assigned to individual attributes. A scale, however, is constructed through the assignment of scores to patterns of attributes. Figure 4.2 illustrates the difference between an index and a scale.

Scaling is a branch of measurement that involves the construction of an instrument that associates qualitative constructs with quantitative metric units. It is an effort to measure "unmeasurable" constructs such as prejudice and self-esteem. Scales are generally divided into two broad categories: unidimensional and multidimensional. At least 100 scaling techniques exist but this chapter covers only 3 of the most popular. Unidimensional scaling was developed in the first half of the twentieth century. Unidimensional items measure the same dimension of the same phenomenon. Multidimensional scales, developed in the 1950s and 1960s, measure several dimensions using various items. They rely on concept mapping to display their data.

Unlike indexes, scales are used to measure intensity. Arbitrary scales are developed by the researcher and are based primarily upon face validity; i.e., the scale appears to measure what the researcher intends to measure. Scales are intended to measure relative degrees of a concept. For example, in using arbitrary scales to measure success in life, you would start with ordinal or interval scales of phenomena that lend themselves to accepted measurements. We could arbitrarily accept the attributes of income level, education, and occupation to determine whether certain individuals are successes in life, assign a value within each attribute, and use the total score to measure success. Figure 4.3 illustrates an arbitrary scale.

We can use the scale to compare individuals. For example, if Joe had a total of 15 points from measuring the three attributes, the

Annual Income	Education	Occupation
Under $25,000 = 1	Grade school or less = 1	Unskilled labor = 1
$25,000 to $40,000 = 2	High school = 2	Skilled labor = 2
$40,001 to $50,000 = 3	Some college = 3	Service = 3
$50,001 to $75,000 = 4	College degree = 4	Professional = 4
Over $75,000 = 5	Graduate degree = 5	High professional = 5

Fig. 4.3 Arbitrary scale showing relationship of annual income, education, and occupation.

researcher could consider him a greater success in life than Tom who scored a total of only 10. [Note: As the example indicates, an arbitrary scale is subject to attack as not being a true measure of the objective; i.e., success in life.]

Attitude scales

The three most popular types of attitudinal scales commonly used in criminology and criminal justice research are the Thurstone, Likert, and Guttman scales.

Thurstone scale—Thurstone developed the first types of attitude scales. He actually invented three different methods for developing a unidimensional scale: (1) the method of equal-appearing intervals, (2) the method of successive intervals, and (3) the most popular method of paired comparisons. His scales represent attempts to develop a format for generating groups of indicators of a variable that have at least an empirical structure among them. The method of paired comparisons is the easiest to implement. Each judge is required to sort the attributes measured into a predetermined number of categories so that the intervals between them are subjectively equal.

Thurstone scaling is a five-step process. First, the researcher composes a large number of statements that are favorable or unfavorable to the subject of the scale. For example, a researcher assessing the contributions of Eric Holder as a U.S. Attorney General could state that, "Holder accomplished a lot of good as attorney general." A group of similar value statements would be constructed regarding performance. Next, a group of judges, generally not less than 50, would be asked to sort the statements subjectively into ordinal scales. The researcher then rates each statement by giving it a score based on the position each judge gave the statement, and computes the average. For example, the lowest score (perhaps 1) would be assigned to the weakest indicator and the highest score to the strongest indicator. Intermediate scores would be assigned to indicators between the two extremes, then a number of ranks would be established to represent each gradation of intensity of feeling about the statement. The researcher would next test the relevance of the items by computation and end up with a scale of 15 to 20 statements about Holder's performance that could be used. Using this procedure, the weak questions or questions that produce vastly conflicting answers are disregarded when selecting the statements to use.

Likert scale—These scales are the most commonly used for conducting attitudinal research. They are named after their developer, Rensis Likert. The scales consist of a simple summation of (usually) a five-point bipolar response ranging from strongly agree to strongly disagree. The scale is an adaptation of the Machiavellian scale. [Machiavellianism is a manipulative orientation toward others.] A number of items are selected. Respondents are asked to answer each item using a five-point scale (strongly agree, agree, no opinion, disagree, and strongly disagree). The total score for each respondent is the simple summation of all items. Items that lack variability or fail to distinguish between high and low scores are usually eliminated from the final scale. Items used in the final index are scored and used for the analysis.

Likert stated that the number of choices used is an important issue. His original paper noted that if five alternatives are used, it is necessary to assign values from 1 to 5, with 3 assigned to the undecided position. Likert also stated that the number of choices should be left to the tastes of individual researchers.[1] In actual practice, researchers often determine the number arbitrarily according to personal taste or convention.

Guttman scale—Also known as scalogram analysis or cumulative scaling, Guttman scaling establishes a one-dimensional continuum for a concept to be measured. The Guttman scaling technique is very popular with survey researchers. Louis Guttman developed the technique based on the facts that (1) some items under consideration may be harder indicators of a variable than others and (2) respondents who accept a given hard indicator will also accept the easier items. A large number of statements are composed and evaluated by a researcher and submitted to a large number of judges for sorting into categories (usually 11). The statements (with Likert-type options) are administered to a large group of subjects. The results are analyzed, nondiscriminating statements are removed, and a scale is constructed using the remaining statements. The important

Number of Respondents in Test Sample	Item 2	Item 5	Item 3	Item 6	Item 11	Item 14
8	Y	Y	Y	Y	Y	Y
13	Y	Y	Y	Y	Y	Y
6	Y	Y	Y	Y	Y	N
9	Y	Y	Y	N	N	N
14	Y	Y	N	N	N	N
15	Y	N	N	N	N	N

Fig. 4.4 Matrix constructed from series of statements.

part of Guttman scaling is the analysis. For example, we construct a series of statements on the value of probation and a matrix is constructed as illustrated in Figure 4.4. The matrix was sorted so that respondents who agree with more statements are listed at the top and those who agreed with fewer statements are listed at the bottom. Next, the items were arranged so that those with more agreements (Y) were listed to the left and those with fewer agreements were listed to the right.

Although the cumulativeness of the scale is not perfect, if respondents agreed with item 5, they always agreed with item 2. The above chart can help a researcher estimate a scale score value for each item. This scale score is then used in the final calculation of a respondent's score. In our example, item 2 would have the highest score and item 14 the lowest. The final scale would consist of a number of responses selected from the original questions about the value of probation. The respondents would be asked to place a check next to each statement with which they agree. Each statement will have an assigned value estimated as the result of an analysis of the matrix. The responses will then be scored by adding the point value of each statement selected.

Scale construction

Researchers have often debated the choices of scale construction and the number of scale choices used. Another issue is the use of equal intervals when placing choices on a scale. Many contend that unless the equality of the intervals can be experimentally verified, scale data may be treated only as ordinal and a measurement error is introduced if used as interval data. How many choices should be used in constructing a scale? Most researchers agree that increasing the number of choices generally increases an instrument's reliability. Several studies suggest that the use of a Likert scale with seven points according to the distances generates data that can be used as interval data with a lower measurement error and correspondingly higher precision as compared to five-point equal interval scales. These studies also conclude that placement of the seven points on the scale produces surprisingly symmetrical but not equal distances.[2]

---

validity and reliability

Error is present in every research project; a careful look at a research project will reveal limitations and possible areas of errors. *Error* is another word for invalidity. For a study to be accurate to an acceptable level, its findings must be reliable and valid. Both factors must be considered in planning any research project. A project lacking or suspect in either area will be a failure. Although the terms **validity** and **reliability** may convey similar meanings to most people, researchers see a vast difference between the two terms. In research, validity refers to the effectiveness of the data measurements based on the question: "What does the test measure and how well does it measure it?" Reliability deals with the accuracy of data measurements. A measurement that yields the same results repeatedly is reliable. The purpose of reliability safeguards is to ensure that remeasuring the same research data will yield the same results.

- Reliability always follows validity.
- If your research findings are valid, then they will also be reliable.
- If your research findings are reliable, you cannot assume that they are valid.

Validity

A validity question is: "Does the study really say what I think it says?" Another way of stating the question is: "Does my measuring instrument in fact measure what it claims to measure and is it an accurate and true measure of the phenomenon under study?" Researchers are worried about several types of validity as briefly described below.

Internal validity is defined as freedom from bias in forming conclusions from data. It seeks to ascertain that the changes in the dependent variable result from the influence of the independent variable rather than from the research design.

External validity is concerned with the generalizability of conclusions reached through observation of a sample to a population; i.e., whether the conclusions drawn from a sample can be generalized to other cases.

Face validity examines whether a measuring instrument or a research appears, at face value, to measure what the researcher intended to measure. In determining face validity, a researcher must depend on his or her judgment rather than empirical grounds. Does the study appear to be a reasonable attempt to measure the point in question? Earl Babbie said that we should ask whether it jibes with our common agreements and our individual mental images associated with a particular concept.[3]

Content validity is concerned with the issue of whether a measure covers the range of meanings included in the concept. It refers to the accuracy with which an instrument measures the factors or situations under study; i.e., how accurately the instrument elicits the information sought. Content validity is often equated with face validity.

Construct validity is measured by external criteria based on logical relationships among variables. *Construct* as used in this context refers to any concept that cannot be directly observed or isolated, such as prejudice or self-esteem. Construct validity is interested in the degree to which the construct is actually measured.

Pragmatic validity takes a practical approach and asks: "Does it work?" The two basic types are concurrent validity and predictive validity. Concurrent validity is interested in whether the measure used helps to gauge the present characteristics of the point in question. Predictive validity attempts to access how accurate the measure is for predicting future results. Predictive validity, also known as criterion-related validity, is based on an external criterion. For example, the validity of a college admissions examination as a predictor of a student's ability to complete college-level work successfully may be determined by the relationship between the grades on the admissions exam and the later grade point averages of the student in college.

Triangulation

Each research method has particular strengths and weaknesses. There is the danger that the research findings will reflect, at least in part, the method of inquiry. Accordingly, if possible, a research design should use more than one method to study the issues. **Triangulation** (also known as convergent validity) involves the use of multiple methods to measure the same phenomenon. The use of different measures to measure the same phenomenon should produce similar results (triangulation). Triangulation is the best method for assessing validity.

Reliability

Reliability is concerned with the precision of the measurement instrument; reliability equals the exactness of the measure. A useful reliability question is: "Will the study yield the same results each time it is repeated?" A quantity of seized marijuana is weighed on the laboratory scales and found to weigh 12 kilograms. If the scales are reliable, the same amount of marijuana weighed on the same scales should again weigh 12 kilograms. If same amount shows a different weight, the scales are not reliable.

---

summary

- Most researchers contend that, "If it exists, it can be measured."
- Measurement is the process of limiting data.
- Precision is not the same as accuracy. An item can be stated with precision and still be inaccurate.
- Before data may be compared, it must be measured at some level.
- The four common measurement scales are nominal, ordinal, interval, and ratio. The nominal scale simply distinguishes the items as different. The ordinal scale assumes that there is a rank order to the data. The interval scale assumes that the distance from one category to another has some meaning. The ratio is the highest level of measurement. It assumes that items may be compared to others as a ratio.
- Variables are continuous or discrete.
- Indexes and scales are used for data analysis; both are data-reduction devices.
- Scaling is a branch of measurement that involves the construction of an instrument that associates qualitative constructs

with quantitative metric units. Scales, unlike indexes, are used to measure the intensity of an item.

- The three most popular attitudinal scales are Thurstone, Likert, and Guttman.
- Validity is concerned with the question, "Does my measuring instrument in fact measure what it claims to measure?"
- Reliability is concerned with the precision of the measurement instrument.

terminology

Measurement
Classification
Nominal scale
Ordinal scale
Interval scale
Ratio scale
Continuous variable
Discrete variable
Index
Scale
Thurstone scale
Likert scale
Guttman scale
Triangulation
Reliability

discussion points

1. How does measuring data limit it?
2. List the four levels of measurements and explain each.
3. What is the difference between face validity and external validity?
4. Describe why researchers are concerned about reliability.

5. How can a measuring instrument be reliable and not valid?

6. Describe the importance of measurements to a researcher.

7. How do scales and indexes differ? How are they similar?

endnotes

1. M. Matell and J. Jacoby. Is there an optimal number of alternatives for Likert items? *Journal of Applied Psychology* 56(6); 506–509, 1972.

2. J. Munishi. A method for constructing Likert scales (unpublished paper), 1990.

3. E. Babbie. *The Practice of Social Research*, 6th ed. Belmont, CA: Wadsworth Publishing, 1992.

analytical and experimental research

This chapter discusses both analytical and experimental research designs. Analytical research design is generally appropriate for data that are quantitative and need statistical assistance to extract their meaning. Analytical research depends largely on statistical investigation of the collected data. Experimental research design is appropriate for data derived from an experimental control situation utilizing two separate groups or a single group from which data is gathered at different times.

analytical research

The **analytical research** design is also known as quantitative research or analytical survey study. It relies heavily on statistical measures to ascertain meanings and display data. The data is analyzed so that researchers may infer meanings from it. Analytical research is concerned primarily with problems of estimation and with testing statistically based hypotheses.

Analytical research is based on inferential statistics. As discussed in Chapter 3, in inferential statistics, characteristics about a population are inferred from analysis of the similar characteristics of a segment (sample) of that population. The result is an estimation type of inference. Inferences may also be made regarding future events or conditions—often referred to as prediction inferences. The Research in Action box describes an example of analytical research.

RESEARCH IN ACTION 2: TEMPORAL PATTERNS OF CRIMINAL HOMICIDE IN SAN FRANCISCO*

The purpose of this section was to test Hypotheses 4, 5, 6, 7, and 8, which deal with the temporal patterns of victim involvement in criminal homicides. The temporal aspects of crime—the month of the year, day of the week, hour of the day—have been studied throughout the last two centuries. One popular thesis is that violent crimes against the person are more prevalent in warm weather, while crimes against property are more prevalent in cold weather. This theory is labeled the *thermic law of delinquency*. Lombroso, after a survey of crime, reached a similar conclusion and found that crimes against the person are more numerous in summer than in winter. He considered this phenomenon an "influence of nature." Wolfgang found that the peak months for murder in Philadelphia were July and December. He concluded that the "positive relationship between temperature changes and variation in the number of criminal homicides is not established." Wolfgang noted that as the two peak months for criminal homicide were also the months when people are more likely to take vacations and have holidays and leisure time, i.e., July and December, the increased criminal homicide rate may be the result of increased leisure time.

The geographic locations of the above studies (France, England, and the city of Philadelphia) are noted for cold winters, whereas the mean temperature in San Francisco is 65°F and the average fluctuation is only 5°. If the difference in homicide rates is the result of the influence of nature, then in San Francisco, where the temperatures are fairly constant, the rate of homicide would be expected to be uniform throughout the year. On the other hand, if the increase is a direct result of the relative index of available leisure time, as concluded by Wolfgang, the rate should increase in the months in which more leisure time is available.

The lowest monthly total for criminal homicides for the combined 3 years considered by the study was June, with a total of 17. The highest combined month was September, with a total of 28. Table 5.1 shows a breakdown of the criminal homicides by

* Excerpted from PhD dissertation of Cliff Roberson; citations omitted.

season in San Francisco: spring, 62; summer, 67; fall, 78; and winter, 80.

From a review of the above data, and on the basis of the chi-square test reported in Table 5.1 for San Francisco during the time period covered by the study, there was no significant association between the ... seasons of the year and the rate of criminal homicides. Thus, Null Hypothesis 5 was not rejected. [Hypothesis 5: There is no significant association between the rate of criminal homicide and the seasons of the year.]

TABLE 5.1: CHI-SQUARE TEST OF ASSOCIATION BETWEEN CRIMINAL HOMICIDE RATES AND SEASONS, SAN FRANCISCO, 1971–1973

Season	Observed	Expected[a]	$(O - E)^2/_E$
Spring	62	72	1.39
Summer	67	72	0.35
Fall	78	72	0.50
Winter	80	72	0.89

Note: Observed = actual number of cases per season. Expected = theoretical equal distribution of total number. Level of confidence (0.05) with three degrees of freedom = 7.81 5.

[a] Error due to rounding.

Role of Statistics in Analytical Research

The tools used in analytical research include many of the statistical tools discussed in Chapter 3. Those tools include the normal curve (a general representation of the distribution patterns generally inherent in populations), hypothesis testing, standard deviation, and correlation techniques. (Note: Not all conclusions made as the result of analytical testing are dependent on the results of statistical tests.) Statistics is a tool and its functions can be reduced to four basic roles:

- **Location of center of data.** The best prediction of when or where something will occur is at the center of the array. For example, if the average response time of the team being measured is at the 50-minute mark, then the best prediction of the response time of the next team to measure will be at the 50-minute mark.

- **Determination of diversification of data.** The more widely the data are diversified, the less likely any fixed-point predictions about them will be accurate. For example, if the response times of the sample teams varied only slightly from the 50-minute mark, the prediction of 50 minutes for the response time of the next team will likely be more accurate than if the response times of the sample varied widely from 10 to 180 minutes.

- **Determination of how closely or distantly related certain data characteristics are.** For example, if there is a close relationship between two or more characteristics, the probability of predicting the presence or absence of a characteristic may be increased. If we conduct a study and determine a close relationship between academic success and noninvolvement in juvenile delinquency, we could probably conclude also that honor-roll students are less likely to be involved in juvenile delinquency than students who are failing.

- **Statistics should help us to determine the probability that (1) any conclusions reached regarding the correlation of certain characteristics were the results of mere chance or (2) they were influenced by some other factor.** Accordingly, in the last example, statistics could help us establish whether the results were caused by mere chance or whether there is some relationship between academic success and noninvolvement in juvenile delinquency.

Developing Analytical Research Projects

The first steps, as in all research projects, are defining the problem and then analyzing whether the problem is appropriate for an analytical research project. Next, should be a review of the literature to find related research projects and determine how they relate to your project. The questions below should be answered before the design of the project is completed:

- What is the goal of the research?
- What are the research hypotheses?
- What null hypotheses will be used, if any?
- How will the hypotheses be tested?
- What data are needed to test the hypotheses?

- What data collection instruments will be needed?
- Is the data collection plan feasible?
- How will the plan be pre-tested?
- After the data is collected, who will analyze and evaluate the data?
- What types of reports will be made at the conclusion of the project?

Hypothesis Testing

Analytical research design involves the use of hypothesis testing. One common problem is the failure of researchers to realize that *hypothesis* has two different meanings. First, as used in research design, hypotheses state the research problems. In this context, research hypotheses refer to tentative guesses or conclusions about a certain phenomenon that the researcher wants to establish or verify.

The second meaning of hypotheses concerns statements tested by statistical techniques. Statistically based hypotheses are narrow and are capable of being tested by quantitative data. The general method of testing statistically based hypotheses is by using null hypotheses. A **null hypothesis** postulates that there is no significant difference between the phenomena being compared. As used in this context, *significant* has a special meaning. As noted in Chapter 3, when analytical researchers use *significant,* it refers to the level of association that has been tested and the results indicate that the possibility of the difference occurring by mere chance or sampling error is less than a given level, normally 0.05, or 5%.

Common Errors

Common errors that occur during analytical research projects include:

- The failure to develop testable and appropriate hypotheses.
- Failing to use a sample of sufficient size.
- The use of inappropriate statistical tests.
- Failing to collect reliable data.
- Forming conclusions and recommendations that are not supported by data analysis.
- Overstating the importance of small differences in data variables.

- Using only one test when others are available and would contribute to the overall validity of the study.
- Using the "shotgun" approach to research and indiscriminately using data from various sources.
- Basing judgments on hasty and unwarranted conclusions.

experimental research

Experimental research involves the conduct of experiments to answer research questions. Experimental research design is also known as the cause-and-effect method, the **pre-test and post-test control group** design, and the laboratory method. The experimental design deals with the phenomena of **cause and effect**. Two matched groups are used: one is considered the **control group** and the other the **experimental group**. After an assessment to establish comparability, an independent variable is introduced to the experimental group. In the classic experimental research design, at least two groups have identical characteristics, values, and status. Although perfect identity exists only in theory, the concept of matched groups is employed. The four general types of experimental research designs are pre-experimental, true experimental, quasi-experimental, and correlational or ex post facto designs.

Estimation

Estimation in analytical research is either a fixed-point estimate or an interval estimate. The statement that a city mayor will be reelected with 56% of the vote is a fixed-point estimate. The interval estimate may take several different forms. A popular form is that the mayor will be reelected by 56 to 59% of the vote. A second form would be that the mayor will be reelected with 56% percent of the vote plus or minus 3%—stated another way, the mayor will be reelected with 53 to 59% of the vote. The third form is that we predict with 90% accuracy that the mayor will receive at least 60% of the vote. Note that point estimates are more precise, but may afford more opportunity for error.

Experiment

There is a difference between an experiment and experimental research. An **experiment** is a test of manipulation made by a researcher to see what difference the experiment will make on the subjects. In experimental research, a factual meaning is behind the experiment and the purpose of the research is to discover that meaning. An experiment merely determines a fact.[1]

The construction of a machine that will read fingerprints is an experiment to determine whether such a machine can be built. The attempt to discover meaning behind this fact would be experimental research. To conduct experimental research, as opposed to experimentation, you need an experimental group, a control group, and an experimental variable.

Variables

Experimental research involves the introduction of a **variable** to a control group. If the researcher has control of the variable and can manipulate it or change it at will, then the variable is considered independent. If the researcher has no control over a variable and it occurs as the result of an influence of the independent variable, the second variable is considered dependent. All experimental designs may be classified as functional designs or factorial designs. If a researcher can control the independent variable at will, the design is classified as **functional**. If the researcher cannot control the variable, the design is considered **factorial**.

Validity Problems

Several factors cause concern regarding the **internal validity** of experimental research. Internal validity indicates whether the conclusions drawn from the results accurately reflect what actually occurred in the experiment. Factors that may affect the internal validity of an experimental research project include:

- **Time span.** Events that occur during a study but are not parts of the project may damage the internal validity of the project. For example, a project studying the effects of a pre-release program may be influenced by the lack of available jobs.
- **Maturation.** This the normal aging process of individuals during the duration of a project.
- **Selection bias.** The biased selection of individuals for to a group may result in distorted data or findings.

- **Other special issues affect the external validity of experimental research projects.** External validity asks whether research conclusions may be generalized to the real world. Those issues include:
  - Reactive effect of testing. Persons in control groups are more aware of the concept involved and thus may act differently.
  - Multiple-treatment interference. The cumulative effects of the pre- and the post-test activities may vary the test results.
  - Selection bias. Biased selection of groups or subjects can affect both external and internal validity.

Experimental Research Categories

As noted earlier, experimental research designs are normally divided into pre-experimental, true experimental, quasi-experimental, and ex post facto or correlational categories.[2]

Pre-experimental design

The **pre-experimental design** may be subdivided into the one-shot case study, the one-group pre-test and post-test design, and the static group comparison. The one-shot case study is the most primitive design. Its aim is to explain a consequent event by an antecedent. It is an approach that created many superstitions and is probably the least reliable experimental approach. Paul Leedy provides this good example of pre-experimental research.[3] If a researcher sees a child sitting on the damp ground in cold weather and the next day the child has a cold, the researcher notes the exposure of the child to cold, damp earth (the variable), and also the observation that the child has a cold. Accordingly, the researcher may conclude that the effect when a child sits on the damp earth in cold weather is that the child gets a cold, thus the design of a one-shot case study is:

- **Pre-experimental evaluation**—the child did not have a cold before she sat on the damp earth.
- **Introduction of a variable**—the damp earth.
- **Post-evaluation observation**—the child has a cold.

The goal of the one-group pre-test and post-test design is to evaluate the influence of a variable. One group is used. After a pre-test, a variable is introduced to the group. The group is then post-tested to determine the effects of the variable. For example, a law enforcement agency evaluates the number of citizen complaints regarding police behavior. The officers are then required to attend sensitivity training. After completion of the training, the number of citizen complaints for a comparable period is evaluated to determine whether the variable (training) had any effect in reducing the number of complaints.

The static group comparison divides the subjects into two randomly selected groups. One is designated the control group and the other the experimental group. No attempt is made to examine the pre-experimental equivalence of the two groups. A variable is introduced to the experimental group, but not to the control group. At the conclusion of the study, both groups are evaluated and a comparison is made between the groups to determine the effect of the variable on the experimental group.

True experimental design

The **true experimental design** offers a greater degree of control and normally yields a higher degree of internal and external validity than the pre-experimental designs. Leedy divides the true experimental design research into (1) pre-test and post-test control group design, (2) Solomon four group design, and (23) post-test-only control group design.[4]

The goal of the pre-test and post-test control group design is to study the effect of a variable on a carefully controlled sample. Many researchers consider this design the "workhorse" of traditional experimentation. Two comparable groups are selected. After a pre-test, an influence is introduced to one of the two carefully controlled groups and the two groups are compared to determine the effects of the imposed influence. For example, individuals released from prison are divided into two comparable groups. One (experimental) group is given pre-release counseling in money management. The other (control) group (control group) does not receive training. After a certain period, the two groups are compared to determine the effects of the counseling on the experimental group. The steps in this design are:

- Two comparable groups are selected.
- The two groups are pre-tested to ensure comparability.
- An experimental variable is introduced to the experimental group.
- The two groups are compared to determine the effects, if any, of the experimental variable on the experimental group.

The **Solomon four group** is designed to minimize the Hawthorne effect and eliminate pre-test influence. The name comes from a series of research studies conducted at Western Electric Company's Hawthorne plant near Chicago in the 1920s and 1930s. The observation was that studying individuals makes them feel important and changes their normal behaviors. A pre-test of a study group may produce a similar effect.

The Solomon four group design is an extension of the pre-test and post-test control group design. R. L. Solomon proposed the design in 1949 to emphasize external validity factors. The design includes two control groups and two experimental groups. Only one control group and one experimental group are pre-tested. A variable is then introduced to both experimental groups. The data are analyzed by performing analysis of variance (ANOVA) of the post-test scores of the four groups. This design helps determine the effects of pre-testing; it requires considerably larger samples because of the need for four matched groups.

The last of the true experimental designs is the post-test-only control group design in which no pre-tests are administered. The samples are randomly divided into two groups, a variable is introduced to one group, and then both groups are post-tested to discover differences, if any, resulting from the introduction of the variable. This design is used in situations in which a pre-test is not practical. Generally, the test for significance in this design is the t-test. Because there is no pre-test, randomness in selecting the two groups is critical.

Quasi-experimental design

The third category, the **quasi-experimental design**, may be subdivided into the nonrandomized control group pre-test and post-test design, the time series experiment, the control-group time series, and the equivalent time samples design. The nonrandomized control group pre-test and post-test design is similar to the true experimental design but the two groups are not equivalent. For example, juveniles released from correctional institutions in New Mexico where certain types of pre-release counseling are provided are compared to juveniles released from correctional institutions in Missouri where the pre-release counseling is different. Circumstances beyond the control of the researchers prevent the two groups from being equivalent. The lack of equivalent groups may affect the validity of the project.

The **time series experiment** involves evaluating a group and then introducing a variable into the system, after which evaluations are made to determine any changes in the group. If a substantial change has resulted, the researcher may conclude that the introduction of the variable was the cause of the difference. A major problem with this design is that extraneous factors appearing during the observation period may have affected the results.

The control group time series is similar to the time series design except that the control group has a similar environment but does not experience the introduction of the variable. The control group helps ensure internal validity in drawing conclusions about the effects of the variable. The equivalent time samples design is a variety of the control group time series that attempts to control history in time designs. A variable is present at some times and absent at other times, thereby creating an on-again, off-again design that allows a researcher to study the differences when the variable is present and when it is absent. For example, a group of juveniles could be introduced to the variable of counseling for 6 months followed by no counseling for 6 months, and so on. After a period of on-again, off-again counseling, the researcher may be able to notice differences while the subjects undergo counseling and when they are not being counseled.

Ex post facto designs

The **ex post facto design** is simply research in reverse. A difference is noted between similar groups. The groups are then studied to determine whether different influences were present or present in different degrees in one or more of the groups. Correlational design studies generally attempt to establish cause-and-effect relationships between two groups of data. They considered deceptive and their use requires caution. As Leedy notes, correlation is too simple an answer for most of the complex realities of life.[5]

Common Errors

Common errors that may occur in experimental research include the failure to select an appropriate control group, the use of too small a control group, and the use of measurements that are not valid or reliable. Another error is the inappropriate use of the results of defined correlations as proof of a cause-and-effect relationship.

summary

- Analytical research depends largely upon statistical investigation of collected data. Experimental research design is appropriate for data derived from an experimental control situation in which data is gathered from two separate groups or from a single group at different times.

- The statistical tools used in analytical research include the normal curve (a general representation of the distribution patterns generally inherent in populations), hypothesis testing, standard deviations, and correlation techniques.

- Experimental research involves the use of experiments to answer questions. Experimental research design is also known as the cause-and-effect method, the pre-test and post-test control group design, and the laboratory method. This design deals with the phenomena of cause and effect.

- Experimental research designs are normally divided into pre-experimental, true experimental, quasi-experimental, and ex post facto or correlational categories.

terminology

Analytical research

Inference

Normal curve

Hypothesis testing

Probability

Null hypothesis

Experimental research

Control group

Experimental group

Cause and effect

Pre-test and post-test control group

Estimation

Experiment

Variable

Functional design

Factorial design

Internal validation

External validation

Pre-experimental design

True experimental design

Solomon four group

Quasi-experimental design

Time series experiment

Ex post facto design

Correlational design

discussion points

1. Distinguish between experimental and analytical research.
2. Explain the principles of analytical research.
3. Discuss the four roles of statistics in analytical research.
4. What is the importance of the phenomenon of cause and effect to experimental researchers?
5. What are the four basic categories of experimental research design? Provide an example of each.
6. Explain the difference between experiments and experimental research design.

endnotes

1. J. A. True. *Finding Out: Conducting and Evaluating Social Research.* Belmont, CA: Wadsworth Publishing, 1983, p. 33.
2. D. Campbell and J. C. Stanley. Experimental and quasi-experimental designs for research on teaching. In *Handbook of Research on Teaching,* N. L. Gage, Ed. Chicago: Rand McNally, 1963, p. 171.
3. P. D. Leedy. *Practical Research Planning and Design,* 5th ed. New York: Macmillan, 1993, p. 297.
4. Ibid., p. 299.
5. Ibid.

6

survey research methods and sampling

introduction

Surveys are the most widely used methods for collecting data in criminal justice research. As techniques of gathering information, surveys describe the nature and extent of a specified set of data ranging from physical counts and frequencies to attitudes and opinions. In the first part of this chapter, we provide an overview of the purposes of survey research. Although the term often refers to a particular type of empirical research, there are many different kinds of surveys. We are concerned specifically with the use of surveys in face-to-face interviews with individuals drawn from a sample. Three types of interviews are discussed: structured, semi-structured, and unstructured. Since surveys can also be administered via telephone and mail, we will also discuss these methods.

After a researcher selects the survey method that is best for the situation, the survey instrument must be constructed. Here we focus on the questionnaire instrument by addressing a number of design issues including decisions about wording, organization, and pre-testing the questionnaire. We follow with a discussion of the major advantages and disadvantages of the use of each type of survey and emphasize which type is best for specific situations.

In the remainder of the chapter, we discuss sampling—a key factor for any type of survey research that involves a process of selecting part of a population to represent the whole population. We cover various terms associated with sampling, such as population and sampling bias. As a final note, we turn our attention to a discussion of the distinctions between probability and nonprobability sampling methods and explore the major types of both techniques.

purposes of survey research

Survey research is a very common activity in our society. You have no doubt been solicited by a survey taker who wanted to ask your opinion about some current event issue. Perhaps you recently completed a customer satisfaction card at a local restaurant or responded to a telephone survey conducted by a major credit card company. Sometimes surveys ask opinions about a product or may pertain to attitudes toward public officials. There are probably as many different reasons for conducting survey research as there are surveys.

During the late nineteenth and early twentieth centuries, census surveys were developed to collect facts about some immediate social problems in communities. Survey takers gathered information that dramatized its pressing nature and turned over the information to public officials in hopes of influencing governmental policy. Surveys gathered facts about housing conditions, employment, health, income and expenditures, crime, and other factors.[1] The broad scope of these studies led to the understanding that the main purpose of a survey is to obtain an overview of a social situation. In common with other research methods, the purpose of survey research depends on the nature of the inquiry. The three general purposes are identified as descriptive, explanatory, and exploratory. Although a survey may aim to satisfy more than one of these purposes, it is useful to examine all three purposes separately.

Descriptive Purpose

Surveys are frequently conducted for the purpose of making descriptive assertions about some population. The researcher attempts to discover the distribution of certain trait characteristics of the sample population. For example, in a March 1999 Gallup Poll of 1,018 Americans, citizens were asked, "If the price of gasoline went up to $1.50 per gallon, would you cut back your driving or not?" Five categories of household income ($75,000 and over, $50,000 to $75,000, $30,000 to $50,000, $20,000 to $30,000, and under $20,000) were used to distinguish the sample population. Seventy-one percent of the highest household income responded "no" while only 29% responded "yes." Conversely, 61% of the $30,000 to $50,000 group responded "yes" and 39% of this group answered "no." By separating responses based on household income, the distribution results of the survey indicated that the impact of gas price increase would be more severe on the less well off.[2]

Explanatory Purpose

Although the intended use of most surveys is to describe, many have the added purpose of making explanatory statements about the population. An explanatory purpose requires **multivariate analysis**, which involves the simultaneous examination of two or more variables. For example, voter preference for certain political candidates may be explained in terms of such variables as party affiliation, education, race, religion, gender, and region of the country. An examination of the relationships between these variables may explain why voters prefer one candidate over another.[3]

Exploratory Purpose

The final purpose of survey research involves exploration. You will recall from discussions in Chapter 2 that the word *exploratory* suggests that little is known about a subject; therefore, the task is to "do some digging," "delve into," or "investigate" an issue. The same concept applies to exploratory survey methods that aim to investigate the "big picture" rather than a specific topic. For example, a group of researchers used a mail survey to examine the attitudes of criminal justice workgroups toward intensive supervised probation in Kansas City, Kansas. The purpose of the study was to explore consumer perceptions of the effectiveness of this corrections program. The findings of the research provided insight into the perceptions of certain groups associated with the program, which was viewed as a requisite first step for overcoming any obstacles or resistance to successful program implementation.[4]

types of survey research

The three types of survey research are classified by their methods of data collection. They are in-person interviews, telephone interviews, and mail surveys. Selecting the type of survey requires a researcher to first consider issues relating to the population sample, nature of questioning, availability of data, and resources. A few preliminary questions can help determine whether a face-to-face interview, telephone survey, or mailed self-administered questionnaire will be the most appropriate survey method.

What are the limitations for identifying persons within a sample population? If a completed listing of every person within a population sample is available, any type of survey method might be a possibility. However, if such a list is not accessible, a researcher will likely have to locate respondents and this will necessarily have some influence on the type of survey method. For example, a researcher interested in conducting a study of inner city drug dealers will not have a list of all the people within the population. The method of data collection will likely involve in-person interviews as mail or telephone surveys are not well-suited for this type of research.

Are there limitations with regard to the respondents when administering the survey? A researcher should consider certain abilities of respondents prior to conducting a survey. Of primary concern is whether the respondents can read and write. If not, a self-administered questionnaire is not an appropriate method. The issue of literacy can be extremely important in research projects involving prisoner populations. Also, language barriers and cultural differences should be taken into account.

What level of cooperation can a researcher expect from a sample population? While the aptitudes of respondents are matters for concern, equally important is whether respondents will be inclined to participate in a survey. Here, good rapport with the population may equate to a high participation. For example, a researcher will likely receive a high return rate of mailed surveys when researching juvenile justice issues if he or she has maintained regular communications with juvenile justice administrators for some time. Also, if sensitive issues associated with the research focus pose a perceived threat to the respondents, they may not cooperate fully.

What types of survey questions will be asked? A researcher should consider how comprehensive a response is needed. If the aim of the survey is to collect aggregate data, perhaps a mailed survey will suffice. However, if very detailed information is required, an interview format is likely to net better response data. Conversely, if it is likely that the respondent will be required to consult with other persons or review records to acquire the data needed for the survey, an interview format may be too time consuming.

What resources and support will be necessary for the survey? A researcher should identify what resources and support will be necessary to carry out a survey. Cost is often a major determining factor in selecting a type of survey. The postage for a mailed survey may be less expensive than long distance phone calls or driving long distances to conduct in-person interviews. Time also becomes a factor. If a response is needed immediately, a mailed survey would, of course, not be a wise choice.

We have noted a few preliminary questions that will help in the selection of a particular type of survey, but sometimes there is no clear choice of which one is best. This is because each method has its advantages and disadvantages and the choice comes down to the preference of the researcher. Some researchers are of the opinion that data collected from self-administered mail surveys are riddled with problems of validity and reliability. Others are less concerned with control issues and prefer interviews that enable them to obtain very detailed data. Still others rely heavily on mailed surveys to capture large amounts of data in hopes of understanding the research problem. Gaining a greater appreciation for each type of survey research requires us to take a closer look at each individual method. We start with an examination of in-person interviews.

in-person interviews

Personal interviewing is a dynamic process whereby an interviewer (the researcher) orally solicits responses from persons identified within a sample population (respondents). The interview is viewed as a fairly straightforward method of gaining information, especially if the conversation is clear and fairly to the point.

Three basic terms are used to distinguish the degrees of formality of an interview: fully structured interviews, semi-structured interviews, and unstructured interviews. Although the approaches differ, all techniques require that the researcher listen to what is said and systematically record the responses.

For a **structured interview**, the researcher develops a predetermined set of questions and asks the respondent for specific replies. The researcher controls the interview and asks all respondents the same questions in the same order. Two examples of structured survey questions are:

Question: In which of the following groups is your household's total annual income before taxes?

_____ Under $20,000

_____ $20,000 to $35,000

_____ $35,000 to $50,000

_____ $50,000 to $65,000

_____ $65,000 to $90,000

_____ $90,000 to $125,000

_____ $125,000 to $200,000

_____ More than $200,000

Question: What is the storage capacity (hard drive size) of your personal computer?

_____ Fewer than 200 megabytes

_____ 500 to 800 megabytes

_____ More than 800 megabytes

_____ Don't know

In each example, the respondent is asked for a specific response to the question. The interviewer does not take the opportunity to probe or ask follow-up questions. This format is probably better described as an in-person survey rather than an interview. In addition to questions, structured interviews may involve provocative statements intended to prompt an immediate response. Each statement or question includes a list of possible responses and only one may be chosen (see Table 6.1). The instruction to the respondents states, "Please indicate your level of agreement with each statement below by placing an X in the appropriate box."

This type of survey is referred to as a **Likert scale** because it contains statements with which respondents show degrees of agreement or disagreement. Scaling is used to code survey responses relating to conceptual constructs such as attitude and belief. The result is that quantitative measurements can be taken from qualitative responses. The use of numeric codes that represent answers to questions saves time and helps to ensure validity and reliability of the data. A discussion of several conventional and special scales used in criminal justice research and strategies for ensuring validity and reliability is provided in Chapter 8.

Like the structured interview, the **semi-structured interview** involves the development of a set of questions in advance. Again,

TABLE 6.1: STRUCTURED INTERVIEW STATEMENTS AND RESPONSES

Statement	Disagree Strongly	Disagree Somewhat	Don't Know	Agree Somewhat	Agree Strongly
1. People in jail are usually guilty.					
2. Bonds should be abolished.					
3. Prisoner privileges should be limited.					
4. Parole rules should be tightened.					
5. Once a convict, always a convict.					

the interviewer is very much in control of the survey, and that is the only similarity. In a semi-structured interview, the researcher possesses greater latitude in deciding how the survey will be administered. He or she is free to relax the rigid procedures of the structured interview and attempt to gain more detailed information by:

- Modifying the order of questions
- Changing the wording of the questions and statements
- Giving explanations
- Omitting some questions
- Including additional questions

The semi-structured interview relies upon the researcher's ability to perceive how the interview is developing and to make changes accordingly. The process is different from the pencil-to-paper structured survey in that the researcher adjusts the questioning based on the respondent's answers. However, the semi-structured survey is still based upon a preconceived agenda—to elicit data for a particular focus. It relies heavily on both closed and semi-closed questions to gather immediate responses.

Consider a semi-structured survey that might be administered to a person who has filed for unemployment benefits (Table 6.2). It is a short (five-question) survey in which the interviewer asks questions based on preceding responses. The objectives of this survey are to obtain a certain kind of data in a short time and to gather information that will be used to determine the respondent's eligibility for unemployment compensation.

TABLE 6.2: QUESTIONNAIRE FOR DETERMINING ELIGIBILITY FOR UNEMPLOYMENT COMPENSATION BENEFITS

Question 1: **Are you currently employed?**

If YES: ☐   If NO: ☐

Part-time Full-time (Circle One)

Where: Job prospects:

How long: Occupational skills:

Job duties:

GO TO QUESTION 5   GO TO QUESTION 2

Question 2: **Are you receiving unemployment benefits?**

If YES: ☐   If NO: ☐

How long: Date paperwork was filled:

Amount:

GO TO QUESTION 3   GO TO QUESTION 3

Question 3: **What methods are you using to find out about job openings? (Check All)**

Newspaper advertising   Employment agencies

Public services   Television

Other:

GO TO QUESTION 4

Question 4: **Have you sought the assistance of a career counseling service?**

If YES: ☐   If NO: ☐

Where: Why Not?

When:

GO TO QUESTION 5

Question 5: **Do you find your present income adequate?**

YES: ☐   NO: ☐

                                   If NO, STATE REASON

This concludes the interview.

Unstructured interviews utilize open-ended questions and are sometimes referred to as clinical interviews. The purpose is to obtain as much detailed information as possible from respondents. Unlike the other two types of surveys, the unstructured format allows the interviewer an opportunity to probe or ask follow-up questions. Also, interviews are generally easier for respondents if they are asked about opinions or beliefs. A few examples of open-ended questions will help distinguish this type of interview from the others.

Why do you want to be a police officer?

Why you are for or against the death penalty?

How would you describe your fellow correctional officers?

In addition to open-ended questions, word association and sentence completion formats are popular ways of conducting unstructured interviews. With **word association**, the researcher presents one word at a time and the respondent replies with the first word that comes to mind. Sentence completion involves presenting an incomplete sentence and asking a respondent to complete it.

Unstructured interviews are conducted on a one-to-one basis or in focus groups. Focus groups represent an increasingly popular way to learn about opinions and attitudes. They involve in-depth interviews with a small number of people (typically 6 to 10) who are brought together to discuss selected topics. The composition of a focus group is based on similarities of the members—they all have knowledge about the subject matter. Sometimes researchers use different groups to get differing views. For example, suppose a metropolitan area voted to consolidate city and county police departments into a single metropolitan police agency. It would be desirable to have separate focus groups for line officers, managers, and administrators. Each group would represent a potentially different perspective on the changes necessary for consolidation. When focus groups are conducted, the researcher's main task is to keep the group focused on the topic of discussion by helping the group generate a lively and productive conversation so that useful information can be gathered to address the objective of the study. Questions should always be open-ended, and the researcher should take care not to ask leading questions.

As a final note, it is important to distinguish between focus groups and group interviewing. The latter is simply a means of assembling several persons in a room and asking each one to individually respond to a set of questions. Ideally, a researcher conducting a focus group poses a question to the group and the members then talk to each other about the topic. The researcher serves as the moderator, primarily listening and facilitating discussions. At the same time, the researcher must record the dialogue by taking notes or audio/video taping the discussion. The dynamic of a focus group is quite different from the dynamic of an interview.

Choosing a Type of Interview: Factors to Consider

Extent of control

In comparing the relative advantages and disadvantages of all three types of interviews, an initial concern is the amount of control that the researcher exerts during the interview. If the focus of the research is to compare responses of a large sample group, the researcher is likely to use a structured or semi-structured interview. He or she maintains strict control of the interview and asks a set of predetermined questions; the respondent's options for answering are limited. In the unstructured interview, the respondent has greater freedom of expression and may seek elaborate responses. This can be understood to mean a shift in control from the interviewer to the respondent. To be sure, there can be a considerable amount of give and take during an unstructured interview. However, the interviewer never actually yields control because the unstructured format enables him or her to capitalize on verbal and other cues observed during the interview process and adjust the questioning accordingly.

Time

Interviewing is time consuming. The length of an interview session varies based on format. Assuming sample sizes are identical, it stands to reason that the unstructured format is by far the most time consuming type of interview. Also, if responses are to be coded for analysis, closed-ended questions are easier to process than open-ended questions because coding narrative responses is very time consuming.

Location

The location of the interview is another general consideration for deciding the type of interview. Interviews are best conducted in a quiet place in order to make the person interviewed feel relaxed and inclined to devote his full attention to the researcher's questions and statements. Unstructured interviews require the utmost attention to this detail, especially if electronic equipment is used during the interview.

Desired information

The choice of a structured, semi-structured, or unstructured approach depends on the information desired by the researcher. The amount of information required may involve multiple stages of interviewing. In this technique, the researcher first conducts unstructured interviews to gather preliminary data that will be used to develop and administer semi-structured interviews. Findings from the second interview stage are then used to develop a final structured survey. For example, in a study of gang violence, Scott Decker and his fellow researchers interviewed 99 active gang members representing 29 gangs in the St. Louis area. They used a semi-structured questionnaire developed from unstructured interviews conducted before the beginning of the study to guide the interviews.[5]

Role of researcher

A final factor to consider is the role of the researcher. The mere presence of an interviewer can increase cooperation rates. Furthermore, the better the interviewing skills of the researcher, the better the quality of data collected from respondents. The interviewer must be self-confident, able to adapt to various situations, and possess a willingness to hear what is said and change direction if necessary. Perhaps most importantly, the researcher must be tolerant of mistakes that will occur during the interview process.

telephone survey

Another way of gathering survey data is by telephone. A telephone interview enables a researcher to gather information rapidly. When comparing it to in-person interviews, the telephone interview is similar in two very important ways. First, it allows some personal contact between the interviewer and the respondent. Second, its purpose is to gather data that assesses the prevalence of some variable under study.

The popularity of the telephone survey method has increased as technological advances in the telephone industry have occurred. It would have been unlikely that a researcher would have chosen a telephone survey as the preferred method of data collection prior to the 1970s, but in recent years, telephone surveys have become common in the United States.

Technological advances in the computer industry have also had great influence on the use of telephone surveys. Today, the computer-assisted telephone interview (CATI) is a viable method of gathering information. CATI surveys are conducted by an interviewer using a computer terminal. The survey questions appear on the computer screen and the interviewer keys the respondent's answers into the computer as they are given.

A popular method of conducting large-scale telephone surveys is through the use of a telephone interviewing facility. A CATI is implemented using a station consisting of multiple stand-alone or networked computers. An interviewer at each station conducts a computer-administered interview. Because a computer controls the questionnaire, skip patterns are executed exactly as intended, and there is no missing data. Also, because answers are entered directly into the computer, data analysis can start immediately. Academic research centers are particularly noted for offering large-scale CATI services. For

RESEARCH IN ACTION 3: PREPARATORY TIPS FOR CONDUCTING INTERVIEWS

Proficiency at conducting interviews can only be achieved through experience. After a researcher has conducted several interviews, confidence begins to build and he or she typically becomes more comfortable with this method of data collection. Good interviewers have good interpersonal communication skills that allow them to correct a respondent's misunderstandings or confusion in interpreting questions. The most successful interviewers follow a well-thought-out game plan. They prepare in advance and have a sense of what challenges may occur during interviews. The following is a list of suggestions to help a researcher prepare to conduct interviews.

- Always have survey questions and statements prepared ahead of time. Know them thoroughly.
- Practice interviewing techniques prior to actually administering interviews. If training is needed, seek the help of an experienced interviewer.
- Always pre-test your survey. Delete questions and statements that are not appropriate and add questions and statements if necessary.
- Develop a procedure that will guide your interview. Include at least the following:
  - Introduction. Make a brief introduction and explain the purpose of the research.
  - Initial commentary. Try to relax the respondent by explaining the format. If conducting unstructured interviews and audio taping the conversation, ask for respondent's approval.
  - Conduct interview. A structured approach requires the research to cover the questions and record the answers exactly. Semi-structured interviews may necessitate changing the question format or adjusting the interview based on a respondent's answers. Unstructured interviews require a great deal of listening and probing. Probing involves asking follow-up questions to further explain a response. Sometimes the most effective way to encourage someone to elaborate is to do nothing at all—just pause and wait.

This "silent probe" suggests that you are waiting and listening for what he next has to say.

- All approaches require a researcher to be straightforward and to conduct the interview in a nonthreatening way. Additionally, the researcher should be aware that certain gestures, facial expressions, or other cues may lead a respondent to answer in a certain way.
- No matter what method is used for recording, the interviewer should capture all responses immediately.
- Closure. Thanking the participants for their time and input should adequately end the interview session.
- Assign a time limit to the interview and practice keeping to this length of time.
- If scheduling interview appointments is necessary, consider the best time of day to call or visit.
- Plan to dress in a fashion similar to those who will be interviewed. If the respondent will be wearing a uniform, attire should be more formal than relaxed.
- Test your recording equipment before the interview to ensure that it is in good working order. Always take additional batteries and tapes when using recording devices.
- Consider the use of visual materials such as cards, charts, and other audiovisual aids that may prove helpful during the interview.
- Decide what follow-up procedures will be needed. If it is necessary to gather additional information, consider how to address this issue with respondents. A respondent is likely to be interested in survey results, so be prepared to make those findings available in an executive summary or similar document.

example, the Center for Survey Research at the Docking Institute of Public Affairs at Fort Hays State University in Hays, Kansas, provides public opinion services using a variety of methods including CATIs.

using computers in survey research

In addition to CATIs, computers have been used to facilitate other types of survey research. The trend in recent years is toward the use

RESEARCH IN ACTION 4: KANSAS CITIZENS JUSTICE INITIATIVE PUBLIC OPINION SURVEY

The Kansas Citizens Justice Initiative Public Opinion Survey represents the first in-depth study of the Kansas court system in 24 years.[6] This study was conducted by the Kansas Justice Commission, composed of 46 members appointed by the Governor, the Kansas Supreme Court, and state legislative leaders. One part of this study is a survey of Kansas citizens to determine their opinions of the Kansas court system.

The findings from this survey of Kansas citizens are based on a random-digit telephone sample of 1,226 respondents. The survey was conducted using a computer-assisted telephone interviewing (CATI) system. The objectives of the survey are to:

- Gauge the types of respondents' previous experiences with the court system and assess their satisfaction with the experience.
- Determine levels of access to the legal system.
- Assess perceptions of fairness regarding the court system.
- Gauge opinions on child custody and child support issues.
- Determine the level of acceptance for alternative dispute resolution and other court system innovations.
- Investigate attitudes toward the selection and/or appointment of judges.
- Ascertain the level of support for increased funding for the Kansas court system.

The survey of 1,226 Kansans found that about 54% of respondents received formal notices that they may be called to jury service, 27% have gone to traffic court, slightly over 21% have been involved in civil suits, and 10% or fewer reported having been parties to small claims suits, serving as witnesses at trials, or involvements in criminal cases. Taken together, over 73% of respondents reported some type of experience with the court system in Kansas. People involved with the Kansas court system within the past 5 years evaluated their experiences as follows:

- Even though those who serve on juries feel that they are performing an important public service, over 45% of these individuals feel that the courts should give them greater compensation for their time and effort.
- Most people who had recent experiences with the small claims proceedings reported that they had few problems with the paperwork, court personnel, or understanding the proceedings.
- About 60% of those involved in civil cases were parties to divorce cases. About 50% said their civil cases took a reasonable amount of time to resolve. Over 60% of respondents reported that they were satisfied with the outcomes of their civil cases, and 65% felt their attorneys' fees were reasonable.
- About 13% of the respondents (153) indicated that in the past they had been unable to obtain legal assistance. Fewer than 10% of these respondents said they frequently needed the help of an attorney and half indicated they needed legal help a few times.

The survey also assessed the opinions of the general public regarding their basic perception of the court system, opinions related to family law issues, their support for various proposed changes in the court system, and their support for increased funding of state courts. The general perception of the court system for most respondents is that the system is fair. Over 70% believe that the courts in criminal cases treat the accused in a fair and just manner. Another 60% agree that the interests of victims of crime are addressed. A majority of the respondents supported more flexibility for judges in sentencing convicted criminals, while 40% said judges should have to abide by sentencing guidelines.

The general perception of most respondents was that attorneys charged too much for their services, and that wealthy litigants had legal advantages. This general perception is at odds with other findings from this survey indicating that 65% of those involved in civil suits felt their attorneys' fees were reasonable.

On family law issues, the survey findings showed that even though men and women differ on whether mothers should be assigned most parental rights in divorce cases, large majorities of both women and men favored automatic deduction of child support payments from their paychecks and protecting children's interests over their parents' interests.

The findings related to the public's support for proposed court system innovations indicate that a majority of survey respondents:

- Have a favorable opinion of using paralegals for minor legal cases as long as the paralegals are supervised by attorneys.
- Approve requirements for mediation in civil cases including divorce and child custody cases, personal injury suits, and landlord-tenant disputes.
- Support the election of local judges.
- Support greater flexibility for judges in sentencing of criminal cases.

The Kansans surveyed were evenly divided over whether to continue the state's practice of having at least one judge residing in each county. They are also fairly equally divided over increasing state funding for more judges and support staff, and favor by a three-to-one margin allowing local communities to pay more for judicial services if they wish to do so. By more than a two to one margin, respondents felt that judges should be paid about the same salaries as attorneys in their communities with similar numbers of years in practice.

of laptop computers for in-person interview surveys. Data collection via a laptop computer is known as the **computer-assisted personal interview (CAPI)**. An important advantage of taking a portable computer into the field is speed and quality. The computer can be programmed to perform a number of functions automatically such as data assembly, editing, and analysis.

Another major method of computer-assisted data collection is the electronic mail (e-mail) survey. A number of commercial software programs are capable of receiving completed questionnaires via e-mail. Files can be attached to e-mail questionnaires to ascertain respondents' reactions to graphic images, sound files, and documents.

Clearly, as the Internet becomes more widely used, traditional methods of gathering data may eventually disappear.

Finally, a number of Web-based companies like mySurveyLab, Zoomerang, and SurveyMonkey offer online survey tools that enable researchers to create their own surveys quickly and easily at minimal cost. A primary strength of these Web survey applications is that each offers intuitive Web interfacing that makes it easy for even nontechnical users to create surveys and export collected data. A brief overview of these tools is as follows:

Application	Website	Features
mySurveyLab	www.mysurveylab.com	Creates surveys tailored to nature of specific business; provides tools to help analyze survey data and store results in spreadsheets
SurveyMonkey	www.surveymonkey.com	Lets users create surveys for businesses, charities, and individuals
Zoomerang	www.zoomerang.com	Tool for creating and sending online surveys and reviewing results in real time; can create custom survey paths, eliminating need to read and respond to eliminated questions; sends reminders to those who fail to respond; cross-tabulates results between groups of respondents

Despite the various ways to use computers in survey research, many researchers prefer to conduct paper-and-pencil telephone surveys. Whether a researcher plans to use modern technology or traditional methods, he or she must understand the value of preparing a detailed plan well in advance of making that first phone call. Many of the factors that should be considered during planning are the same as those listed for personal interviews. However, a unique feature of the telephone survey is the absence of visual contact between interviewer and respondent. This represents a disadvantage for an interviewer because gestures and other nonverbal cues cannot be seen. This potential obstacle should be considered when planning the protocol to be followed, with a great deal of attention given to the development of very detailed verbal explanations. To that end, it may be wise to include a clear and concise introductory remark that the phone call is not for telemarketing purposes, Unsuspecting citizens are inundated daily with solicitation phone calls, some of which are fraudulent. It has been estimated that telemarketing fraud costs consumers $40 billion a year and that 92% of adults in the United States have received fraudulent telephone offers.[7] It is important then that a respondent clearly understands that the intent of the call is to gather survey data and not sell merchandise.

mail surveys

Criminal justice researchers conduct a large number of mail surveys each year. The most common type of mail survey is the self-administered questionnaire. This method of data collection enables a researcher to survey a large group of respondents in a minimum time. For example, a researcher interested in studying the attitudes of police administrators may choose to send a questionnaire to all sheriffs in a particular state. The advantage of this type of survey is that the questionnaire can be mass mailed, completed, and returned to the researcher in much less time than it would take to conduct interviews of only a few respondents. In addition to saving time, a mail survey is an affordable method of gathering information. Typically, only printing and postage costs are necessary to initiate a self-administered mail survey.

Although the method has clear advantages, three problems may occur. The first is lack of response. Without follow-up, a mailed survey may unfortunately net only a small percentage return rate in a one-time-only distribution. Second, although a self-administered questionnaire may have been addressed to a certain person, a researcher has few ways to determine who actually completed the document. The third problem with this type of survey is little or no possibility of checking the honesty or seriousness of responses.

Increasing Return Rates

It is not unusual to receive a low return on the initial mailing of a survey. Reasons for this vary but a universal cause for failure to return surveys is that completing questionnaires is not high on anyone's priority list. Because the general nature of people and businesses tends to be reactive to problems, it is often the case that other tasks require immediate attention. Personnel, operational, and political matters are important matters, require attention daily, and likely will take precedence over answering questions.

Additionally, many people have the perception that completing surveys is a bothersome chore. Perhaps a questionnaire is lengthy and will take a lot of time to complete or perhaps three other surveys were also received in the mail. A respondent may have a perception that there is no value in providing the requested information. To overcome this problem, researchers have developed several ways of making the return of questionnaires easier. The popular **total design method** is based on a social exchange theory of why people choose to respond to surveys. Attention is given to every administrative detail that may affect response including the length and appearance of a questionnaire, the ease of following instructions and responding, and the sequence and timing of mailings. A reminder postcard follows an initial mailing; then a second mailing is sent. For those who still have not responded, a special delivery mailing is sent. In some cases, telephone contact is made with the respondents to further enhance the data collection effort.[8]

Another method of increasing response rates is to accompany a survey with a cover letter that should include important details. First, it must clearly explain the important features of the survey. The letter is essentially a brief message of the purpose of conducting a survey, how and why the respondent was chosen, and why it is important for the respondent to complete the questionnaire. A statement of confidentiality should also be included.

A third important feature of a cover letter is the format. The letter must clearly show affiliation with or sponsorship by an institution or organization. A common approach is to print a cover letter on the official letterhead of an institution that the respondent knows and respects. For criminal justice students conducting survey research, it is common practice to print a cover letter on university letterhead. Figure 6.1 is an example of a cover letter generated by a university student.

One of the best historical overviews of survey research is provided by Don Dillman, the Thomas S. Foley Distinguished Professor of Public Policy in the Departments of Sociology and Rural Sociology and deputy director of the Social and Economic Sciences Research Center at Washington State University. His article titled, "Presidential Address: Navigating the Rapids of Change: Some Observations on Survey Methodology in the Early Twenty-First Century,"[9] addresses factors that have reshaped survey research, the various survey modes in extensive use today, and the need for new research perspectives and concepts that flow from the long-term trend toward greater use of self-administered survey procedures for collecting survey data.

WASHBURN UNIVERSITY
School of Applied Studies
Criminal Justice Department

Jarett Lee, Sheriff   [Date]
Topeka, Kansas

Dear Sheriff Lee:

   A research project directed by the Department of Criminal Justice at Washburn University is under way to gather important information about the relationship between correctional practices and juvenile prisoners who are confined in adult jails throughout the state. The larger urban jails are being asked to participate in this project.
   Enclosed you will find a survey questionnaire containing a total of 20 questions regarding classification, programs, staff training, and other related issues. You will not find anything unusual in this questionnaire. This is a typical survey that asks standard questions and provides you with an opportunity to describe the correctional practices at your facility. Likewise, please find the enclosed self-addressed, stamped envelope that has been provided for the convenient return of your questionnaire.
   You may be assured of complete confidentiality. As you will note, space is not provided on the questionnaire for you to give your name. Furthermore, your name will never be placed on the questionnaire.
   The results of this research will be available this fall, and I will gladly send you a copy of the executive summary report.
   I truly appreciate your willingness to participate in this important research. If you require additional information, or have any questions, please write or call.

Sincerely,

Amanda Loren
Project Director
1700 SW College Avenue
Topeka, Kansas 66621
913-231-1010, Extension 1411

Fig. 6.1 Questionnaire transmittal cover letter.

designing questionnaires

Whether research involves face-to-face interviews, telephone interviews, or self-administered mail surveys, several design features should be considered when constructing a survey questionnaire. The first consideration is to determine the purpose of the questioning. Michael Patton suggests that four major kinds of questions are common to evaluation questionnaires.[10] These questions (behavior, opinion, feeling, and knowledge) are also applicable to research questionnaires because they address precisely the information needed from the respondents. According to Patton:

- **Behavior questions** ask about what a person does or has done. These questions are aimed at descriptions of actual program experiences, activities, actions by participants, and respondent behaviors that would have been observable had the evaluator been present when the behavior took place.
- **Opinion questions** are aimed at finding out what people think about something, usually various aspects of a program in which they have participated. Opinion questions tell us about people's goals, intentions, desires, and values.
- **Feeling questions** elicit information about the emotional responses of people to their experiences and thoughts. Feelings occur within people; they are natural, emotional responses to experiences. Feelings tap the affective dimensions of human life and program experience.
- **Knowledge questions** are asked to determine what factual information the respondent has. The assumption in asking knowledge questions is that certain facts are considered to be known or true. The facts are not opinions, feelings, or actions. Rather, they represent what's known: the facts of the case.[11]

Figure 6.2 provides examples for each type of questioning purpose. Note that the response categories are formatted to solicit structured responses. If more detailed information were sought, the questioning purpose would remain the same but the format would require open-ended questions. Another feature to consider when constructing a questionnaire is the scope of the questioning. If the extent of the questioning is to be limited, dichotomous questions may be in order. These questions have only two possible responses, typically yes-or-no, true-or-false, or agree-or-disagree responses. Consider the following public opinion question and statements about capital punishment:

Do you believe that the death penalty deters crime?
     __ Yes __ No

I believe that the death penalty deters crime.
     __ True __ False

The death penalty deters crime.

___ Agree ___ Disagree

Sometimes the scope of the questioning is greater and requires a researcher to ask multiple questions. The respondent is first given a filter question to determine whether a subsequent question will be necessary. For instance, a study of juvenile delinquency may involve asking teenagers about their behavior. Depending on the response to the first question, a second question can be asked to collect more explicit information.

Question 1: Have you ever shoplifted?

___ Yes ___ No

Question 2: If Yes, how many times? (Check one)

___ Once

___ 2 to 5 times

___ 6 to 10 times

___ More than 10 times

A third design feature is the organization of the questionnaire. Two key issues are aesthetics and the ordering of the questions. A questionnaire should not appear gaudy; it should be simple and neat. Font sizes should be easily readable. Likewise, the placement of the questions is an important design consideration. Generally, the initial

---

1. Behavior questions are aimed at learning about what a respondent has actually experienced. This type questioning calls for responses such as:

   Always — Often — Sometimes — Seldom — Never

2. Opinion questions are geared toward what a respondent thinks or believes. This type of questioning calls for responses such as:

   Strongly Agree — Agree — Disagree — Strongly Disagree

3. Feeling questions are intended to obtain information about a respondent's emotions. This type of questioning calls for responses such as:

   Confident ____ ____ ____ ____ Scared

4. Knowledge questions ask what a respondent knows to be a right or wrong answer. This type of question calls for responses such as:

   True — False — Don't know

Fig. 6.2 Response categories for closed questions.

questions set the tone of the survey and therefore should be easy to answer. Keep in mind also that the more questions on a survey, the more apt the respondent is to get tired of answering. This requires that important questions requiring some thought should be placed near the beginning of the questionnaire. Conversely, questions that could be perceived as threatening should be placed near the end. A low response rate is guaranteed if extremely personal questions are asked in the beginning of a questionnaire.[12] For example, the following questions may be perceived as too personal:

How old are you?

Are you a college graduate?

How much money do you earn?

Have you ever committed a crime?

The last design feature of the questionnaire to consider is the wording of the questions. It is very important for a researcher to pay close attention to how the survey questions are worded so that the respondent cannot misinterpret them. If the survey questions are too vague or if each question is worded differently, a respondent may become confused or may not understand the questions. As a result, the respondent may become frustrated and decide not to take the questions seriously. The following list concerning the wording of survey questions covers problems and suggestions.

- A question is not definitive enough. Avoid words such as *frequently*, *regularly*, and *occasionally*. One respondent may understand *frequently* to mean daily, while another respondent may comprehend it to mean once a week.

- A question contains words that require specialized knowledge. Never assume that respondents will understand extremely technical words. Likewise, keep the use of jargon to a minimum.

- A question is leading. Questions should not begin with phrases like "Wouldn't you agree that...?" and "Isn't it true that...?" because a respondent may perceive that agreement is the sought-after or favored response.

- A question is loaded. Avoid questions that contain personal biases. For instance, "What do you see as the most important benefit of capital punishment?" conveys to the respondent that capital punishment is beneficial—and linked to a personal view of someone who favors capital punishment.

- A question is double-barreled. Compound questions that constitute two questions should be asked separately; for example, "Do chapter discussion questions and instructor review notes help you to prepare for examinations?" A respondent who finds that only one measure helpful would have a difficult time answering this question.

The best way to ensure that a respondent understands questions is to **pre-test** a questionnaire by conducting a "pilot" test of the questionnaire using subjects who are similar to the group to be studied. The researcher administers the survey to a small group of subjects who then critique the instrument, paying close attention to its wording and organization. Upon completion, the pre-test subjects suggest changes to improve the questionnaire's content and appearance. Questions that will help facilitate a discussion with the pre-test subjects include:

- How long did it take you to complete the survey?
- Were the instructions clear and easy to follow?
- Were any questions vague or misleading?
- Did you find any of the questions to be offensive?
- Were there any questions that you didn't answer?
- Do you have any other comments?

After the pre-test, the questionnaire can be revised based on the comments of the subjects and then administered to the sample population. The results from the pre-test, however, should not be included when the final results are tabulated.

comparison of types of survey research

Each type of survey method has advantages and disadvantages. Choosing which one will work best for collecting the necessary data depends on factors such as the research purpose, resources available, and nature of the sample population (Table 6.3). The task for the researcher is to determine what is most important among the factors for the design selected and choose accordingly.[13]

TABLE **6.3**: COMPARISON OF INFORMATION GATHERING TECHNIQUES

Technique	Strengths	Weaknesses
1. In-Person Interview	a. Allows in-depth, free responses. b. Researcher can see respondent's facial expressions, gestures, etc. c. Visual presentations are possible. d. High percentage of return. e. Responses are accurate.	a. High costs. b. Time consuming. c. Requires skilled interviewers. d. Open to interviewer bias. e. Summarizing data may be more difficult.
2. Telephone Interview	a. Less costly than in-person interviews. b. Amount of time to secure data is low. c. Computer technology can be used. d. Verbal comments are easier responses for most respondents than written ones.	a. Unlisted phone numbers unavailable. b. Can be confused with a telemarketing call. c. Visual presentations not possible. d. Interviewer can bias based on verbal cues or voice inflections
3. Mailed Surveys	a. Inexpensive. b. Offers privacy and anonymity. c. Respondent accustomed to the format. d. Interviewer bias is eliminated. e. Data are easier to summarize.	a. Low response rate. b. Respondent literacy may be problematic. c. Open-ended questions unfeasible. d. Validity of responses. e. No control over who actually completes the survey.

sampling

Survey research involves the collection of data from a sample population via a process known as **sampling**: selecting a portion of a population that is representative of the entire population. The alternative to sampling (enumeration) is to gather data from every member of the total population. Sampling is a key factor for all types of survey research for several reasons. First, it is usually too costly and time-consuming to survey an entire population. Second, the amount of data collected from a total population that requires analysis can be overwhelming. Finally, a sub-unit of a population ordinarily provides sufficient representation of a group as a whole and enough accurate data to base decisions on the results with confidence.

Data collected by sampling is useful only if gathered from respondents who are typical of a population as a whole. Moreover, it is essential that a researcher obtain a sample size large enough to generalize to the entire population. This means that statistically valid inferences must be able to be made about the population. The field of inferential statistics (Chapter 3) includes specific procedures that allow valid inferences to be made.

Probability Sampling Procedures

A **probability sampling** procedure is any method of sampling that utilizes some form of random selection. Further, it requires that each member of the population have an equal chance of selection. The result is that when the respondents are picked from a population at random, the probability of any one person being included in the sample is precisely equal to the probability of including any other individual. A fundamental necessity is a complete and accurate list of all persons within the population. This list is referred to as the **sampling frame**.

Simple Random Sampling

A **simple random sample (SRS)** is a form of probability sampling that:

- Gives all members of a population equal chances of selection.
- Is the standard against which other methods are sometimes evaluated because it is most representative of an entire population and least likely to result in bias.
- Is especially suitable for populations that are small to moderate in size.
- Requires the sampling frame to be comprehensive and current.
- Allows researcher to make inferences about a population based on results obtained from a sample.

Simple random selection begins when a researcher identifies the population to be surveyed. For example, suppose he or she is interested in conducting a survey to measure the attitudes of citizens toward local police. The population to be surveyed would include all persons within the community. Does the community include only people who live within the city limits? What about those who work in the city and live elsewhere? Should only adults be included in the population? This initial procedure of identifying the survey population is not always an easy task but it is a crucial one because the population must consist of people who possess the information sought by the survey. After the target population is identified, the researcher then obtains a complete sampling frame.

The next step in SRS is to assign a number to each person in the population. Using the above example, assume the community is defined as all adults who live within the city limits. The community consists of a total of 50 such persons, each of whom can be identified by name. Having this information in hand, the researcher assigns each person a number from 1 to 50.

Next, sample size is determined based on tables available in standard statistical texts.[14] A table of random numbers (also found in statistics textbooks) is then used to identify persons to be drawn from the desired sample. For example, suppose that we want a 40% sample from the 50 adults who live within the city limits. Using a list of our theoretical population and an illustrated table of random numbers, we can determine which persons will be in our sample (Table 6.4). Note that each person's name has a number.

We know that our sample will consist of 20 people (40%). We then select 20 persons by using the table of random numbers and choosing a random start point. Suppose we start at the top left of the table. Because the entire population consists of 50 people, two-digit numbers (00 to 99) in the table will allow each person a chance of being selected. Numbers 51 to 99 are unusable and should be skipped. The

TABLE 6.4: LIST OF 50 ADULTS LIVING WITHIN CITY LIMITS

1–Alex	2–Amanda	3–Aaron	4–Ardith	5–Carolyn
6–Cathy	7–Carl	8–Cheryl	9–Cliff	10–Connie
11–Curtis	12–David	13–Dennis	14–Derek	15–Dorothy
16–Gary	17–Jack	18–Jarrett	19–Jason	20–Jennifer
21–Jerry	22–Joan	23–John	24–Joshua	25–Ken
26–Kevin	27–Kiel	28–Kim	29–Kristen	30–Leroy
31–Margie	32–Marlin	33–Marla	34–Mark	35–Marilyn
36–Mary	37–Mathew	38–Nancy	39–Ollie	40–Sam
41–Scarlett	42–Sharon	43–Sonny	44–Tanner	45–Theodore
46–Thurston	47–Toak	48–Tyron	49–Wayne	50–Winston

23713	01639	20182
18167	08823	21473
75748	18302	63827
19173	91191	01669
11539	20183	52819
70163	34210	73720
64114	38010	48302
26120	24181	81620

first number is 23 and corresponds with the name John. The second number is 71 and is not usable. We skip to the next number (30) and note that the second person chosen in our sample is Leroy. The next number is 16 and matches Gary. This procedure is followed until all 20 persons have been identified and selected for the sample.

Systematic Sampling

An alternative random procedure that is especially useful for large populations is **systematic sampling**. This method involves moving through the sampling frame list and choosing every *nth* name. To illustrate systematic sampling we return to Table 6.4. Suppose we want a 20% sample from 50 adults. We know that the sample size will consist of 10 persons (20% of 50) and determine which 10 persons by selecting the proper sampling interval first. Sampling intervals are selected by the ratio of sample size to population size. Therefore, we take every fifth name (5 represents the ratio of 10 to 50). Next, we choose a start point from the table of random numbers by selecting a number between the intervals of 1 to 5 (every fifth). In the random table, the first number within the interval is 2 and corresponds with Amanda. Every fifth person is determined by adding 5 and is included in the sample list. This procedure continues until 10 persons have been identified and selected for the sample. Thus, the sample list comprises the names that correspond to 2, 7, 12, 17, 22, 27, 32, 37, 42, and 47.

Stratified Sampling

In **stratified sampling**, all people in the sampling frame are divided into strata (groups or categories). Within each stratum, a simple random sample or systematic sample is selected. Demographic characteristics such as age, sex, and race are often divided into categories.

When the same sampling fraction is used within the strata, the method is known as **proportionate stratified random sampling**; that is, strata are sampled in proportion to their rate of occurrence in the population. When different sampling fractions are used in the strata, the technique is called **disproportionate stratified random sampling** in which a larger than proportionate number are taken from the strata because the strata represent a smaller proportion of the population. Again, returning to the example in Table 6.4, suppose we want a 30% proportionate stratified sampling from the 50 adults. We know that our sample will consist of 15 persons (30% of

50). We determine the 15 persons by first separating the population into age groups, for example, the population can be divided into four age groups: 19 to 29 (10%), 30 to 40 (40%), 41 to 60 (40%), and older than 60 (10%). Note that both the 19 to 29 and older than 60 groups are small (10% or 5 persons). The other two age groups are much larger (40% or 20 persons each). The sample size for each group is then calculated:

$$19 \text{ to } 29 \text{ age group} = (15/50) \times 5 = 1.5$$

$$30 \text{ to } 40 \text{ age group} = (15/50) \times 20 = 6$$

$$41 \text{ to } 60 \text{ age group} = (15/50) \times 20 = 6$$

$$\text{Older than } 60 \text{ age group} = (15/50) \times 5 = 1.5$$

Obviously, we cannot survey 1.5 persons, so we round the number up to 2 persons in the 19 to 29 age group and 2 in the older than 60 group. This means that our sample size has changed from the targeted 15 persons to 16. The final task is to use the table of random numbers to identify the 16 persons based on the criteria set forth by the age categories.

While a proportionate stratified sampling is representative of a whole population in terms of categories, the sample size may prove insufficient if a researcher wants to make comparisons between the groups. For example, the results of two surveys from the 19 to 29 age group would not be a fair comparison with the results of six surveys from the 30 to 40 group because the responses from the 30 to 40 age group would carry three times more weight than the younger group. To rectify this problem, a disproportionate stratified sample can be used. A researcher might take all 5 persons from the 19 to 29 and older than 60 groups and only 5 of 20 persons from each of the larger age groups. This method allows comparisons of the four categories.

Cluster Sampling

When a sample population is dispersed across a wide geographic region, cluster sampling is a popular method for conducting research. The population to be interviewed is divided into clusters, usually along geographic boundaries, and then a random sample of clusters is taken for study. Suppose we wanted to conduct in-person interviews with police throughout the state of Texas. Conducting SRS of all 254 counties requires covering the entire state. Instead, we employ cluster sampling by dividing the 254 counties into six geographical areas (Northeast, North-central, Northwest, Southeast, South-central, and Southwest) and randomly select one county in each area. After the counties are selected, we interview police agencies in all six counties. Cluster sampling provides an economical way of conducting interviews when sample subjects are spread over a large geographic area.

Nonprobability Sampling Procedures

A **nonprobability sampling** procedure does not involve random selection. The researcher selects respondents from the population. While the goal may be to select a sample size that is representative of the population, it is extremely difficult for a researcher to know effectively whether he or she has accomplished this feat. This is especially true when a researcher does not possess an accurate and complete sampling frame.

Convenience Sampling

In **convenience sampling** (also called accidental sampling), a researcher simply chooses a certain number of respondents who are readily available. For example, consider the television news reporter who conducts in-person interviews of shoppers at a local mall to conduct a quick survey of public opinion. If a shopper is at the right place at the right time, he or she will likely be asked to participate. The potential of being included in the sample size is merely a matter of chance. The problem with this type of sampling is that the researcher has no evidence that those who volunteer to participate are representative of the population. Thus, the results of the survey pertain only to the sample size and cannot be generalized to the entire population.

Purposive Sampling

Another type of nonprobability sampling is **purposive** (or judgmental) **sampling**. In criminal justice research, this type of sampling is popular because it allows a researcher to use his or her experience to select a sample typical of the population under study. Purposive sampling is very useful in situations in which a researcher must reach a targeted sample quickly and sampling for proportionality is not the primary concern. For example, in a study of job satisfaction among police officers and differences by gender, Dantzker and Kubin used a purposive sampling strategy to conduct a survey of officers from 14 municipal police agencies in 7 states (Illinois, Texas, California, Nebraska, Alabama, Georgia, and Massachusetts).[15]

Quota Sampling

In **quota sampling**, a researcher selects respondents according to some fixed quota. The objective is to select a proportional number of the major characteristics of a population such as gender, age, race, and geographical location. The researcher uses external data such as a census to estimate the proportion of each characteristic in the population as a whole and a small sample size is selected based on these proportions. This method of sampling bears a resemblance to proportionate stratified random sampling except that the respondents are chosen nonrandomly.[16] Suppose, for example, a researcher is interested in conducting a survey of 100 persons in a community composed of 55% women and 45% men. The researcher would continue to select individuals in each gender characteristic for the sample until the same percentages are met (45 men and 55 women).

Snowball Sampling

The final type of nonprobability sampling is **snowball sampling**. It essentially involves selection of a first subject, then building a list of other persons who could potentially become part of the sample. Normally this is accomplished when a researcher asks a respondent to recommend others who meet the criteria for inclusion in the sample. This method of sampling is useful for researchers conducting exploratory research in which respondents are hard to find or chance meetings are unlikely. For example, Gossett and Williams used snowball sampling to identify and interview 27 female police officers in an exploratory study of gender-based discrimination in a large metropolitan area of the southwestern United States.[17]

summary

- The purpose of a descriptive survey is to describe a population based on information gathered from a group of respondents.

- Explanatory surveys build on the descriptive value of the findings by attempting to provide explanations about information collected from the respondents.

- The final purpose of survey research involves exploration, in which the researcher is more interested in understanding the big picture than in a specific topic.

- The three types of survey research classified by methods of data collection are in-person interviews, telephone interviews, and self-administered questionnaires.

- Another way of gathering survey data is by telephone. As telephone and computer technologies advance, it is likely that the computer-assisted telephone interview (CAT1) will be a preferred method of gathering information. Moreover, computer-assisted personal interviews (CAPIs) and electronic mail (e-mail) surveys have gained popularity as efficient methods of data collection.

- The mailed questionnaire is a common way for a researcher to survey a large group of respondents in a short time. These self-administered surveys can be problematic, particularly in the area of response rate.

- Whether research involves in-person interviews, telephone interviews, or mail surveys, several design features should be considered in constructing a questionnaire.

- The purpose of the questioning, the scope of the questioning, and the organization of the questionnaire are discussed.

- Sampling is the process whereby a representative sample is drawn from an entire population.

- Probability sampling utilizes some form of random selection. Within this category, we examinee simple random sampling (SRS), systematic sampling, proportionate and disproportionate stratified sampling, and cluster sampling.

- In simple random sampling, an individual has an equal chance of being selected.

- Systematic sampling involves moving through the sampling frame list and choosing every *nth* name. This procedure is especially useful for sampling large populations.

- In stratified random sampling, the population is divided into strata and random samples are drawn from each stratum.

- Sample size may be proportionate or disproportionate to the rate of occurrence in the population.
- In cluster sampling, the population is divided into areas and a random sample of clusters is drawn. The greatest benefit is that cluster sampling reduces costs of interviewing respondents located in a large geographical area.
- A nonprobability sampling includes convenience, purposive, quota, and snowball samples.
- Convenience sampling does not involve random sampling. Instead, the researcher simply chooses a certain number of respondents who are readily available.
- Purposive sampling involves selecting a sample typical of a population. This method relies heavily on the researcher's knowledge of the population.
- Quota sampling allocates quotas for a certain number of population characteristics, then employs nonrandom selection to fill the quotas.
- In snowball sampling, respondents are asked to identify others who could potentially be included in the sample.

terminology

Multivariate analysis

In-person interview

Structured interview

Semi-structured interview

Likert scale

Unstructured interview

Word association

Telephone survey

Computer-assisted telephone interview (CATI)

Computer-assisted personal interview (CAPI)

Mail survey

Total design method

Pre-test

Probability sampling
Sampling frame
Simple random sampling (SRS)
Systematic sampling
Proportionate stratified random sampling
Disproportionate stratified random sampling
Cluster sampling
Nonprobability sampling
Convenience sampling
Purposive sampling
Quota sampling
Snowball sampling

discussion points

1. Contrast the objectives of structured, semi-structured, and unstructured interviews.
2. What factors should be considered in deciding which type of interview to conduct?
3. What are probing questions?
4. Why is CATI a popular method of conducting large-scale telephone surveys?
5. What is the total design method?
6. Describe the pre-test.
7. What information should be included in a cover letter?
8. List the four major kinds of questions common to questionnaires.
9. Compare the strengths and weaknesses of in-person interviews, telephone interviews, and mail surveys.
10. What is a sampling frame?
11. Distinguish between features of probability and nonprobability samples.

endnotes

1. J. P. Dean, R. L. Eichhorn, and L. R. Dean. The survey. In *An Introduction to Social Research*, 2nd ed., J. T. Doby, Ed. New York: Appleton-Century-Crofts, 1967.

2. Gallup Organization. March 19–21, 1999.

3. E. Babbie. *Survey Research Methods*. Belmont, CA: Wadsworth Publishing, 1973.

4. G. J. Bayens, M. M. Manske, and J. O. Smykla. Consumer attitudes of ISP work groups in a Midwestern county. *American Journal of Criminal Justice* 22(2): 189–206, 1998.

5. S. H. Decker. Collective and normative features of gang violence. *Justice Quarterly* 13(2): 243–264, 1996.

6. J. A. Aistrup and S. Bannister. Kansas Citizens Justice Initiative Public Opinion Survey. Docking Institute of Public Affairs, Center for Survey Research. Fort Hays State University, Hays, KS, 1998.

7. *Report of National Association of Attorneys General*, November 1997.

8. D. A. Dillman. *Mail and Telephone Surveys: The Total Design Method*. New York: Wiley Interscience, 1978.

9. D. A. Dillman. Presidential address: navigating the rapids of change: some observations on survey methodology in the early twenty-first century. *Public Opinion Quarterly* 66(3): 473–494, 2002.

10. M. Q. Patton. *Practical Evaluation*. Newbury Park, CA: Sage, 1982.

11. Ibid., p. 144.

12. F. E. Hagan. *Research Methods in Criminal Justice and Criminology*. 4th ed. Boston: Allyn & Bacon, 1997.

13. For additional comparisons, see D. C. Miller, *Handbook of Research Design and Social Measurement*, 5th ed. Newbury Park, CA: Sage, 1991.

14. D. R. Anderson, D. J. Sweeney, and T. A. Williams. *Introduction to Statistics: Concepts and Applications*, 3rd ed. St. Paul: West Publishing, 1994.

15. M. L. Dantzker and B. Kubin. Job satisfaction: the gender per-
    spective among police officers. *American Journal of Criminal
    Justice* 23(1): 19–31, 1998.
16. R. Singleton, B. Straits, and M. Straits. *Approaches to Social
    Research*, 2nd ed. New York: Oxford University Press, 1993.
17. J. L. Gossett and J. E. Williams. Perceived discrimination among
    women in law enforcement, *Women in Criminal Justice* 10(1):
    53–73, 1998.

7

participant observation and case studies

introduction

The research methods of participant observation and case studies fall within the category of qualitative research. Recall from discussions in Chapter 2 that this type of research differs considerably from quantitative and evaluative methodologies. Generally speaking, qualitative researchers attempt to describe and interpret a human phenomenon, with specific focus on the research paradigm, methods, and assumptions. In the first segment of this chapter, we describe the fundamental characteristics of the qualitative approach. This sets the stage for an in-depth discussion of the participant observation and case study methods of research.

characteristics of qualitative research

Qualitative research is essentially viewed as field research in which the inquiry process is based on understanding the complexity of a social problem. It is characterized by data collection in a natural setting where the researcher becomes personally involved in the research process in order to appreciate the depth and richness of the problem as a whole. The researcher is more concerned with process than with specifying outcomes, and therefore data are commonly analyzed by an inductive process. Some distinguishing features of qualitative research are:

- It takes place in the field where the inquiry is carried out in natural settings. The emphasis is on studying the whole setting to understand reality.
- Qualitative researchers are interested in the meaningful experiences of people and situations—how people navigate in everyday living.
- Qualitative research is language intense.
- Qualitative research greatly relies on a researcher's ability to observe rather than on measurement instruments (i.e., paper tests). People are the primary data-gathering instruments.
- Qualitative researchers use judgmental rather than random sampling to select atypical subjects.
- Qualitative research involves inductive data analysis (from specific to general). The researcher studies the data inductively to discover unanticipated outcomes.
- Qualitative research attempts to understand reality from the subject's point of view. Therefore, the subject of study plays an important role in interpreting the outcomes.
- Qualitative research methods are most appropriate for answering four questions:
  - What events are occurring in the field setting?
  - What do these events mean to the people involved with them?
  - How are the people able to do what they do in the setting?
  - How do the dynamics among people in this field setting relate to what is occurring in similar settings?

qualitative research strategies

Qualitative research strategies are used when variables are complex, commingled, and difficult to measure. Generally, these types of field studies end with generation of hypotheses and development of theories. As a researcher interacts within the research environment, the emphasis is often to provide a descriptive, sometimes first-person, account of the event studied.

A wide range of research strategies are commonly used in field research. One of the best methods of data collection is **participant observation** in which a researcher actively participates for an extended time in the lives of the people and situations under study. This method assumes that the researcher will be accepted by the group and thus able to acquire detailed information by speaking with the people.[1]

Another exploratory research method is the **case study**. Case studies take a variety of forms, most of which do not involve participant observation. The researcher in a case study explores a single phenomenon (person, activity, etc.) defined or bounded by specified conditions. We now thoroughly examine each of these qualitative, methodological approaches to research.

participant observation

We define participant observation as field research in which the researcher studies a group of individuals in their natural setting by actively participating to varying degrees in the daily lives of the people and activities under study. Researchers often adopt the methodology of participant observation when little is known about a phenomenon. The researcher immerses himself or herself into a particular situation to investigate and describe issues such as:

- Who is in the group or situation?
- What is happening?
- Where do things take place?
- When does the group interact?
- How are the identified elements connected or interrelated?
- Why do things occur as they do?

By virtue of active involvement in the situation observed, the researcher often gains insight and develops interpersonal relationships that are virtually impossible to achieve through any other method.

Types of Participant Observation

Previously, we defined participant observation in terms of the varying degrees in which the researcher participates with a group of individuals in their natural setting. Typically, the participant observer functions in three ways: as **complete observer**, **observer as participant**, and through **complete participation** in the group (the role of observer is concealed).

A common form of qualitative research is participant as complete observer. The researcher informs the group members of his or her research activity and simply observes the activities of the group under study. There is no attempt on the part of the researcher to manipulate the environment; his or her duty is to observe and record.

An example of observer as participant is a one-visit interview.[2] Although it may not be readily apparent, when a researcher conducts an interview with a respondent, he or she is actually performing the role of participant observer. The researcher observes the respondent's demeanor during conversation and can gauge the extent to which further inquiry is necessary and possible.

Complete participation takes place when a researcher joins the activities of the group and begins to manipulate the direction of group activity. Often the researcher must disguise himself or herself to be accepted into the group, thus allowing for maximum interactions. **Disguised observation** is research in which the researcher hides his or her presence or purpose for interacting with a group. For example, criminal justice students at the University of Alabama used disguised observations to examine whether citizens would assist drunks in unlocking the drunks' car doors at two large shopping malls. Students were assigned various roles. Some acted drunk (they were spattered with whiskey on their hands, necks, and faces). Others were observers (they interviewed citizens), safety persons (responsible for the overall safety of participants), and police officers (two were actual policemen who were also students). Of the 85 persons approached by the drunks, 53 helped unlock the car doors, while 32 refused or ignored requests for help.[3]

Participant Observation in Criminal Justice Research

To illustrate participant observation design and how it is used in criminal justice research, we provide excerpts from a National Institute of Justice Research Report titled "Systematic Observation of Public Police: Applying Field Research Methods to Policy Issues."[4] This report describes **systematic social observation (SSO)**, a field research method used to study police. Originally developed in the 1960s and 1970s, SSO has recently been used by the Project on

RESEARCH IN ACTION 5: SYSTEMATIC OBSERVATION OF PUBLIC POLICE[5]

INTRODUCTION

American police are entering a period of experimentation and self-examination that may surpass any other during this century.[5] Police are showing great openness to researchers—both to obtain rigorous evaluations of their work and to demonstrate accountability to constituents. The news is filled with anecdotal accounts of police successes and failures, but policymakers and the public need systematic evidence about what police do and accomplish. They want to know the advantages and disadvantages of traditional methods and how new approaches affect the quality of service delivery. Most importantly, people want to know what is really going on between the police and the public. This report describes systematic social observation, a field research method well suited to answer many questions posed about policing today.

WHAT IS SYSTEMATIC SOCIAL OBSERVATION?

Observation is fundamental to all forms of data collection. The forms differ primarily in how techniques of investigation are organized, how observations are made and recorded, and in their validity and reliability. Systematic observation of natural social phenomena (systematic social observation or SSO) has specific features. First, researchers observe the object of study in its "natural" setting; for example, they may observe directly how an officer responds to a citizen's request for service by being present as the officer interacts with the citizen.

SSO requires that the researcher see and hear an event directly without relying upon others to describe it. Second, researchers make and record their observations according to procedures that can be duplicated. These procedures are made explicit before observation and may be followed by other researchers to produce the same results when they observe the same event. For example, if a researcher wants to know whether an officer was respectful to a complainant, the researcher must define *respectful* and *complainant* in such a way that if other researchers were to follow these rules observing the same situation, they would use the same criteria. This makes it possible for many researchers to conduct observations, rather than relying only upon the observations of a single researcher. Third, these rules are constructed so that researchers can use them to make scientific inferences. For example, suppose one wishes to measure the amount of public disturbance observed by police serving a specific beat. The unit of observation—what is being observed (e.g., a public disturbance)—must be defined in such a way that it can be distinguished from other kinds of events (i.e., citizens engaged in activities that are not public disturbances).

After the unit of observation is defined and distinguished from the stream of other citizen behaviors that might be observed, the researcher may begin to make decisions about how to obtain a representative sample. Finally, the method of observation does not rely upon the event disturbed; i.e., the observation is independent of the event, thereby making it possible to assess the effects of the method of observation. For example, a researcher does not rely upon an officer's report as to whether he or she treated the complainant with respect; the researcher makes that observation and judgment.

SSO has a number of benefits for the study of public policing. Because researchers observe policing in natural settings, they need not rely on the accounts of others to learn what happened. In addition to their observations of the police, SSO researchers may draw from observations made by police of events and may even accompany officers. Obtained at the scene, these "fresh" observations by police are difficult to document in any other way. Official reports often fail to give researchers the kind of information they need, and sometimes the official records are suspect because those who recorded the data intentionally or unintentionally misrepresent what happened. Citizens whom researchers question with surveys may also misrepresent events. A disinterested researcher who focuses on objective observation and accurate recording of observations is likely to obtain the needed information. When a participant or interested party is the sole source of information, biases are more likely to color observations.

SSO draws from a tradition in police research that relies upon direct observation in the field. It is like the work of anthropologists who observe people from a distinctive tribe or culture by being with them. This form of field research is sometimes called ethnography and was used in some classic studies of policing in the 1960s and 1970s. Ethnographers strive to describe not only what their research subjects do, but how they do things and how they feel about their experiences. Ethnographies are used frequently to explain the motivations and rationales of the people studied. Ethnographers do not systematize their field research methods before they go into the field. They assume that their experiences in the field dictate whom and what they study and how they conduct research. They derive data structures from their field experiences and systematize them after their field work. This approach is especially useful when researchers are performing exploratory research on a topic to generate a hypothesis, but it is harder to use ethnographic data for hypothesis testing and establishing the internal and external validity of findings.

HOW SYSTEMATIC SOCIAL OBSERVATION IS DONE

The main procedures for SSO include selection of problems for investigation, preliminary investigation by direct observation (optional), definition of the universe to be observed, sampling for observation, development of instruments to collect and record observations systematically, provision for measuring error, pretesting instruments, organization for direct field observations, processing observations, and quantitative analysis.

Basics of SSO

SSO of police patrol work is accomplished by trained observers who accompany officers at work in police cars, on foot, or even on bicycles. The expectation is that the observer will accompany the assigned officer everywhere the officer goes. Officers are told that they may direct their observer not to accompany them if they believe observer safety is at issue.

While accompanying an assigned officer, an observer may make field notes to help reconstruct events observed. Notes are usually written on a small notepad that is easily carried in a pocket or purse.[9] Observers quickly develop their own shorthand for recording information that will assist their recall of the "who, when, where, and how" details. Officers are allowed and even encouraged to read the notes made by observers, but the notes may not be shown to or discussed with those outside the research team. Because the observed officer may ask to read the observer's notes at any time, an observer must be careful not to record anything the officer may find objectionable. While some might think that observer note taking is too obtrusive, perhaps making observed officers nervous or self-conscious, others find that when done judiciously it can enhance rapport. Observers simply explain it as part of their job, likening it to the reports that officers are required to complete. Most officers readily understand and accept this.

In recent studies we have added post-event interviewing to field researchers' responsibilities. After some events, researchers debrief observed officers to obtain the officers' perspectives on what happened and have them reconstruct the rationales behind their decisions. Our debriefings are informal. There is no questionnaire because the range of events we wish to capture is too great for one set of questions to apply. Also, we want to make the field worker's questions seem as natural as possible, coming from him or her as an individual, rather than some remote scientist. Other research purposes may make a structured debriefing more desirable (with predetermined questions and even listed response options). Some SSO studies have observers debrief one or more citizen participants at a scene after the police–citizen interaction is completed.

Following each observation session, field researchers begin entering observations in formats amenable to data analysis. First, they complete extensive, semi-structured narrative descriptions of the ride and the events that occurred—often 15 to 20 single-spaced pages. Second, they enter data in a highly structured format, using computer software that administers a questionnaire to them about what they observed. Observers must complete data entry for each ride or shift before conducting another observation session. Finally, the narratives and coded data are checked carefully by field supervisors, who are assisted by data checking software. Corrections and clarifications are made quickly before memories fade and events become confused.

CONCLUSION

SSO offers many advantages for gathering and analyzing information about police at work. It can be designed to suit very specific information needs and does not rely on recordkeeping accuracy, candor, or recall of those observed. It offers a scope and depth of data seldom available through official records and survey questionnaires. It can generate rich data sets for both quantitative and qualitative analyses. The largesse from the Violent Crime Control and Law Enforcement Act of 1994 has supported thousands of police department programs to change practices at the street level. This legislation has also supported many evaluations of these efforts. Police departments and those who evaluate their efforts now, more than ever, need rigorous social science tools to measure what matters. SSO can be a valuable tool for those who can commit to its demands.

Policing Neighborhoods (POPN) to study the behavior of police in Indianapolis, Indiana, and St. Petersburg, Florida. The findings of the Project on Policing Neighborhoods in Indianapolis, Indiana, are available electronically at www.ojp.usdoj.gov/nij/pubs.htm.

features of observation

While the extent to which the researcher interacts within the environment may vary, the one element that remains constant is observation. At every level of participation, a researcher always fulfills the role of observer and should consider certain preliminary matters prior to observation. The goal, of course, is sufficient preparation to ensure that observations will be meaningful.

The first issue is the research question. The researcher must formulate a general definition of the problem before the actual field contacts begin. Following this, the researcher determines the method of gathering information. There is a continuum of recording methods (covered in the next section) to document observations as narrative accounts. However, as an alternative, observable data may be documented by means of coded schedules. This involves developing a schedule of codes (symbols) that the researcher uses to categorize events. Recording what is observed simply involves making notes (using a checklist) when a particular event has occurred. The result is that the researcher has more time to observe while still being able to collect all incidents of a particular kind. Although this method tends to quantify events rather than provide a narrative account of a field experience, it provides frequency data, both in absolute (how many times an event occurred) and relative (the relative frequency of different events) terms.

Another important preliminary consideration is deciding whether the observations will take place in public or private areas. Public areas are normally open to everyone. Access to private areas is denied to all but authorized personnel. It should come as no surprise that of the two, it is much easier to conduct an observational study in a public area. Nonetheless, gaining access to private areas may require no more than a phone call or letter of request. The crucial issue regarding location is ensuring that the observations occur in a natural setting. This "real world" feature distinguishes observation studies from other methods. For example, a researcher wanting to study prisoner supervision techniques is likely to gain a better perspective of the dynamics among prisoners and correctional personnel using an observational method in a corrections setting rather than by relying on survey results.

A final item to consider prior to beginning an observational study is **observer effect**—the extent to which the observer is exposed to persons in a natural setting. While the original intent may be to unobtrusively carry out an observational study, even the best laid plans cannot guarantee that the observer will not become exposed to the observed. If this happens, the observer becomes to an extent a participant in a situation, which in turn may in some way change what he or she seeks to observe. This possibility should be considered up front and a contingency plan developed. In most cases, the researcher considers whether it is feasible to become an active participant without overly influencing the setting.

Recording Observations

While conducting an observational study, a researcher must maintain a high level of attention and still be able to accurately record the necessary data. The first task in the collecting effort involves a descriptive account of the research setting. Basically, the aim is to describe the setting, the people, and the events that have taken place. It may also be important to record initial impressions of the setting, people, and events. Several dimensions on which this descriptive account may be collected are identified below. See Table 7.1.

TABLE 7.1: DIMENSIONS OF DESCRIPTIVE OBSERVATION

Space	Physical layout of setting including rooms, climate, etc.
Objects	Furniture, equipment, and other objects within space
Actors	Names of people in setting and distinguishing labels such as rank, job classification, etc.
Activities	Various activities of actors
Acts	Specific actions of individual actors
Goals	What actors are striving to accomplish
Events	Occasions such as meetings
Time	Sequence of events

Source: Adapted from Spradley, J. P. *Participant Observation.* New York: Holt, Rinhart, and Winston. 1980.

Recording Options

There are many options for making records of field observations. The choice of which option(s) to use depends on the limitations of the research setting and preferences of the researcher. The main recording techniques are (1) **field notes**, (2) audiotape recording, (3) videotape recording, and (4) laptop computing.

While actively observing the research setting the researcher prepares **field notes**. Where possible, field notes should cover on-the-spot observations during an event. This common form of data collection in observational studies consists of writing short phrases and using abbreviations. The primary purpose of field notes is to help the researcher recall what happened so that a more detailed document can be produced later. As a routine matter, field notes should be reviewed as soon as possible to add detail and substance. Field notes may not be practical if too many events occur too quickly for a researcher to quickly note observations. If this situation is expected to occur, a researcher might instead use audiotape recording.

The option of using audiotape-recorded observations is very attractive because the devices are handy and versatile. Microcassette recorders are relatively inexpensive and small enough to be carried in a shirt pocket. If necessary, accessories can be purchased to outfit the recorder for hands-free operation. Finally, recorders can be easily concealed if desired. The disadvantage of audiotape recordings is, of course, a malfunction. If batteries become weak or the device does not function, the data collection effort is jeopardized.

Another observational data collection technology is videotape recording. Portable, handheld, video cameras are affordable and can be used in a variety of research settings. The greatest advantage of videotaping is that it produces a definitive re-creation of events that can be viewed several times over. The disadvantage is that video-taping may distract the researcher, thus limiting his or her abilities to record "big picture" events; for example, while a researcher is engrossed with videotaping one event, another of equal importance may go undetected. Also, as with audio devices, video equipment is susceptible to malfunction.

Laptop computers (also known as notebooks) can be very effective for recording data in the field. This is especially true if a researcher possesses good typing skills and is computer literate. As with the previous two options, equipment failure is always a possible menace to the data collection effort.

The four options we discussed are viable data recording methods only as long as the researcher is involved in complete observation. If he or she is engaged in some form of participation, on-the-spot recording may not be feasible. In this case, observation notes should be processed as soon as possible after the field experiences. A good rule to follow is to always process notes of the first field experience before you embark on a second observation.

Analysis and Presentation of Observational Data

After raw data have been collected, how should a researcher go about analyzing them? As a preliminary note, he or she must understand that data collection and analysis are not totally separate functions. In other words, a researcher should conduct ongoing analysis during the data collection effort. Reviewing field notes and tapes immediately after observation gives the researcher a sense of the general picture of what occurred and allows an initial dissection of the collected data. Also, because data are continually collected, organizational skills are essential. Finally, adequate typing skills for anyone contemplating observational data analysis are a must. If **computer data analysis** is planned, there is much to be said for using the laptop computer option to record all data from observations.

Typically, researchers using observational data proceed directly from their written notes to a study report in the form of a narrative text. The initial step is to review all field notes and other recorded materials and condense the information. It is likely that an abundance of information has been recorded, so data reduction ensures that data is non-repetitive and manageable. After these tasks are accomplished, valid conclusions may be drawn from the data. The researcher can then analyze the data and present the findings. As part of the narrative report, the findings can be displayed using graphs, histograms, and other visual presentations.

Matrix, Flow Chart, and Organizational Diagram

In addition to the graphic presentations mentioned above, three other tools may prove useful to display observational study data. The first is the **matrix**, usually a two-dimensional table with rows representing one dimension and columns the second dimension. Table 7.2 is an example of a matrix that provides a synopsis of the overall ratings of 50 correctional agency employees in four job performance categories. The matrix is a useful tool to substantially reduce data derived from a large volume of field notes. In this example, 50 individual job performance appraisals were analyzed and presented as a single matrix.

The **flow chart** is another tool that may prove useful to display observational study data. This is particularly true if a researcher wishes to display all the steps of a process. Moreover, flow charts can be useful to clearly show differences between the way a process should occur and the actual process observed. In such cases, the flow charts of both processes are illustrated and comparisons of presuppositions versus practice are noted.

When the research setting is within a structured organization, an **organizational diagram** that reflects relationships between persons may be useful to display observational data. This pictorial presentation consists of labeled boxes with arrows linking individuals. The focus of the diagram is to display relationships that occur on a regular basis, rather than emphasize the hierarchical structure of posi-

TABLE 7.2: OVERALL JOB PERFORMANCE RATINGS MATRIX

Job Performance Category	Excellent	Acceptable	In Need of Improvement	Unacceptable
Attitude	More than 40%	50%	Less than 10%; 33% of night shift	0%
Resourcefulness	15%; 100% of clerical staff	45%	30%; 50% of line supervisors	0%
Quality of Work	30%	55%	10%; 50% of admission staff	5%
Quantity of Work	35%; 100% of day shift	35%	25%; 75% of night shift	5%

tions within the organization. Some associated text is coupled with the diagram to explain the networking.

case studies

Another qualitative methodological approach to research is the **case study**. Earlier we noted that a case study explores a single phenomenon (e.g., person or activity) defined or bounded by specified conditions. By concentrating on a single phenomenon or entity, the researcher aims to uncover the interactions of significant factors characteristic of the phenomenon.

As in participant observation studies, the orientation of most case study researchers is interpretive: understanding the meaning of a process or experience constitutes the knowledge to be gained from an inductive (theory generating) mode of inquiry, rather than a deductive (theory testing) mode. To some extent, this explains why researchers in the social sciences are fond of the case study method. Social scientists are interested in gaining knowledge of people in their natural settings and their interactions with other people and the environment. The case study is an acceptable and often preferred method of obtaining such insights. Moreover, case studies are particularly useful in criminal justice for a variety of reasons including:

- Assessment of the effectiveness of intervention at an individual level
- Examination of specific issues and analyzing problems
- Influencing policy formulation
- Examining unusual cases
- Evaluation of programs

Characteristics

The case study is an appropriate method for answering research questions that ask "how" and "why" and do not require control over events. In other words, little may be known about a topic, so the researcher exchanges the ability to generalize with an in-depth focus on a small number of representative cases to developing a full understanding of the subject he or she is interested in studying.[6] Exploratory research of this nature is popular with some researchers who see the case study as a diagnostic tool to develop a range of objective possibilities that could occur. When the purpose of research is descriptive, the researcher looks for and describes salient features of a case. Finally, in an explanatory case study, the researcher attempts to identify patterns in which one type of observed variation is systematically related to another type.

Another characteristic of the case study involves population sampling. Case studies are limited in terms of sampling because they focus on such small units of analysis. Probability procedures such as random sampling are rarely used in case study research. Typically, the case study method relies on a researcher's ability to identify cases that are representative of the research problem under study. Another way to characterize a case study is by its special features. These features are not mutually exclusive. They can combine as defining traits. The special features include:

- An empirical inquiry investigating a contemporary phenomenon within its real-life context
- Phenomenon assessed to have boundaries and constitute a case
- Exhaustive collection of data about all aspects of a situation, event, program, or person
- Multi-method strategy of data collection, usually involving interviewing, observing, and analyzing documents
- Simultaneous data analysis with data collection

Types

When identifying types of case studies, we often think of research as a study of an individual person. In this type of research, a detailed account focusing on one person is the objective of a simple case study. For example, a case study might focus on a probationer placed under community supervision for a lengthy period. Multiple case studies, however, may involve several individual cases. When a set of individual cases is studied, the number of individuals is fairly small and all the individuals have certain features in common.

In addition to case studies of individual people, a case study can involve a group, institution, service, event, relationship, or other entity. While a case study can be used to study virtually anything, its focus is always the central aim of the research study; that is, the case study addresses a fundamental research problem.

Research Questions

The case study method may be chosen on the basis of a problem identified prior to research in a field setting. The researcher may have a general idea about what is to be studied and the issues involved from knowledge gained through literature searches and previous observations. Often a research problem is derived from personal interest. Sometimes other stakeholders (i.e., policymakers or governmental officials) determine the research problem.

The researcher may realize that the initial problem is somehow inappropriate (i.e., it may not make sense in terms of the realities of everyday life) or that many important issues in need of study were not anticipated at the outset. If this occurs, the researcher can usually refine the research questions. Whether developed prior to implementation of the study or refined later, the questions must be researchable by case study means. The critical question to consider is whether empirical data obtained by the case study methodology will adequately address the research problem.

Data Collection Strategy

Ways of collecting information via case study vary and range from fairly open, unstructured approaches to closed, structured ones. The nature of a data collection effort often depends on the researcher's personal preference but should always consider the type of study undertaken. If the purpose of the study is exploratory, an unstructured approach is most appropriate. Conversely, a highly structured approach is required if the purpose is explanatory. Table 7.3 summarizes the main data collection techniques commonly used in case studies. By using a combination of observations, interviewing, and document analysis, a researcher is able to use different data sources to validate and cross-check findings.[7]

Analysis and Presentation of Data

Data generated from case studies typically include documents, observation field notes, and interview responses. Because the aim is to make a case study as objective as possible, computer organization of the data is recommended. This involves compiling the data, entering it into a database, and assigning a number to each line of data. The researcher then creates categories to combine the data, assigns labels, and codes all information in the data set. The next step is to

TABLE 7.3: DATA COLLECTION TECHNIQUES COMMONLY USED IN CASE STUDIES

Interview Responses
- Unstructured/open-ended: Characterized by little or no direction from interviewer. Goal is to gain insight into a person's perceptions in a situation.
- Semi-structured: Use of interview guide specifying key topics.
- Structured: Standardized set of questions.

Use of Documents and Records
- Includes wide range of written or recorded materials; i.e., case records, diaries, historical accounts, etc.

Observation Field Notes
- Simple observation: Passive, unobtrusive observation.
- Systematic observation: Use of standardized observation instrument.
- Participant observation: Researcher takes on a role other than that of passive observer and participates in event studied.

determine the meaning of the data, find constructs, themes, and patterns, and decide which elements are most important to the study. As noted earlier, a researcher may consider a computer software system for coding and analyzing case study data.

Presentation of the results of a case study involves both description and interpretation of the findings in an interesting and informative narrative. Three components are recommended for inclusion: particular description, general description, and interpretative commentary.[8] A particular description consists of quotes from interviews and field notes and narrative vignettes. General description informs the reader whether the quotes and vignettes are typical of the data as a whole and relates the parts to the whole. Interpretative commentary provides a framework for understanding both forms of description by explaining the salient characteristics of the case.

Two dominant styles for presenting case study findings are analytic reporting and reflective reporting. The major characteristics of analytic reporting are (1) using an objective writing style and (2) organizing the information into the conventional headings of introduction, literature review, methodology, results, and discussion. Reflective reporting, on the other hand, describes data based on a researcher's intuition and judgment. The researcher attempts to depict a phenomenon by re-creating it contextually. The report on a multiple case study should include the results for each case and also provide a cross-case analysis, noting consistencies and differences in constructs, themes, and patterns.

summary

Qualitative research is essentially field research in which data is collected in a natural setting. It is distinguished by such features as language intensity, inductive data analysis, and understanding reality from the subject's point of view.

- Participant observation is defined as a method of research whereby the researcher actively participates to a degree in the research environment. We typically think of participant observation occurring in one of three ways: complete observer, observer as participant, or complete participation in the daily lives of the people and activities under study.

- Systematic social observation is offered as a principal example of a field research method used to study police behavior in Indianapolis, Indiana, and St. Petersburg, Florida. Researchers utilize participant observation to record events as they see and hear them and do not rely on others to describe or interpret events.

- Fieldwork requires a researcher to be a skilled observer and certain issues must be considered prior to observation.

- A fundamental matter to be considered prior to observation is the research question. Another consideration is deciding where the observations will occur. Great emphasis is placed on ensuring that observations take place in their natural setting.

- A final consideration involves observer effect. If a researcher becomes exposed to those under observation, a contingency plan developed before the start of the study may be considered for implementation.

- Field notes are on-the-spot writings that help a researcher recall what was observed.

- Audio and videotape recordings may also be viable options. Both present the potential for equipment malfunction. If coding and analysis will be performed by a computer program, the researcher should seriously consider using a laptop computer to record data.

- After raw data are collected, the researcher decides how to analyze and present the data. Self-analysis followed by a well-written narrative is one way to determine the features of the data and show the findings. Matrices, flow charts, and organizational diagrams are excellent ways of graphically displaying results. Another way of analyzing the data is via computer.

- The final qualitative approach is the case study. This methodology is especially responsive to research questions of how and why a phenomenon occurs in its natural state.

- Researchers who can tolerate ambiguity and are willing to refine design features, even from the onset of the study, are most skillful in conducting case studies.

- The design of a case study can be customized to address a wide range of research questions and incorporate a variety of data collection, analysis, and reporting techniques.

terminology

Participant observation

Case study

Complete observer

Observer as participant

Complete participation

Disguised observation

Systematic social observation (SSO)

Observer effect

Field notes

Computer analysis

Matrix

Flow chart

Organizational diagram

discussion points

1. What are the fundamental characteristics of the qualitative approach to research?
2. Distinguish the three ways participant observation occurs.

3. What is systematic social observation (SSO)?

4. Is it ethical to deceive the people you are studying in the hope that they will confide in you as they would not confide in an identified researcher?

5. Identify several options available for making records in the field.

6. In what ways could a researcher present data using graphic displays?

7. What are the two dominant styles for presenting case study findings?

endnotes

1. R. Bogdan and S. J. Taylor. *Introduction to Qualitative Research*, 4th ed. Needham Heights, MA: Allyn & Bacon, 1997.

2. F. E. Hagan. *Research Methods in Criminal Justice and Criminology: A Phenomenological Approach to the Social Sciences*. New York: John Wiley & Sons, 1975.

3. W. A. Formby and J. O. Smykla. Attitudes and perceptions toward drinking and driving: a simulation of citizen awareness. *Journal of Police Science and Administration* 12(4): 379–384, 1984.

4. S. Mastrofski, R. Parks, A. Reiss, Jr., et al. *Systematic Observation of Public Police: Applying Field Research Methods to Policy Issues.* NCJ 172859. Washington: U.S. Department of Justice, December 1998.

5. Albert J. Reiss. Systematic observation of natural social phenomena. In *Sociological Methodology*, H. L. Costner, Ed. San Francisco: Jossey-Bass, 1971, pp. 3–33.

6. J. P. Spradley. *Participant Observation*. New York: Holt, Rinehart and Winston, 1980.

7. M. Q. Patton. *Qualitative Research Methods*, 2nd ed. Thousand Oaks, CA: Sage, 1990.

8. F. Erickson. Qualitative methods in research on teaching. In *Handbook of Research on Teaching*, 3rd ed., M. C. Whittrock, Ed. Old Tappan, NJ: Macmillan, 1986.

descriptive, historical, and archival data analyses

introduction

Use of historical and archival data is a relatively neglected area of criminal justice research. Research based on examining existing sources of information is considered archival or documental analysis. While we tend to study social phenomena at a single point in time, we tend to forget that each phase of society has a history. This omission may be due to the tendency of researchers to view history as a mere chronicle of unique events. As C. Wright Mills noted, "Whatever else a person may be, he or she is a social actor and an historical actor who must be understood, if at all, in a close and intricate interplay with historical structure."[1]

descriptive research

The two general purposes of research are description and explanation. **Descriptive research** looks only to describe the facts and characteristics of a phenomenon and is often described as observation with insight. The purpose of descriptive research is to ascertain and describe the facts and characteristics surrounding a phenomenon. The *Uniform Crime Reports*[2] and the national census compilations are classic examples of descriptive research.

One of the earliest examples of recorded descriptive research dates back to John Howard, the High Sheriff of Bedford, England, in 1773.[3] Howard was unhappy with the conditions of the jail when he was appointed High Sheriff. His proposed jail reforms were opposed on the grounds that all prisons in England operated under substantially the same conditions and that his jail should not be any different. To counter these arguments, he conducted a descriptive study of the conditions of jails in England and presented his findings to a committee of the House of Commons. As the result of his study, two new laws were enacted. The first provided for the release of prisoners who were not charged within a certain period. The second required that jails be kept clean, medical care be provided for prisoners, and initiated jail inspection requirements. Howard later conducted similar studies of jails in France, Germany, and the Netherlands, combined the data, and published a comparative survey of jail conditions in Europe. He described conditions in the jails and corrective action ensued as a direct result of his research.

Functions

The goal of descriptive research is to identify problem areas and evaluate current conditions and procedures. Descriptive research is also known as the normative survey method because the researcher using the method obtains data by observation. Descriptive research does not attempt to identify or explain relationships, make predictions, or develop theories. Accordingly, many procedural steps required for other methods may not be necessary. The data is collected for descriptive purposes only. Because this type of research deals with inquiries, the most popular methods of data collection are questionnaires and interviews.

Strengths and Limitations

Strengths: The ability to generate a broad range of data about the characteristics of a phenomena is one of the greatest strengths of descriptive research. Because the principal data sources are questionnaires and interviews, this method is more cost efficient than other types of research and the design of a descriptive research project is normally less complicated. In addition, data collection instruments are generally more flexible and adaptable than the data collection instruments utilized in other research projects.

Limitations: One of the major limitations of descriptive research is that the accuracy of data gathered during interviews and questionnaires depends on the accuracy of the information provided by respondents. In addition, the ability to check the accuracy of the responses is limited. Although the data collection instruments are generally more flexible and adaptable, their design is critical. Inappropriate data collection instruments can easily distort results. In addition, while the structure of the project is generally less complicated, the conduct of the research may be more difficult because of this lack of structure.

Descriptive research depends on definitions. Changing the definition of an event may produce different descriptive conclusions. For example, changing the definition of theft in the *Uniform Crime Reports* would yield different conclusions about the numbers and types of thefts occurring in any one year. Descriptive research seldom deals with the context of life. Although it provides information on aspects, it rarely develops a feel for total context.

Common Errors

Common errors noted in descriptive research projects include the failure to formulate clear and specific objectives, using data collection instruments that introduce bias, and inappropriate selection of units of analysis and samples. In many cases, the unit and sample selections are based on convenience. Another common error, especially in projects involving descriptive methods, is the collection of the data prior to planning the analysis procedures.

Designing Descriptive Research Projects

The normal steps in designing a descriptive research project are:

- Defining the objectives.
- Determining the facts and/or characteristics needed.
- Deciding whether the endeavor will produce the desired results and whether the descriptive procedures are appropriate.
- Ascertaining the need for and importance of the study. Is the study of sufficient need or value to make the project worthwhile?
- Developing a clear statement of data needed and determining its availability.

- Devising a systematic data collection plan.
- Pre-testing the plan and making necessary revisions.
- Collecting data.
- Determining and describing existing conditions.

historical research

Historical research involves the use of historical data to analyze and develop conclusions about the latent meanings of history. Scientific research relies on data gathered during the collection phase of a project. Historical research depends on data observed and reported by others. Accordingly, a historical researcher must examine the original methodology and rationale under which the data were collected. Although the techniques of criminal justice researchers and historians in accessing data are similar, the emphasis is different. The historian is generally interested in obtaining a set of credible statements about particular historical occurrences. The criminal justice researcher tends to be more concerned with using the data to develop and test propositions that explain and predict human behavior.

Purposes

Historical research is not limited to library searches about famous events or people. It can focus on organizations or events limited to a local area. An example of a local research project is a historical examination of the administrative organization of a local police department. For historical research on a local topic, official files of the research subject, if available, are valuable resources. The most common purposes of historical research include:

- Determining why an event happened.
- Discovering the meanings of past events.
- Studying the relationships of past events to each other or to the present.
- Establishing long-term trends.
- Testing theoretical ideas or propositions.
- Studying institutional changes over time.

Historical data is never petrified or static; history is dynamic and that quality defines the role of the historical researcher whose task is not merely to relate what events happened but to present a factually supported rationale to explain why events happened.[4]

Research Problems

While scientific researchers generally attempt to test specific hypotheses developed prior to the data collection effort, a historical researcher will usually develop broad open-ended questions in lieu of hypotheses and is often looking for conceptual themes. In most cases, the significant results of historical research are generalizations and principles derived from documentary data.

Time and Space Dimensions

History is dimensional. Its dimensions are time and space. Historical research generally focuses not on events of history, but on why they occurred. The historical method may follow a time or space dimension.

In looking at the time dimension of a series of events, a researcher must examine the time continuum—a linear chronology of events similar to a yardstick that illustrates the series of events under study at the precise points of their relative occurrence. The time dimension of a study emphasizes chronology. It is not, however, merely a list of a series of events. We need to look at the series and explain the meanings of the events in relation to each other and to the problem under study. For example, to study the growth of the police department in your city, create a time continuum. If your city is 100 years old, draw a line 10 inches long. Divide the line into 10 equal (inch) subdivisions; each inch represents a 10-year span. Then plot the significant events pertaining to your study along the line at the precise points of their occurrences. The time continuum will reveal the slowness or rapidity with which key events happened. A researcher tries to discover why the events happened slowly during some periods and very rapidly during others.

The **space dimension** emphasizes the role of a place in history and is a form of historical geography. The aim of a researcher in examining the space dimension of events under study is to understand the spatial significance of the events. One common method of examining spatial dimensions is to plot the locations of occurrences on a map. This technique may reveal new insights into a project.

Designing Historical Research Plan

The research method selected depends to a great extent on the data available and the purposes of the research. For example, to ascertain the present state of policing in New York City, a historical approach would be inappropriate. One of the first steps in designing a historical research project is defining or selecting the problem that will serve as the subject of the research. A clear definition of the problem is required. Without it, the project will fail. Evaluate the significance of the study. Is this research important? If not, why waste time on it?

Next, consider the availability of data. If the required data is unavailable, the project cannot be researched. Formulate the research problem or question and subquestions if necessary. As in all other types of research, a data collection plan should be developed, followed by a pre-test to determine the availability of data and the soundness of the research question; then revise as necessary.

archival or document research

Archival research based on analysis of existing sources of information is also known as document analysis. The two principal types are secondary analysis and content analysis. Secondary analysis involves examining the results of earlier reported research. During secondary analysis, the researcher may reexamine the methods, data, and results. Often a researcher will attempt to reexamine the research in new ways or attempt to find possible sources of error or bias in the earlier research. An area of caution in secondary analysis is that the original researcher is likely to have been selective in recording data and reporting the results. Much of the information contained in a report may consist of the original researcher's reconstructions or interpretations. Also, clerical or typographical errors or omissions may appear in earlier reports.

Content analysis is a technique for making inferences by objectively and systematically identifying specified characteristics of messages.[5] Content analysis is used in two contexts. The first is an analysis of the content of various documents as part of the research process. The second context is the use of the technique to provide a predetermined coding scheme and categories for tabulating the contents of documents. In this context, the researcher can determine by the number of entries tabulated in each category the direction or weight of the archival evidence. For example, we may want to determine whether the newspaper accounts of police handling of the "Rodney King riots" in Los Angeles were negative, positive, or neutral. This could be accomplished by researching the newspaper articles about the riot, classifying the articles found as favorable, neutral, or unfavorable to the police, and then tabulating their direction. Document analysis can be used effectively to conduct research, especially when used in conjunction with other techniques. It may be the only way to collect data of past events, and is relatively inexpensive.

Secondary Sources

Most document analysis involves **secondary sources** containing information originally collected for purposes other than the present research project. Secondary sources have the advantages of being ready-made and generally available. Because they were generated independently of the present research, the research plan must be tailored to fit the existing available data. Another major feature of secondary sources is that generally they are not limited in time and space.

Secondary source data also has disadvantages because it may not contain all the data items preferred for a research project. A researcher has no way to reconstruct the missing data and may have to speculate about the meaning of language in the various documents. The strengths of using secondary sources, however, far outweigh the disadvantages, and the use of secondary sources is widespread in criminal justice research.

Credibility

The inability to control the accuracy of collected data means that the researcher must carefully weigh, double check, and, if possible, verify from other sources any data obtained from historical documents to ensure the **credibility** of his or her study.

Document, as used in this chapter, refers to any written material that may be used as a source of information about a research project. As noted earlier, one of the major problems in historical or archival analysis is credibility. To overcome credibility issues, researchers have developed various techniques for document analysis. The techniques used to measure or establish credibility may be divided into external and internal criticisms. **External criticism** involves attempts to distinguish legitimate research from hoaxes and misrepresentations. Frauds are not uncommon. Famous hoaxes include Thomas Chatterton and his famous eighteenth-century forgeries known as the "Rowley Manuscripts." A few years ago, a spurious biography of Howard Hughes fooled the editors of a major publishing houses.

Internal criticism is concerned with establishing the degree of credibility of a particular document. In conducting external criticism, a researcher must carefully evaluate many documents and their sources. Establishing the authenticity of documents is a study in itself and may involve carbon dating, handwriting analysis, identification of ink and paper, vocabulary usage and writing style, and other considerations. While most researchers are not equipped to conduct such authenticity studies, each document used in research should be evaluated:

- How reliable is the author?
- Do other sources agree with the author?
- Does the document make sense?

In conducting an **internal review** of a document, the main question is: "What do the words mean?" During an internal review, a researcher should ask:

- Was the ultimate source of the facts or details reliable?
- Does the reporter have sufficient insight into his or her own behavior or the behavior of others to be able to provide certain types of information?
- Did the primary source accurately report the facts or details?
- If the primary source of data is not available, how accurate are the secondary sources?
- Are external corroborations of the facts or details under examination available? This test is based on the general rule to accept only facts or details based on independent testimonies of at least two witnesses.

Personal and Institutional Documents

Documents are personal in the sense that they are produced by humans and most reveal something about human behavior. We tend, however, to think of personal documents as those that reveal something personal about those who wrote them—autobiographies, diaries, personal letters, and memoranda. It is difficult to establish the credibility of personal documents. Their importance, however, should not be neglected. Most researchers require less corroboration when dealing with personal documents. Although it is conceivable that a diary or letter may have been written with the intent to deceive future readers, the chances are that most such personal documents are valid. The situations in which individuals write diaries and personal letters indicate a willingness to tell the truth that tends to be stronger than the motivation to tell the truth in the production of many other documents. Autobiographies may, however, be self-serving and that may cast a doubt on their credibility.

Researchers may obtain a great deal of information by analyzing written documents kept by institutions for administrative or governmental purposes. Articles in newspapers and magazines such as *Time* and *Newsweek* may also be used to conduct historical and documental research. Other available sources include letters, videos, memoirs, and diaries. Information about individuals including birth, death, marriage, school, military, police, and census records is readily available. Emile Durkheim, in a classic study of suicide, used several kinds of government documents to test his propositions despite the inadequacy and lack of reliability of government documents. Modern researchers have thousands of more reliable government documents at their disposal.[6]

replication of previous research

Researchers are in the habit of carefully scrutinizing and criticizing research of others under the common generic process known as **peer review**. One recognized hallmark of research is that no view remains immune to challenge. During peer review, we point out the strengths and weaknesses we see in others' research designs, data collection techniques, and analysis. Often during peer review, hidden biases are revealed and faulty reasoning exposed. **Replication** is another method to check the accuracy of prior research. Replication in different locations or at different times may provide additional data about research questions. It involves repeating the research of others by studying the same questions and using the same methodology. If the replication produces similar results, confidence in the original research may be increased.

Probably the most famous replication research involves the findings of Swiss psychologist Jean Piaget. In 1932, he reported a series of studies involving playing games with children and asking them about the rules. He also conducted informal interviews in which he told the children about an incident involving right and wrong and asked for each child's opinion. Piaget concluded that moral judgment develops in a sequential process, with three major stages. Young children see adult rules as sacred and unchangeable. Around age eight, children begin to shift toward regarding the rules as products of group agreements and instruments for achieving cooperative purposes. Later, the concept of equity is modified in the direction of relativism, taking into account the specific circumstances. Piaget concluded that moral judgment is not taught, but rather develops spontaneously from children's attempts to make sense of the social interactions in their world. He also noted that, in more mature stages, children develop moral judgments from their interactions with other children rather than with adults.[7] Piaget's conclusions were received with mixed emotions because they contradicted existing theories. His conclusions were not accepted until his research had been replicated by others. For example, in 1937, Learner repeated Piaget's study in the United States.[8] The study has been repeated many times—sometimes using the same hypothetical incidents and sometimes using different ones.

Another classic example of replication research involves Marvin Wolfgang's analysis of criminal homicides in the city of Philadelphia.[9] His study was replicated by Voss and Hepburn for homicides in Chicago,[10] by Pokorny for homicides in Houston,[11] and partially by Roberson for homicides in San Francisco. Studies of the four cities, using similar research plans, allowed researchers to determine significant differences in the homicide patterns of the various cities.

locating documents

Researchers have conducted studies of human behavior for many years. Modern researchers can consult major archives, universities, and governmental depositories that make copies of previous research available. For example, when Roberson conducted his replication study, he obtained microfilm copies of the reports of the other researches from University MicroFilms, an archive in Ann Arbor, Michigan. Major research archives are also located in Berkeley, New Haven, and Williamstown.

When beginning a document search, it is often useful to start with a broad perspective on a topic by consulting an abstract service such as Criminal Justice Abstracts or Sociological Abstracts. Subject matter indexes such as the Criminal Justice Index, the Social Sciences Index, and the International Encyclopedia of Social Sciences are also useful. The three major criminal justice journals (*Criminology*, *Journal of Criminal Justice*, and *Justice Quarterly*) contain reports of criminal justice research. *Criminology* is published by the American Society of Criminology. The *Journal of Criminal Justice* is an independent publication distributed by the University of Michigan. *Justice Quarterly* is published by the Academy of Criminal Justice Sciences. All three enjoy considerable prestige in the criminological and criminal justice academic communities.

Another excellent starting place to search for documents is the National Archive of Criminal Justice Data sponsored by the Bureau of Justice Statistics (BJS), an agency of the Department of Justice. The archive was established in 1978 under the auspices of the Inter-University Consortium for Political and Social Research (ICPSR) with the central mission of facilitating and encouraging research in the field of criminal justice through the sharing of data resources. The ICPSR is a membership-based organization with over 350 member colleges and universities in the U.S. and abroad. A catalog of the National Archive may be obtained via the Internet. Its Website is www.icpsr.umich.edu/NACJD.

reviewing related literature

In earlier sections of this chapter, we examined historical research. This section covers the review of related literature that constitutes an important part of any project. Although historical research has many similar attributes, it is more exhaustive and tends to cover more extended periods. A review of the literature precedes the research phase of a project; a literature review *is* the project in historical research. Instructors of research courses generally agree that students do not understand the purpose of reviewing the literature related to research projects. Fundamentally, the more you know about related research, the more knowledgeably you can approach your research project. Note that the review covers related (collateral) research, not necessarily research identical to yours.

Purpose

A review of related literature serves several purposes. The primary purpose is to assist in attacking a research problem. In any research project, the problem or question is central to the research. Any effort that assists in researching the problem should be made. By looking at what others have done in related areas, you are better prepared to resolve your problem. The review may reveal investigations similar to your own and demonstrate how other researchers handled similar situations. A review can also suggest avenues of approach for dealing with a problem situation and may also reveal additional sources of data that you may not have known existed.

A review will also provide you with new ideas and approaches that may not have occurred to you. In addition, it can help you evaluate your own research by comparing it with the similar efforts of others. A review may also help you see your own study in historical and associated perspectives and in relation to earlier attacks on the same research problem.

Conducting a Search

Although the specific methods of a search for related literature depend to a great extent on the nature of your research problem, certain general procedures apply. Start by reviewing indexes and abstracts that will provide you with information about important current studies and related projects. For current events, do not overlook *Facts on File*, *The Los Angeles Times* and *The New York Times* indexes. Information services such as MED, LARS, ERIC, and University Microfilms may also be useful. The Internet provides an inexhaustible list of resources available to researchers. For example, you may electronically search major university libraries from the comfort of your home. Chapter 10 contains more information. Vast sources of information about government publications are the Depository Libraries maintained by the federal government, which has been described as the largest source of information on earth. When researching the related literature, the steps below are recommended:

- Be systematic and thorough. Do the job right the first time.
- Use your computer as much as possible.
- Be accurate. Making photocopies is a common means of obtaining accurate data quickly.
- Make sure your bibliographic notes of references are complete.
- Keep your research problem-related. Ask how a literature item relates to your problem.

Writing Reviews

After reviewing the related literature, the next step is to write a review of the literature. Before you begin writing, form a clear view of what you are going to do. The review should discuss the related research reports, studies, and writings that bear directly upon your own effort. Often, in their eagerness to proceed with research, students consider the review section an unnecessary appendage to a project. However, a conscientious and thorough review may reveal new possibilities and new ways of looking at a research problem that may have otherwise been overlooked. One way of looking at the review is to consider it a discussion with another researcher about what others have written about your topic.

Formulate a plan for writing the review section; otherwise, your review will look unplanned and disorganized. Outlining the review is an excellent method of developing a plan. The outline should suggest relevant areas for discussion and indicate the direction the review should take. A good approach is to base your review outline on an inverted pyramid. Start at the bottom with broad-based literature, then move upward to the more specific or localized studies that focus more intensely on your specific research problem.

Remember that the review section covers only related literature. It is not the place to reproduce previous studies. What you say about the related research is more important than what the original authors wrote. Present the reviews in your own words. Paraphrase rather than use long quotations. Long quotations represent a last resort; use them only for good reasons. The review should be a synopsis of important related literature, not conventional filler in a report.

In writing a review, it is important to establish that the related literature is connected to your research. One recommendation is that a researcher writing a review should position the statement of the research problem in plain view as a constant reminder that the central axis of the review is the research problem. Group related research into groups that pertain to various sub-parts of your research problem. Write section heads that include words that are identical to those found in the statement of the research problem. At the end of each section, make sure your review answers "What does it mean?"

Remember that at some stage of the literature review process, you will have to be satisfied with what you have as a foundation to move forward with your research. However, you will continually add to your review and may rewrite it a number of times. Chapter 11 provides an in-depth discussion of literature reviews.

**RESEARCH IN ACTION 6: SUGGESTIONS FOR
PREPARING LITERATURE REVIEW***

When you begin the review of the literature you should give readers a basic idea of how you intend to treat him or her. You are not writing a mystery. Be a loudmouth! Tell readers "who done it." Reveal your plot! Reviewing literature may be particularly difficult because some topics make it hard to "hedge" at the beginning and end of your review. The more extensive the previous work, the more difficult the preparation of the literature section. The following suggestions may be of help.

If you have chosen a topic on which there is little previous research, do not panic. It is acceptable to review only two or three closely related studies. You may find, on the other hand, two or three areas of investigation that relate to what you are doing. You may have to decide which of these you will review in depth or determine it is necessary to review all of them. Generally, the solution is worked out in the following sequence.

First, review in depth those studies that are similar to yours, indicating their strengths and weaknesses and how their findings may be incorporated or improved upon in your research design. Next, note those aspects that have a bearing on your problem (but are not directly related) into a general review of several paragraphs or pages to bring readers closer to your research problem. In that case, you may cite summaries that others pulled together on the topic. It is highly unlikely that any area of "investigatory saturation" has not been reviewed earlier in a professional journal or a doctoral thesis. Remember, however, that you are responsible for the authenticity of the summary, so you should read the original accounts of investigation that are particularly germane to your study.

It is especially desirable to include a discussion section at the end of the literature review to pull together the implications of the previous studies and indicate the direction you take in the third chapter (research design) of the report. Some of you will find that a separate section labeled "Discussion of Previous Research" is a comfortable way to handle the discussion section.

---

* This information was taken from a thesis course syllabus frequently used by the authors.

Others will prefer to put their overall observations in the summary section. A table or figure that summarizes the major research components and findings can serve as a useful device to help your readers comprehend the various elements of the studies you reviewed.

summary

- The purpose of descriptive research is to ascertain and describe the facts and characteristics of a phenomenon.

- Research of historical and archival data is a relatively neglected area of criminal justice research.

- Research based on analysis of existing sources of information is considered archival or documental analysis.

- Historical research involves the use of historical data to analyze and develop conclusions about the latent meanings of history. This type of research depends on data observed and reported by others.

- Historical research is not limited to library searches for information about famous events or people. It can examine local organizations or events.

- Although a scientific researcher generally attempts to test specific hypotheses developed prior to the data collection effort, a historical researcher will usually develop broad, open-ended questions in lieu of hypotheses.

- History is dimensional; its dimensions are time and space. Historical research generally focuses on why events occurred instead of focusing on the events. The historical method may be based on a time or space dimension of history.

- Research based on analysis of existing sources of information is also known as document analysis. The two principal types are secondary analysis and content analysis.

- Content analysis is used in two contexts. The first is analysis of the contents of various documents as part of the research process. The second context is devising a predetermined coding scheme and categories for tabulating the contents of the documents.

- Most document analysis involves the use of secondary sources. Secondary sources include any information originally collected for purposes other than those related to the present research project.
- The inability to control the accuracy of the collected data means that a researcher must carefully weigh, double check, and, if possible, verify from other sources any data obtained from historical documents.
- Research replication is another method to check the accuracy of prior research. Replication in different locations or at different times may provide new or additional data about research questions.
- The more you know about related research, the more knowledgeably you can approach your project. The review of related literature describes related research, not necessarily research that is identical to yours.
- A review of related literature has several purposes. The primary purpose is to assist in attacking your research problem.
- Before you begin writing, get a clear view of what you are going to do. The review covers related research reports, studies, and writings that bear directly upon your efforts.

terminology

Descriptive research

Historical research

Time continuum

Space dimension

Archival research

Secondary analysis

Content analysis

Secondary sources

Credibility

External criticism

Internal criticism

Internal review

Replication

Peer review

discussion points

1. How does historical research differ from others types of research?
2. Distinguish between time and space dimensions of historical research projects.
3. List four common examples of historical research.
4. Describe how to write a review of related literature.
5. What are the general goals of historical research?

endnotes

1. C. W. Mills. *The Sociological Imagination.* New York: Oxford University Press, 1968, p. 146.
2. The Uniform Crime Reports (UCR) contains official data on crime that is reported to law enforcement agencies across the United States who then provide the data to the Federal Bureau of Investigation (FBI). UCR focuses on index crimes, which include homicide and non-negligent manslaughter, robbery, forcible rape, aggravated assault, burglary, larceny/theft, motor vehicle theft, and arson. UCR is a summary-based reporting system, with data aggregated to the city, county, state, and other geographic levels. FBI Crime in the United States: Uniform Crime Reports (2007). Washington, D.C.: U.S. Department of Justice.
3. P. D. Leedy. *Practical Research Planning and Design,* 3rd ed. New York: Macmillan, 1985, p. 173.
4. Ibid., p. 224.
5. O. R. Holsti. *Content Analysis for the Social Sciences and Humanities.* Reading, MA: Addison-Wesley, 1969, p. 14.
6. E. Durkheim. *Suicide: A Study in Sociology.* New York: Free Press, 1897.
7. J. Piaget. *The Moral Judgment of the Child.* Glencoe, IL: Free Press, 1932.

8. B. Rotman. *Jean Piaget: Psychologist of the Real.* New York: Cornell U. Press, 1977.

9. M. E. Wolfgang. *Patterns of Criminal Homicide.* Philadelphia: University of Pennsylvania Press, 1958.

10. H. L. Voss and J. R. Hepburn. Patterns of criminal homicide in Chicago, *Journal of Criminal Law, Criminology, and Police Studies* 59: 499–508, 1968.

11. A. D. Pokorny. A comparison of criminal homicide in two cities. *Journal of Criminal Law, Criminology and Police Science* 56: 479–497, 1965.

ethics in research

introduction

In 1989, an award-winning scientist was charged with falsifying laboratory reports to reflect that laboratory tests that were never performed had been performed. He was also charged with basing his research findings on those phony tests.[1] This conduct was clearly a breach of ethical duties. Unfortunately, not all such breaches are this obvious.

The primary subject of criminal justice researchers is human behavior. Ethical concerns can arise from almost all aspects of the research process. What do we mean by ethics? **Ethics** is defined as the principles of morality, including both the science of the good and the nature of the right. It is also defined as the rules of conduct recognized in respect to a particular class of human actions.[2]

In this chapter, we examine the ethical standards of conduct surrounding research processes. For researchers, most ethical issues arise from three situations. First, a researcher has an ethical obligation to conduct research in a neutral and impartial manner, without personal moral judgments clouding observations. Second, certain standards of conduct are required in dealing with human subjects. The third issue is honesty in reporting. The **Academy of Criminal Justice Sciences** (ACJS) Code of Ethics will be examined in relation to all three of these areas.

Academy of Criminal Justice Science (ACJS) code of ethics

The academy adopted a **code of ethics** at its annual meeting in 1999. The code is divided into three sections:

- General principles
- Ethical standards that underlie members' professional responsibilities and conduct
- Policies and procedures for enforcing those principles and standards

The code states that membership in ACJS commits members to adhere to its code of ethics in determining ethical behavior in the context of their everyday professional activities. The code also provides that activities that are purely personal and not related to criminal justice as a profession are not subject to the code. The ethical standards in the code are broadly written in order to apply to applications in a wide variety of roles and contexts. According to the general principles, academy members should be very careful to avoid incompetent, unethical, or unscrupulous use of criminal justice knowledge. The code recognizes the great potential for harm associated with studying criminal justice. Members should not knowingly place their well-being or the well-being of others in jeopardy in their professional work.

At the 1999 annual meeting, the academy approved a new code of ethics after using the American Sociological Association's Code of Ethics as a model. Section III B of the ACJS code provides guidance regarding the ethical duties of researchers. The complete text of the code appears on the ACJS Website: www.acjs.org.

neutral and impartial research

In 1918, Max Weber made the classic statement on **objectivity** and neutrality when he coined the phrase **value-free sociology**. He stated that sociology, like other sciences, must not be encumbered by personal values if it is to make special contributions to society. Earl Babbie contends, however, that social research can never be totally objective because researchers are humanly subjective. Both Weber and Babbie are concerned about political views influencing the conduct and reporting of research projects. Babbie states: "Although you are permitted to have political views, you are expected to hold them aside when you enter the realm of science." He also said that both liberals and conservatives should recognize the facts of social science research, regardless of how those facts accord with their personal politics.[3] The ACJS Code of Ethics indicates that members of the academy as researchers should maintain objectivity and integrity in the conduct of criminal justice research.

research involving humans

The need for researchers studying human behavior to involve human subjects in their research raises questionable issues. Most present-day restrictions on using human subjects can be traced to the **Belmont report**. The National Research Act of 1974 created a **National Commission for the Protection of Human Subjects (NCPHS)**. The commission reviewed the U.S. Department of Health, Education and Welfare (HEW) guidelines developed in 1971 and issued the Belmont report as a result. The report proposed the alteration of the guidelines and the roles of institutional review boards so as not to interfere with an investigator's freedom of research. The report also recommended revisions of the HEW guidelines and advocated three basic principles:

- Respect for individuals accomplished through informed consent and treating individuals as autonomous agents. If their autonomy is diminished, they are entitled to protection.
- Beneficence in that subjects should not be harmed and that one should maximize benefits and minimize potential harm.
- Justice, which seeks that both the benefits and burdens of research be distributed equitably through the selection of subjects.

The HEW guidelines were revised in 1981, took into account the criticisms of the original regulations by social scientists, and excluded most social science research from the regulations. The regulations were again revised by the publication in 1991 of the Federal Policy for the Protection of Human Subjects. Much of the research excluded by the 1981 revision was again included under the guidelines. In October

1995, President Clinton issued Executive Order 12975 establishing a National Bioethics Advisory Commission. A recurring theme of the regulations is the requirement for an institutional review board to monitor individuals within institutions that conduct research using human subjects.

Stuart Cook compiled the following list of ethical issues to avoid during research involving human subjects.[4] You will note that more than one ethical issue may arise during a study.

- Involving human subjects in research without their knowledge or consent
- Coercing people to participate
- Withholding from human subjects the true nature of the research
- Deceiving or misleading human subjects
- Leading subjects to commit acts that lessen their self-respect
- Violating the right of **self-determination**; for example, by research on behavior and character change
- Exposing subjects to mental or physical stress
- Failing to treat research subjects fairly; not showing them consideration and respect
- Withholding benefits from participants in control groups

The ACJS Code of Ethics provides that all research should meet the human subject requirements imposed by educational institutions and funding sources. Study design and information gathering techniques should conform to regulations protecting the rights of human subjects, regardless of funding source. The code also provides that members should take culturally appropriate steps to secure informed consent and avoid invasions of privacy. Special actions are required of members studying individuals who are illiterate, are under correctional or judicial supervision, are minors, have low social status, have diminished capacity, are unfamiliar with social research, or otherwise occupy positions of unequal power. In addition, members should try to anticipate potential threats to confidentiality. Techniques to protect confidentiality such as removal of direct identifiers, use of randomized responses, and other statistical solutions to ensure privacy should be used where appropriate. Care should also be taken to ensure secure storage, maintenance, and/or destruction of sensitive records.

The code requires that any confidential information provided by research participants should be treated as such by members, even when the information enjoys no legal protection or privilege and legal force is applied. The obligation of confidentiality also applies to members of research organization such as interviewers, coders, and clerical staff. The code places the responsibility on administrators and chief investigators to instruct staff members on this point and make every effort to ensure that access to confidential information is restricted.

Involving Human Subjects without Their Knowledge or Consent

Should any individual serve as a subject in a research project without knowing about it in advance? Some researchers will argue that lack of knowledge of involvement is required in some situations. Others contend that a researcher who involves an individual in research without the latter's consent has infringed upon the individual's right to decide whether or not to participate.

A researcher may feel that seeking the consent of a human subject would completely change the behavior of the subject and render the research meaningless. In this case, the researcher is left with the choice of abandoning the project or conducting it despite the ethical considerations involved. Accordingly, the researcher faces a value conflict between the duty to add to knowledge and the duty not to infringe upon a subject's freedom of choice. The value conflict should be examined on the basis of how much the effects of the research would impact the subjects. If the extent of the imposition is slight, the ethical concerns are smaller and the ethical question about engaging them in research without their knowledge less serious. As the extent of the imposition increases, the ethical costs increase correspondingly and the questions become more severe.

In many cases, where humans are used as subjects in research without their knowledge or consent, unobtrusive (secretive and non-reactive) observations are used. The advantage of using unobtrusive observation is that data collection does not influence the actions of the subjects. Many researchers contend that the only accurate method to study human behavior is to observe humans in natural settings without their knowledge or assistance. Self-reported descriptions of behavior are considered by many to be unreliable.

People tend to recount their actions in a light most favorable to them and they forget material facts. In addition, people who are watched act differently from those who are unaware that they are observed. The ethical dilemmas in unobtrusive observations should be considered by asking: "Is the value of the data collection sufficient to override the fact that the humans were the subjects of a research project without their knowledge and consent?" This question may be easier to answer if the behaviors under observation would have occurred without the researcher's involvement. A more difficult question occurs when a researcher creates a study situations; for example, studying a witness's reaction to an apparent crime (the crime is staged by actors and the sole purpose of the production is to study the witness's reactions). While staged situations such as this may be the only way to judge certain responses, the stress or trauma of observing a crime may have a considerable impact on a witness.

B. A. Meltzer studied juror deliberations by the use of hidden microphones. When news of his research became public, many congressmen were upset because they saw the jury recording as a threat to fundamental institutions.[5] A congressional investigation resulted. Congress then passed a statute mandating that anyone who attempts to record the proceedings of a jury in the United States while the jury is deliberating or voting is guilty of a felony.[6]

Coercing People to Participate

In the 1970s, the state of New York allowed eight inmates to be inoculated with a venereal infection to test for possible cures. For their so-called voluntary participation, the prisoners received, in their own words, "syphilis and a carton of cigarettes."[7] Encouraging student participation in a research project by promising extra credit to be applied to a course grade is considered a questionable practice by many. Such questionable actions arise because researchers need people to participate in their research.

Individuals are ordered on occasion by their employers, commanding officers, wardens, or professors to participate in research. These situations clearly involve coercion. In some cases, it is more difficult to distinguish between coercion and a fair exchange of a reward. Examples are the college professor who gives extra credit to students to take part in research or the prisoner who participates in research to increase his or her chances of parole. Are these individuals coerced or are they involved in a fair exchange of a reward? The ethical concerns of coercion include the loss by the subject of the freedom to choose and the fact that the subjects may be forced to participate in projects involving causes they do not embrace.

Informed Consent

Should consent given to participate in a research project be informed consent? **Informed consent** had its origin in medical treatment. It means that a patient has a right to know the risks involved before consenting to medical treatment. When applied to research in the social sciences, the term has acquired connotations extending far beyond its original meaning. According to Stuart Cook, the withholding of information about research in which a person consents to participate is a questionable practice and, as a result, freedom of choice and human dignity are diminished. Cook also contends that social scientists are obliged to avoid such acts if possible and if they cannot, they must give careful consideration to the ethical costs of carrying out the research and the values to be served in so doing.[8]

Informed consent means consent given by an individual who received adequate information about the nature of the research and who has the ability to decline without prejudice. One of the problems with informed consent is that a full explanation of the research may in some cases defeat the purposes of the research or distort the results. Informed consent also implies that no coercion is involved in participation. Many researchers are reluctant to provide too much information about the nature of the research to human subjects. As noted by Belinda McCarthy, in obtaining consent, researchers are reluctant to provide too much information, especially in the early stages of a project when the need to develop rapport and willingness to cooperate are important.[9]

Informed consent should precede involvement in a research project, so that the individuals are given meaningful opportunities to decline participation. A consent should include information about any risks that subjects may reasonably expect and any discomfort or loss of dignity that may result. Individuals should be informed about all aspects of the study that might reasonably influence their willingness to take part.

A related issued in dealing with the problem of informed consent is whether all subjects are equally deserving of informed consents. For example, public figures can be observed by anyone and are less vulnerable than nonpublic figures in private places.[10] Finbarr O'Connor claims that the application of standard guidelines for protection of human subjects to Woodward and Bernstein's Watergate investigation would have changed the course of American history."[11] John Galliher contends:

While all people may be worthy of the same respect as human beings, it does not necessarily follow that their activities merit the same degree of protection and respect ... it is questionable whether the files of the American Nazi Party are deserving of the same respect as any other data source; must one secure the active cooperation of the Ku Klux Klan, or for that matter the Pentagon, before conducting research in their organizations or with their personnel? The question is, how much honor is proper for the sociologist in studying the membership and organization of what he considers an essentially dishonorable, morally outrageous, and destructive enterprise? Is it not the failure of sociology to uncover corrupt, illegitimate, covert practices of government or industry because of the supposed prohibitions of professional ethics tantamount to supporting such practices.[12]

Murray Wax identifies "six paradoxes of consent" applied to field work:[13]

- Many people studied may be semiliterate and not accustomed to the legal argot.
- Many will distrust a situation requiring their endorsement on a piece of paper.
- Consent of subjects is a continual process dependent on mutual learning and evolution.
- Knowing nothing of ethnography, they have no basis upon which to decide to give, or not to give, consent.
- Ethnography involves observation and discussion and not a rationalistic a priori analysis.
- Field work is an evolving process; thus the subjects of investigation are likely to shift during the course of study.

Withholding True Nature of Research

Similar to the concerns about individuals involved in research projects without their consents is the concern for individuals who are involved in a project with their consents but are unaware of the true nature of the research. The subjects are generally given a brief overview of a project and a "cover story" about their participation. The concept of informed consent discussed earlier applies to these situations and the individuals cannot be considered true volunteers. Prior to conducting research in these situations, a researcher must carefully consider the ethical costs and concerns of conducting the research. The ACJS Code of Ethics declares that human subjects have the right to full disclosure of the purposes of the research as early as appropriate to the research process. They also have a right to have their questions answered about the purpose and usage of the report.

Deceiving Participants

In a 1970s study, a researcher observed homosexual activity in public restrooms in a manner so that the individuals were unaware that they were watched. The researcher noted the participants' automobile license numbers and from that information obtained their home addresses. Later, he visited their homes, explaining that he was conducting a health survey. He did not inform them that he observed them in the restrooms. He asked the individuals many personal questions that eventually became a part of his research on public homosexual conduct.[14]

Is there a difference between a conscious effort to hide part of the available information (failing to inform the subjects they were observed in homosexual activities) and deliberate lying (the purpose was a health survey)? Would the researcher's conduct have been more acceptable had he not lied to the individuals? As noted by Stuart Cook, deception may be considered an affront to individual autonomy and self-respect, or an occasionally legitimate means to be used in the service of a higher value.[15]

Alternatives to deception may include providing only general information with full disclosure after the research has been completed or having subjects take part in role playing after the nature of the research has been explained. There are serious doubts about the validity of using role playing techniques. Before using deception in research, a researcher should evaluate the nature of the project and weigh its value against the impact of deception, the sensitivity of the behavior involved, and the degree of privacy invaded.

Violating Right of Self-Determination

The concept of the right of self-determination is interwoven with informed consent. Researchers who produce significant changes in the behavior of human subjects without their informed consent are violating the individuals' own rights to self-determination in action and character. This right is violated even when the change produced is one others might consider desirable.

Exposing Subjects to Mental or Physical Stress

The ACJS Code of Ethics provides that the conduct of criminal justice research should not expose respondents to more than minimal risks of personal harm. Academy members should make every effort to ensure the safety and security of respondents and project staff. Informed consent should be obtained when the risks of research are greater than the risks of everyday life.

Inconsiderate and Unfair Treatment

Any researcher involved with human subjects is obligated to treat them fairly and show them consideration and respect. During research, a tendency to treat participants as objects rather than human subjects may develop. Certain steps may be taken to minimize unfair and inconsiderate behaviors. One step is to recognize the situational context in which the researcher and the subject have accepted their differences in status. Another step is for the researcher to follow up after the project is completed to ensure that the subjects received the benefits promised for participation.

Withholding Benefits from Participants in Control Groups

Assume a researcher is convinced that her new treatment will benefit people who have a certain disease. She establishes two groups of human subjects who are afflicted with the disease. One group receives the treatment; the treatment is withheld from the control group. If the researcher believes that the new treatment will benefit all subjects, are there ethical concerns in withholding it from the control group? A similar ethical concern occurs when members of a control group in a study measuring the value of a benefit are deprived of a benefit they had before the study.

One horrible example of withholding treatment was discovered in the 1970s. Several decades earlier, a government-supported experiment was conducted to evaluate the effectiveness of a new treatment for syphilis. Members of the control group did not receive the medicine. After the experiment ended, members of the control group were forgotten until the appearance of reports that the health of many of the control group members deteriorated as a result of the disease.

In one experiment, about 600 families received government payments that raised their annual incomes to about $5,000. Another 600 families in the same communities constituted the control group and received no assistance although they were in equal need. The purpose of the study was to determine the effect of a guaranteed annual income on incentive to work. The researcher concluded that the results indicated no reduction in work incentive among those receiving payments.

Questionable Practices

In the examples listed below, the human subjects were not told the purposes of the research. While they may not have been deliberately misled, they were not told the whole truth. Which of the following examples do you consider ethically permissible? Which do you consider borderline or unethical? Why?

- To test restaurant discrimination against African-Americans in the area of the United Nations headquarters in New York, researchers sent two same-sex pairs of diners (one pair was white and one black) to the same restaurants. In many of the restaurants, the black pair received inferior service, such as delays in seating, delays in service, undesirable seating, and other inconveniences.

- A social scientist ran for mayor of his hometown. Without the knowledge of the voters, he distributed "emotional" campaign literature in one part of town and "rational" literature in other parts of the town. From the size of the votes in the two sets of precincts he inferred the relative effectiveness of the two types of appeal.

- An individual played the role of a handicapped person with a flat tire to determine what types of individuals would stop and render assistance.

- A group of mothers with children under the age of seven gave consent for researchers to observe the children. The researchers were in fact observing the interactions of the mothers and children.

- Subjects were told that they were selected at random, when in fact they were purposely selected.

- A college instructor, in attempt to test the effects of an unfair berating, administers a 1-hour examination to two sections of a specific course. The overall performances of the two sections were essentially the same. He artificially lowers the grades of one section and then berates them in class. He later administers a final examination to both sections. The section subjected to berating performed significantly lower on the final exam.

analysis and reporting

In 1989, the University of Utah held a press conference to announce that two of its researchers succeeded in producing excess energy by fusing deuterium nuclei in a palladium lattice (cold fusion). Normally, an announcement of such importance would have been preceded by a careful review by the scientific community and making a detailed report available to other scientists. Those steps were not taken. Two months later, hundreds of scientists from all over the world gathered in Santa Fe, New Mexico, to discuss efforts to confirm the claim. The meeting was beamed live by satellite to thousands of other scientists. The two Utah professors were expected to be the first speakers. At the last minute, the two professors canceled their appearance, claiming that they were too busy in the laboratory to attend. Attempts to replicate their experiment were unsuccessful. Why was their laboratory off-limits to other scientists? Why were they unwilling to reveal the details of their research? Why were the standards of scientific conduct ignored? Most scientists now conclude that their report was merely the wishful interpretation of sloppy and incomplete experiments.[16]

In another case, the National Institutes of Health (NIH) levied severe sanctions against a professor of biological sciences at Purdue University for plagiarizing the work of scientists at Harvard University. The NIH alleged that while at Baylor University, the professor patterned his experiments after those detailed in a manuscript sent him for peer review, used the information to publish his own work, and falsified his records to claim credit for discovering a key enzyme in the retina. The NIH stated, "To purloin willfully the ideas of another investigator ... raises the worst fears and concerns among the members of the scientific community."[17]

Researchers have a duty to present their research in a fair and accurate manner. Their roles include being objective and value-free in approaching and reporting the subject matter. Any problems and weaknesses of a project should be disclosed, including any mistakes that may have affected the results of the study. There is a corresponding duty to report negative findings.

In 1992, a report by the American Association of University Women (AAUW) swept though the world of education. The report described the American classroom as a "hell hole" for girls (females were alleg-edly invisible, ignored, silenced, and broken by loss of self-esteem). The text of the report was basically an expression of hard-line cam-pus feminism. The report contended that, "School curricula should deal directly with issues of power, gender politics, and violence against women." Many school curricula were changed as a result of the report.

Judith Kleinfeld, a professor of psychology at the University of Alaska, was one of the first researchers to undertake an in-depth analysis of the report and opined that the AAUW's synthesis of 1,100 studies in the field ignored or suppressed studies that didn't fit the woman-as-victim thesis. She concluded that the report con-stituted "politicized research" and "false political propaganda." Other researchers agreed with her.[18]

The ACJS Code of Ethics states that members should acknowl-edge persons who contribute to their research and their copy-righted publications. Any claims and ordering of authorship and acknowledgments should accurately reflect the contributions of all main participants (including students) in the research and writ-ing processes, except where such ordering or acknowledgment is determined by official protocol. Data and material taken verbatim from another person's published or unpublished writings should be explicitly identified and referenced to their author. Citations to original ideas and data developed in the work of others, even if not quoted verbatim, should be acknowledged. Conversely, the code also provides that while generally adhering to the norm of acknowledging the contributions of all collaborators, members should be sensitive to harm that may arise from disclosure and respect a collaborator's need for anonymity.

American Association for Public Opinion Research (AAPOR) code of ethics

In addition to the Academy of Criminal Justice Sciences Code of Ethics referenced earlier in this chapter, the American Association for Public Opinion Research (AAPOR) developed a code of ethics for researchers. The key parts specify that:

- Researchers will exercise due care in gathering and process-ing research data and take reasonable steps to ensure the accuracy of the results.

- Due care will be exercised in the development of research designs and in the analysis of data.
- Only suitable research tools and methods of analysis will be used.
- Research tools and methods of analysis will not be selected because of their capacity to yield a desired result.
- Researchers will not make interpretations of research results nor tacitly permit interpretations that are inconsistent with the data available.
- Researchers shall not knowingly imply that interpretations should be accorded greater confidence than the data actually warrants.
- The findings and methods shall be accurately described in appropriate detail in all research reports.
- Researchers shall cooperate with legally authorized representatives of the public by describing the methods used in the research projects.
- Researchers shall retain the right to approve the release of information about their findings. When misinterpretations appear, researchers shall publicly disclose necessary information to correct the problem.
- Researchers shall hold confidential information obtained about a client's general business affairs and the findings of research conducted for a client, except when authorized by the client.
- Researchers shall accept only those assignments that he or she is capable of accomplishing.
- Researchers shall not lie to respondents or use practices and methods that abuse, coerce, or humiliate them.
- Researchers shall respect the anonymity of every respondent unless the respondent waives such anonymity for specified users.
- Researchers shall hold as privileged and confidential all information that tends to identify the respondent.

summary

- The primary subject of criminal justice researchers is human behavior. Ethical concerns can arise from most aspects of the research process. Ethics is defined as the principles of morality, including both the science of the good and the nature of the right.

- Ethics is also defined as the rules of conduct recognized in respect to a particular class of human actions.

- For researchers, most ethical issues arise from three situations. The first is the ethical obligation to conduct research in a neutral and impartial manner, without personal moral judgments clouding observations.

- Second are the certain standards of conduct required when dealing with human subjects.

- Third is the issue of honesty in research reporting.

- The Academy of Criminal Justice Sciences adopted a code of ethics at its annual meeting in 1999. The three sections cover (1) general principles, (2) ethical standards that underlie members' professional responsibilities and conduct, and (3) policies and procedures for enforcing the principles and standards.

- The ACJS Code of Ethics indicates that members of the academy as researchers should maintain objectivity and integrity in the conduct of criminal justice research.

- Many questionable issues arise because researchers studying human behavior need human subjects in their research. Most current restrictions on using human subjects can be traced to the Belmont report.

- Stuart Cook compiled a list of ethical issues present in any research involving human subjects: involving human subjects in research without their knowledge or consent; coercing people to participate; withholding the true nature of the research; deceiving or misleading human subjects; leading them to commit acts that lessen their self-respect; violating their rights of self-determination, particularly during research on behavior and character change; exposing subjects to mental or physical stress; failing to treat them fairly and not showing them consideration and respect; and withholding benefits from control group participants.

- Researchers have a duty to present their research in a fair and accurate manner. Their roles include being objective and value-free in approaching and reporting the subject matter.

Any problems and weaknesses of a project should be disclosed by the researcher.

terminology

Ethics

Academy of Criminal Justice Science (ACJS)

Code of Ethics

Objectivity

Value-free sociology

Belmont report

National Commission for the Protection of Human Subjects (NCPHS)

Self-determination

Informed Consent

American Association for Public Opinion Research (AAPOR)

discussion points

1. What problems are associated with the use of human subjects?
2. Are there any situations in which a researcher is justified in deceiving a human subject?
3. Ned Polsky once stated, "If one is effectively to study adult criminals in their natural settings, he must make the moral decision that in some ways he will break the law himself."[19] Do you agree? Justify your answer.
4. A researcher is opposed to abortion and birth control. She wants to conduct a study on the popular opinions regarding the problems caused by overpopulation. What ethical issues would she face and how should she handle those issues?

endnotes

1. *Chronicle of Higher Education*, January 25, 1989, p. A44.

2. *American College Dictionary*. New York: Random House, 1964.

3. E. Babbie. *The Practice of Social Research*, 6th ed. Belmont, CA: Wadsworth Publishing, 1992, p. 476.

4. S. W. Cook. Ethical issues in the conduct of research in social relations. In *Research Methods in Social Relations*, 3rd ed. C. Sellitz et al., Eds. New York: Holt, Rinehart and Winston, 1976.

5. B. A. Meltzer. Projected study of the jury as a working institution. *Annals of the American Academy of Political and Social Sciences* 287: 97–102, 1953.

6. Cook, 1976, p. 205.

7. G. Geis. Ethical and legal issues in experiments with offender populations. In *Criminal Justice Research: Approaches, Problems and Policy*. S. Talarico, Ed. Cincinnati: Anderson, 1980.

8. Cook, 1976, p. 210.

9. M. C. Braswell, B. R. McCarthy, and B. J. McCarthy. *Justice, Crime and Ethics*, 3rd ed. Cincinnati: Anderson, 1998.

10. B. Thorne. You still takin' notes? Fieldwork and problems of informed consent. *Social Problems* 27: 284–297, 1980.

11. F. W. O'Connor. The ethical demands of the Belmont report. In *Deviance and Decency*, C. Klockars and F. W. O'Connor, Eds. Beverly Hills: Sage, 1979, pp. 225–228.

12. J. F. Galliher. The protection of human subjects: a re-examination of the professional code of ethics. *American Sociologist* 9: 93–100, 1973.

13. M. Wax. Paradoxes of consent to the practice of field work. *Social Problems* 27: 272–283, 1980.

14. L. Humphreys. *Tearoom Trade*. Chicago: Aldine, 1970.

15. Cook, 1976.

16. *Chronicle of Higher Education*, June 14, 1989.

17. *Chronicle of Higher Education*, July 19, 1989, p. A4.

18. J. Leo. Truth sinks AAUW's big lie. *Victoria Advocate*, February 15, 1999, p. 13A.

19. N. Polsky. *Hustlers, Beats and Others*. Chicago: Aldine, 1967, p. 139.

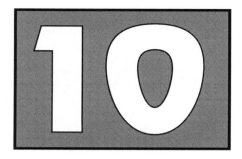

developing research plans

introduction

In Chapter 2, we began addressing several matters that must be taken into account when considering a research design. We progressively expanded our discussion of this topic by exploring the various methodological strategies available to a researcher considering how to carry out a research project. Although it is true that choosing a research design method is a major undertaking, it is also true that this choice is only one of many tasks required when developing a research plan.

This chapter explores several equally important tasks to be performed when developing a **research plan**. We begin by considering **topic selection** and examine five important issues. We discuss how to refine the direction of research by writing a topic statement. Next, we further refine our topic by discussing how to focus the research by composing a purpose statement. In a later section, we explore literature review and how to begin a search for literature on a particular topic. Much of our discussion centers on the purpose of the literature review and using library resources.

topic selection

Successful research begins with choosing an area of study of interest to the researcher. The idea is that if the researcher is interested in a particular topic, he or she will remain motivated throughout the project. This is an important quality because research can take considerable time and may become tedious or even burdensome. For the beginning researcher, the choice of a research topic is typically based on previous knowledge he or she brings to a project. This is particularly true if that knowledge is the result of an original interest in the subject. It is not unusual to find that a researcher's mastery of a certain area of study originated in part due to a keen interest in that area.

Another feature to consider when selecting a research topic is that research should be challenging. If a researcher possesses a certain amount of knowledge about a topic, the goal should be to broaden that knowledge. Conversely, some researchers select a research topic based on a desire to gain knowledge in a related but unfamiliar area. Limited knowledge about a topic often stimulates greater interest. Whether the goal is to expand on previous knowledge or delve into unfamiliar territory, research should be viewed as a quest that will ultimately result in new knowledge for the researcher. When selecting a research topic, the topic should be broad enough to yield sufficient information, but not so broad that it involves multiple issues or overwhelming amounts of information.

Another consideration in selecting a topic is whether the topic is researchable. Obviously, if a researcher will be hampered by problems throughout his or research, it should be dismissed as impractical. Below are three important questions that should be answered in determining researchability.

- Is the area of interest focused enough? After a topic has been selected, determine whether it involves a single issue or multiple issues. If it involves multiple issues, identify all the issues involved and select one issue of interest.

- Are the necessary resources readily available? In addition to considering the costs associated with conducting the research, it is equally important to examine whether the research can be concluded within a specific time frame.

- Is access to data restricted? The environment in which the research will be conducted may exert tremendous influence on the initial decision of topic selection. If severe limitations may hinder data collection, an alternative topic is in order.

A final matter to consider when choosing a research topic is the ability to conduct research. The strengths and weaknesses of a researcher, especially in the collection and analysis of data, should be assessed.

RESEARCH IN ACTION 7: LOCALLY INITIATED RESEARCH PARTNERSHIPS IN POLICING: NIJ'S FACTORS FOR SUCCESS[1]

The traditional approach to most major policing research projects has been for a police department to cooperate with a researcher who wrote a proposal and submitted it. The researcher controls all steps of the process. The department cooperates by providing access to records and staff or conducting experiments on some aspects of police operations.

This approach is changing. A program developed by the National Institute of Justice (NIJ) with support from the U.S. Department of Justice's Office of Community Oriented Policing Services enables police to participate as equals with researchers. Through locally initiated research partnerships, the police and research partners share responsibilities throughout a project by jointly selecting (locally initiating) a topic of interest to the department and collaborating on the research design, its implementation, and interpretation of the study findings.

AIMS OF PROGRAM

Begun in 1995, the NIJ partnership program in policing currently encompasses several research projects. The new approach complements the basic premise of community policing: working as partners achieve more than individuals working alone. A project in Philadelphia exemplifies how the police can establish productive partnerships with researchers just as they establish relationships with the community. Philadelphia police worked in concert with Temple University researchers to evaluate the department's community policing initiative. Using multiple methods (surveys, observation, and interviews), the partners documented exemplary community-oriented and problem-solving policing and discovered factors that facilitated or hindered implementation.

What happened in Philadelphia also illustrates the aim of the partnership approach. The university-based researchers gained experience in the field and a better grasp of the realities of police operations. The department was able to tap the expertise of the researchers and apply it to solving operational problems. The findings served as a basis for mid-course corrections in the department's approach to community policing—evidence that research partnerships can produce change in police policy and practice. The long-term aim is for the partnerships to extend beyond the lives of the initial projects and become ongoing collaborations that will build the research capacity of police departments, enabling them to become more efficient and effective in reducing crime. Encouraged by the program's potential to improve research and practice, NIJ applied the concept to other topics and is now sponsoring locally initiated research partnerships in domestic violence, juvenile justice, and other areas. In an evaluation of the partnership program conducted by the Institute for Law and Justice, NIJ set out to discover how the projects are working and what factors lead to success.

LEARNING ABOUT PROSPECTIVE PARTNERS

Police executives and researchers interested in establishing a partnership are likely to raise a number of questions before they make a commitment. They will want to determine, for example, what police practitioners should know about researchers to work effectively with them and how researchers should approach police they see as prospective partners. Because one of the chief objectives in a partnership program is to build foundations for ongoing police-researcher collaboration, an additional question raised is whether and how a particular partnership can be sustained as a routine way to conduct research. The evaluators addressed these questions through the broader question of what constitutes a successful collaboration. The evaluation findings indicated that several factors, from cultivating the police–researcher relationship to ensuring the adequacy of information systems are essential. The evaluators also developed practical measures of success.

WHAT LEADS TO SUCCESS?

It is no surprise that partnerships of police departments and researchers have greater chances of succeeding if the relationships are built on a foundation of trust and open communication, but careful cultivation of the relationship is only one component in the inventory of factors that achieve success.

The partners must develop good working relationships— Conducting research as a partnership calls for individuals to work together to develop common objectives and define roles and responsibilities. Most project participants have found that to achieve these and other ends it is advantageous to establish several modes of communication during the course of the research such as frequent meetings, e-mail exchanges, telephone calls, and brief progress reports. In some projects, inclusion of police union members has been essential. In the Oakland, California, project, for example, in which the effects of officer stress on family life were studied, union representatives formed part of the research team and contributed ideas about how to persuade officers and their spouses to be interviewed. Cultivating this relationship paid off because the research resulted in a better understanding of the effects of stress on families and provided the department with ideas on how to reduce the problems that stress can create.

Trust between partners must be cultivated—Building trust is especially important when the participants have not previously worked together. In such instances, researchers have found it to their advantage to "pay their dues" to achieve acceptance from police; for example, by accompanying police officers on ride-a-longs, conducting department-wide interviews instead of confining interviews to a single unit, and accommodating departmental requests for help on issues and problems outside the immediate scope of the research project. The key researcher in one project spent the first 6 months interviewing sergeants and commanders. She felt that winning the trust and confidence of the police managers would lay a foundation for the research she would conduct.

Researchers should invest in understanding local police culture—Parallel with building trust, and as a foundation for it, researchers must understand the local police culture whose elements include officers' attitudes toward their jobs, the role of sergeants in community policing, the history of the department's personnel relationships, and the political environment. Especially important for researchers is understanding how the philosophy of community policing and its implementation are perceived through the lens of the local police culture. The amount of effort required to understand the local police culture should not be underestimated. That culture is likely to have developed over a long period and may therefore not be as receptive to new ideas as researchers might like to believe. Familiarity with the department's culture helps a researcher formulate realistic recommendations from the research findings.

Graduate students can be used effectively—In several projects involving universities, graduate students played key roles. They performed a variety of tasks including collecting data, providing assistance in developing the research design, analyzing information systems, and interpreting results. In some projects, graduate students were assigned independent research projects such as determining the feasibility of computer mapping in a police department and identifying information systems needs. The primary author of one project shared responsibility with a graduate student on the report of a major evaluation of community policing. Such use of graduate students can be a win–win situation—they benefit from the real-world experience of working in a police department while the partnership gains by acquiring cost-effective support.

Information systems must be able to support research—In several projects, researchers found that the police departments' information systems were unable to fully support the research. The records may not have contained the amount of detail needed for analysis or a system may not have had an information system. In these situations, the project timetables had to change to accommodate the dearth of available information. For example, in some projects, the researchers found it necessary to establish a system for collecting the records needed or substantially change an existing system before useful analysis could proceed. In other projects, the information systems contained the data needed, but considerable manipulation was necessary before analysis was possible. Ironically, the analysis usually generated ideas for improving the information systems for both operational and research purposes.

Local research projects must fit their audiences—The primary aim of partnership projects is to solve local problems and secondarily to contribute to the general knowledge about a topic. For that reason, the final product must be tailored to a local audience. In general, police commanders are not interested in the details of a research design. Instead, they want to concentrate on the impacts of results on policies and operations. Experience with the partnership projects reveals that the findings can be presented in a variety of formats—brief written or oral presentations, slide presentations, memoranda, or summary tables, to name a few—with the selection tailored to audience needs. Reports geared to scholars, containing literature reviews and extensive bibliographical references, usually are not appropriate for or well received by practitioners. In fact, researchers must do double duty if they intend to publish in peer-reviewed journals. They must develop one type of product for police practitioners and another for the journals.

Key staff must remain in place—Retaining the same core group of people over the life of a multiyear research project is especially important to success, but can be difficult. During the normal course of events, police may be transferred to other assignments, retire, or earn promotions (which may mean reassignment). Their participation in the research project rarely blocks such changes. Conversely, some researchers have left the projects to accept positions at other universities. Because turnover means assigning a new person to a project, it almost always disrupts the research schedule. Participants in stable projects have generally expressed satisfaction with the research process.

MEASURES OF SUCCESS

Close observation of the partnership projects suggests that their "bottom-line" success includes at least one of three measures:

- Whether the department changes as a result of the research
- Whether information systems have been developed or improved
- Whether the partnership continues beyond the life of the initial research project

Change—Because the immediate aim of the partnership is solving a local problem, a change in operational procedures or policies obviously signals success. In some cases, project evaluations have produced mid-course corrections in the way community policing is implemented. Philadelphia (noted above) is an example. Los Angeles is another. There, a survey of police officers by the department and its partners, University of California at Los Angeles and University of Southern California, led to changes in the community policing initiative. Community policing in Charleston, West Virginia; Hagerstown, Maryland; and Racine, Wisconsin, has also been influenced by partnerships with researchers. The police departments in Rapid City, South Dakota; Pocatello, Idaho; and Eureka and Redding, California, that work with the LINC research firm improved their procedures for reporting domestic violence as a result of the partnership. Results of a single project may serve several purposes. One commander noted the use of survey results "as the basis for this year's strategic plan, as input for a continuing education program for middle managers, and to show that morale in [his command] area is not as bad as believed."

Managing information—Upgrading existing information systems or installing a system is a sign of success because information lies at the core of research and can drive a department's policy decisions. The Seattle Police Department's partnership with the University of Washington to address domestic violence illustrates this. As part of the partnership project, the department established an information system to obtain and manage domestic violence data. A researcher commented on the advantages for both researchers and practitioners by noting, "We helped the police department set up the database for domestic violence, and they've been entering data for more than a year. And we also get access to that data." A database created to meet the daily operational needs of the department also generates high-quality data for research purposes.

Sustaining the partnership—Local research capacity increases as the partnership develops and achieves success in individual projects. That improvement is a product of the joint effort of equal partners. In other federal initiatives, by contrast, the aim is to train police practitioners to conduct research on their own. Several partnerships have been sustained beyond the initial study when the partners were asked, on the basis of their experiences, to tackle other projects. For example, researchers from the University of California at Oakland who worked with the Oakland Police Department were subsequently asked to evaluate a federally sponsored project on reducing gang-related crime. In New York City, the partnership of the police and researchers from the City University of New York continued when additional federal funding was provided to improve computerized crime mapping.

SEATTLE: IMPROVING POLICE RESPONSE TO DOMESTIC VIOLENCE

The partnership forged in Seattle to improve police handling of domestic violence exemplifies the way locally initiated research can change a department's approach to reducing crime. The internal view of the ability of the police department's domestic violence unit was that reporting and analysis of incident data were inadequate. Based on that view, the partnership focused on evaluating the unit.

Origins—The Seattle partnership, created in 1996, brought researchers from the University of Washington School of Public Health, the Harborview Injury Prevention and Research Center, and units of the city government that handled domestic violence together with the police department's domestic violence unit. The unit was organized two years earlier as part of the newly created Family and Youth Protection Bureau to provide specialized follow-up investigation of domestic violence crimes. Thus, the partnership was a logical extension of an already established arrangement among the organizations whose key members collaborated on other projects, among them improving the medical release forms used by officers in handling domestic disputes.

Results—As noted above, one result was upgrading the existing system of collecting information about domestic violence. Other results were:

- Designing and refining a domestic violence incident report used by the police
- Obtaining physician assistance in designing the incident report
- Improving access to medical information from hospitals and physicians
- Assigning more investigative responsibility to the domestic violence unit

Partnership extension—The Seattle partnership continued the following year, this time with the aim of developing a lethality scale risk assessment tool that would enable the department to work smarter in investigating domestic violence cases. This was done by expanding the officers' reporting form to enable them to cite risk factors (e.g., use of alcohol and/or drugs) for the escalation of violence in certain situations. As of this writing, data collected from the risk assessment tool by means of the reporting form are being analyzed.

Pluses for both sides—Even if the immediate problem defined by the partnership is not fully resolved, both police and researchers gain from their experiences. Working with researchers encourages police departments to approach issues more systematically than they otherwise might, critically assess the quality and utility of their information systems, and understand research findings in a broad context. On the other side of the partnership, researchers have the opportunity to apply the tools of their trade in an operational setting, see the findings of empirical research influence local policy making, and assess whether operational changes made under community policing are producing the desired results. If the attitudes of participating police and researchers are indications, the partnership projects will build a firm foundation for lasting police-researcher relationships. One commander recognized the value of the resources available to the department and was especially enthusiastic about continuing the partnership: "We've traditionally been a closed department ... solving our problems on our own. The doors of the local university were open, but our eyes were closed." One researcher expressed the value of the partnership in helping researchers better understand the challenges faced by police departments: "The policy decisions that police make are some of the most difficult that I've seen, and have major implications. I think I can help."

Some researchers have excellent interpersonal communication skills. Those who do not have these skills have limited capabilities to conduct interviews. Others have a good grasp of statistical concepts and applications. Lack of this skill inhibits a researcher's abilities to translate numerical data into meaningful conclusions. A critical self-examination of your abilities to gather and examine data is vital for selecting a topic for research (see Figure 10.1).

A topic should be:

- Interesting to researcher
- Familiar to researcher
- Challenging to researcher
- Researchable
- Realistic within researcher's abilities

REMEMBER: Be willing to explore and reject several topics before choosing the one just right for you!

Fig. 10.1 Tips for beginning researchers: deciding on a topic for research.

refining topic and narrowing focus of research

After a topic of research has been selected, the next task is to refine it. The first step is to develop a **topic statement**—a single sentence that helps the researcher establish the direction of the research, for example:

Topic: Youth and drugs

Topic Emphasis: Relationship between youth crime and drug usage

Topic Statement: Increases in youth crimes are directly attributed to drug usage

After a topic statement has been articulated, the next step is considering the purpose of the research. When the purpose is established, a purpose statement can be written. This single sentence states the focus of the study in terms of the overall objective. It should be written as concisely as possible to clearly convey the central idea examined in the study. Among the several ways of developing a purpose statement, one of the better ways is to use a script by completing blanks (based on leading words) in a sentence. For example, "The purpose of this research is to _____ (describe? explore? examine? explain? understand?) the _____ (central idea to be studied)."

Using our topic statement above (increases in youth crimes are directly attributed to drug usage), we can write a preliminary purpose statement using a scripted format. For example: The purpose of this research is to examine the relationship between drug usage and increases in youth crime.

It is important to remember that refining a topic may occur several times before the final draft is complete. Likewise, establishing the purpose of a study requires that other elements be considered. One element is the unit of analysis. The task here is to define and explicitly state the population or site to be studied. Also, occasionally definitions must be established with regard to the central idea to be studied. Finally, the research must remain focused on the methodological approach.

---

literature review

As noted in Chapter 8, one of the most important functions of research design is the **literature review** that often serves as a starting point for a researcher to begin exploring aspects of an original research idea or concept. Moreover, the review provides valuable information about existing research that in turn can prove useful in refining a research topic. By performing a literature review, a researcher can also gain a better appreciation of several hurdles likely to be confronted during the proposed study. Two basic issues to consider in planning to use literature in a research study are: (1) understanding the purpose of a literature review and (2) knowing how to access research materials.

Purposes

Literature review has several purposes. The fundamental purpose of a review is serving as the primary means of gathering resource information about the research topic. Thus, the review is an important tool for gathering data that the researcher does not have or may not know exists. A literature review also adds historical perspectives by clarifying the relationship between the researcher's work and the work of other researchers who performed similar studies. Moreover, it provides a gauge by which a researcher can evaluate his or her individual research effort in comparison with earlier efforts of others.

The final purpose of the literature review relates to the written documents of a study. Typically, a literature review is a separate and unique section of a journal article, thesis, or dissertation that informs readers of the findings of other studies that are closely related to the study reported. In most documents, the literature review immediately follows the introduction and precedes the methods section.

Accessing Research Materials

The two most common ways of accessing literature are visiting a library and via computer link to Internet resources. The line that separates these methods of gathering documents erodes constantly as more and more information is stored electronically and made available via computers. We address the use of the Internet for conducting criminal justice research as a separate and final section of this chapter and first focus on the use of library resources.

Using Libraries

The key to a successful library search of the literature is to know how the library operates. While this may seem to be a rudimentary comment, it is remarkable how many students do not take the time to educate themselves about their local libraries. To learn how a library functions, only one rule applies: learn to use the library by visiting it. Investing hours is the best way of becoming familiar with the library. Several guidelines will help make the hands-on experience successful:

- Know the layout of the library. It is a good practice on the first few visits to simply walk around and explore. The goal is to understand where the books, periodicals, and other documents are located.

- Learn to use the card catalog or online catalog. In libraries that still use card catalogs, the cards are arranged alphabetically by author, subject, and title. The main collection of books will likely be organized by Dewey Decimal Call Number or Library of Congress Classification and can be checked out for a specific period. Reference books such as encyclopedias and almanacs provide quick facts and normally cannot be checked out because of their constant use. Online catalogs involve accessing books and periodicals via computer. For example, MAGIC2 is the Michigan State University Library online catalog system accessible through two interfaces: a graphic version available through the Web and a text interface accessible through a telephone network connection.[2]

- Learn to use online index databases that allow access to hundreds of journals, magazines, and newspapers—many in full text. One of the best sources for criminal justice abstracts is Silver Platter Information. This global company publishes reference databases in electronic formats to provide librarians and knowledge workers in research-oriented organizations with excellent searching, accurate results, and seamless links to full content.[3]

- Become familiar with a library's microfiche system, which usually consists of a collection of thin plastic cards, each containing reduced images of hundreds of library cards in alphabetical order. This is a particularly important system to know when seeking dated books and periodicals.

- Know the interlibrary loan policies and procedures. Also be aware that some libraries levy charges when they provide materials.

Gathering information for a literature review will become easier after you master the use of a library. Although library materials are useful in a variety of ways, the inevitable task will be to decide how much of the information should be shared with readers in the literature review. This matter is addressed in Chapters 8 and 11.

Virtual Libraries

Several universities and government agencies offer virtual library services to criminal justice students. These are electronic resources that access databases, electronic journals, and other criminal justice materials. For example, the virtual law library at the University of Indiana is a Web catalog maintained by experts in the legal field.[4]

The World Criminal Justice Library Network (WCJLN) is an international list intended to provide a forum for discussion among librarians, documentation specialists, researchers, faculty, professionals, and others interested in criminal justice information. Activities include the publication, dissemination, exchange, processing, accessing, management, and evaluation of criminal justice information and resources in any format.

The National Center for Victims of Crime Virtual Library contains materials addressing informational needs in the area of crime victimization.[5] The Library of Congress, America's oldest national cultural institution, is the largest repository of recorded knowledge in the world and a symbol of the vital connection between knowledge and democracy.[6]

Google

Google (www.google.com) is perhaps the most popular American public corporation specializing in Internet search. Founded by two Stanford University PhD students in 1996, Google created services and tools (Web applications, advertising networks, and business solutions) for the general public and business environment alike. This Internet search engine indexes billions of Web pages, so that users can search for information through the use of keywords and operators.

summary

- Successful research begins with choosing an area of study of interest to the researcher.
- The research topic should be challenging.
- Research should be viewed as a quest that will gain new knowledge for the researcher.
- The topic must be researchable.
- A researcher should evaluate his or her abilities to conduct research.
- The first step is the development of a topic statement, a single sentence that helps establish the direction of the research.
- The literature review serves as the starting point to begin exploring aspects of an original research idea or concept.

terminology

Research plan

Topic selection

Topic statement

Literature review

discussion points

1. List several issues that a researcher should consider when choosing a research topic.

2. According to the NIJ article, what issues were raised by police and researchers in jointly selecting a topic of interest to the department? Collaboration on research design? Shared responsibility for implementation? Interpretation of findings?

3. Write a purpose statement using a scripting method.

4. What are the purposes of a literature review?

5. What is a virtual library?

endnotes

1. Adapted from T. McEwen. *National Institute of Justice Journal,* Vol. 238, January 1999.

2. www.lib.msu.edu

3. www.silverplatter.com

4. www.law.indiana.edu/law/v-lib/lawindex.html

5. www.ncvc.org/vroom/main.htm

6. www.lcweb.loc.gov/library

writing research reports

introduction

For some, the most difficult task involved in research is writing the report. One reason is because writing is time consuming. It entails the preparation of an initial draft, revising and editing, and then revising again. Another reason is that a researcher's writings must typically conform to a specific manuscript format associated with the field of study. This especially applies to students in academic institutions, and such requirements may create problems for a novice researcher who possesses little or no experience in writing an objective research report.

The difficulties associated with writing the research report can be eased if the researcher views report writing as a process that starts when the researcher begins generating ideas and simply makes notes. These notes evolve into outlines and eventually into a rough draft of the report. Initially, it is common to focus on the introduction, literature, and methodology chapters. After data collection has been completed, it is time for the remaining results and discussion chapters to be written. This chapter briefly explores the process of writing a research report and discusses some of the more important issues associated with this endeavor. We provide several guidelines for writing a research report and take a close look at each of its sections.

when to begin writing

The writing of the research report starts at the beginning of the research process. That is, the writing starts when the researcher begins making notes about the research study. The notes will serve as the foundation for the actual report. Typically, a researcher's first notes pertain to research ideas and possible hypotheses, potential resource materials for the literature review, and possible methodological approaches. This is particularly true if the researcher plans to write a **research prospectus** (the preliminary first half of a research report that includes the introduction, literature review, and methodology chapters). Opportunities to make notes and prepare draft writings occur throughout a research study as a researcher performs related tasks. Consider the following tasks relating to the composition of a research prospectus:

- When contemplating a title for the study, several titles can be proposed and discussed with fellow researchers or an academic supervisor.

- When a researcher begins gathering previous research documents related to the subject under study, it is a good idea to begin writing a preliminary draft of the literature review, which is commonly the second chapter of a research report. Likewise, an annotated bibliography can be started for later use on a reference list.

- When research is to be grounded on theory, it is important to formulate theoretical constructs. The need for theory-generating or theory-testing research to investigate a certain physical, psychological, or social problem is commonly part of the introductory chapter.

- When conceptual definitions are to be specified in a report, the researcher should keep account of the definitions found in the literature review. While it is acceptable to cite definitions previously offered by another researcher, it may be more appropriate to write definitions that better represent the general concepts of the study.

- When deciding on a methodology, a researcher should begin drafting ideas about sample size, design, procedures, and data analysis plans to be included in the methods chapter. It is likely that the methodology will be modified later because of necessary adjustments to the original data collection plans.

preparatory tips

The most successful researchers develop well-thought-out plans before they start writing. They prepare in advance and have a sense of what challenges may lie ahead. The following suggestions concern preparation for writing a research report:

- Think about the research topic and purpose. To prepare to write, review the topic statement and consider the purpose of the research.

- Identify your audience and consider how that will affect your paper. Never assume that the audience has prior knowledge of the topic. Know what style and tone of writing are required— informal, scholarly, first-person reporting, or dramatized.

- Review a copy of a "model" research report. Read other research reports that have been accepted to see how they were organized.

- Establish a process and stay focused. Writing the paper is the ultimate goal, but several tasks must be completed before the end product can be written. If you focus too quickly on what the results may show or the possible implications of your research, you may miss some of the important details that should have been covered earlier in the study.

- Use time management skills. Make good use of your time by establishing a schedule for your research writing and deter-mine how much you will write. We suggest producing three to five rough draft pages during each writing session. After you establish a schedule of writing sessions, try to adhere to it.

- Designate a proofreader. Identify fellow researchers, academic supervisors, or others to read your preliminary writings and offer their reactions and ideas. Another person often has a fresh perspective and may say something that triggers new ideas. Furthermore, it is often difficult to identify corrections needed to one's own paper.

components of report

The customary sections of a research document include:

1. An introduction to the research problem
2. A thorough review of the existing literature on the subject
3. The methodological approach for collection and analyses of the data
4. Disclosure of the findings
5. Discussion of the findings
6. References

We discuss each of these sections as separate and distinct chapters of the research report.

Chapter 1: Introduction and Statement of Hypothesis

Introduction

The main purpose of the **introduction** is to provide an overview of the research problem or questions under inquiry. The format and content of the introduction depend upon a number of variables including the style of the discipline and the expectations of your academic supervisor. There are guidelines to keep in mind, however, when composing the initial chapter. In general, your introduction should:

- Catch the attention of your readers while introducing the topic.
- Provide relevant context for your topic and establish its importance.
- Clearly state the purpose or aim of the research.
- Provide conceptual definitions as necessary.
- Provide the theoretical context of the study.
- State the hypotheses or research questions.

Examine the following excerpts taken from the introduction sections of several research reports. Note how these paragraphs fulfill one or more of the general guidelines listed above.

Perhaps no problem in America is more serious than the unequal treatment of racial and ethnic groups by the institutions responsible for administering justice. Two of the professed values of the American judicial system are equal protection and fundamental fairness of the law; they may represent the central aim of our entire judicial system. With respect to these values, however, the professed and the operational have differed seriously at times.[1]

A number of different theories have been developed that attempt to explain the increased level of crime in society. Two of these theoretical perspectives—routine activities and social disorganization—tend to overlap and complement one another in their explanation of crime causation. The present study tests some of the basic premises of these two theories.[2]

In the abundant literature on occupational or workplace stress, various definitions and conceptualizations of stress have been used. Sometimes stress refers to the sources (i.e., stressors), though stress (or strain) more usually is viewed as an inner state reflected by anxiety or frustration, or as a response characterized by behaviors such as yelling or adrenaline flow (Ellison and Genz, 1983). In this paper, the sources of stress are called "causes" or "stressors." We indicate problematic occupational stress by self-reports that the informant is in an emotional state of stress, experiencing consequences unfavorable for physical or emotional wellbeing.[3]

Measuring the amount of force or the frequency with which police use either reasonable or excessive force is not the focus of this study. Nor is it the purpose of this study to examine when officers should use deadly force. Instead, by focusing on the various kinds of situations that officers face every day, this study seeks to develop insight into two major components that influence use of force outcomes. The first component concerns officers' perceptions of the threat level or risk inherent in a police-citizen encounter to either the respondent or others in the immediate area. The second component is to understand more fully how officers respond given the totality of the situation. The study also seeks to explain factors that contribute to variations in officers' collective responses concerning when and how much force is appropriate. Thus, this effort seeks to explain the factors that officers believe contribute to their estimation of the dangers inherent in police-citizen encounters.[4]

Statement of hypothesis

A well-written **statement of hypothesis**, usually expressed in one sentence, is one of the most important sentences in the introduction. It states the position of the researcher, reflecting the full scope of a phenomenon that the researcher will go about proving or disproving.

When writing a hypothesis, be sure that it is not too broad to be defended within the scope of your paper. The hypothesis should be as specific as possible and devoid of confusing language. Also, a hypothesis should indicate what will actually be studied, not the value judgments of the researcher. A simple statement of the hypothesis includes the two variables under study and the type of relationship the researcher expects to demonstrate. If a report will cover more than one hypothesis, both should be stated clearly and distinctly.

In regard to where the hypothesis appears in the research report, it may initially emerge toward the end of the introduction chapter. However, it is important to restate the hypothesis in a paragraph toward the end of the literature review chapter. Doing so connects the statement of the hypothesis to the next (methodology) chapter that establishes the approach used to test the hypothesis. The following abstracts contain well-written statements of hypotheses. Note that the final example states two hypotheses.

This study used quantitative data from Japan and the United States to test the hypothesis that the Japanese public has higher confidence in their police than does the American public.[5]

The authors tested the hypothesis that greater enforcement of existing laws against carrying concealed weapons would reduce firearms violence in Kansas City, Missouri.[6]

Using cost estimates for the homicide rate in a number of cities, this study tests the hypothesis that the war on illicit drugs has diverted police resources from other law enforcement activities, resulting in a higher rate of violent crimes than would otherwise have been the case.[7]

This study tested the hypothesis that the presence of guns in the home, the type of gun, and the method of gun storage are associated with risk for adolescent suicide.[8]

This study of gender differences in police physical abilities tested two hypotheses: (1) female applicants would fail the physical ability test more often than male applicants, and (2) the physical ability selection test administered by the police agency would not measure critical tasks.[9]

Chapter 2: Literature Review

Before addressing several issues relating to writing the literature review, it is important to reiterate that the **literature review** is the starting point for many research projects. During or after the development of a research topic, the researcher initiates a literature review to obtain a sense of the entire area of study. The review helps the researcher appreciate the previous contributions of others in the field, thereby identifying the major researchers in the discipline, and shows how other researchers present their studies and address the strengths, weaknesses, and significant contributions of previous studies. The key to writing a good literature review is to read books, periodicals, and other documents, and then isolate the materials that are most relevant to your area of study. While masses of literature may be relevant to your research, you must focus on the classics and contemporary literature directly linked to your subject.

Perhaps the best way to begin is to develop an outline of what is to be accomplished. First, consider the classics—historical research that established the framework for a particular area of study. One of the best ways to identify a classic is to note how many times certain studies are cited in other researchers' literature reviews. Consider how these historical research efforts connect to your own research and note the similarities with regard to theoretical framework, research agenda, and problem orientation. Next, organize all other relevant documents and specifically identify contemporary research documents that are most closely aligned to your own work because you will probably want to show trends and themes in the literature. Noting the contemporary literature last can be an excellent way of building up to your own study and establishing a need for such research. Typically, a literature review is presented chronologically or thematically. Next, identify the various ways that your study differs from the previous research. This necessarily means that you have identified the variables to be studied and established a research methodology. Finally, develop a standard method to summarize the previous research. At a minimum, the research problem, methodology, and findings of each study should be detailed.

When writing the literature review, your task is to educate readers on the extant literature relevant to your research question. It may be helpful to visualize this chapter in terms of a spiral or a coil. The outer edge of the spiral represents the foundational literature (Figure 11.1) generally associated to your topic. As you follow the coil inward toward the center, you begin to refine your review to include

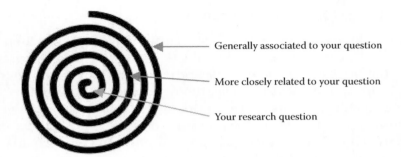

Generally associated to your question

More closely related to your question

Your research question

Figure 11.1 Spiral concept of literature review.

prior study areas more closely related to your topic. The center of the spiral addresses the area that contains your particular research question. The following sources can provide more information about literature reviews:

- www.writing.utoronto.ca/advice/specific-types-of-writing/literature-review
- The literature review: a few tips on conducting it:
  - www.unc.edu/depts/wcweb/handouts/literature_review.html
- American Psychological Association literature review samples:
  - http://faculty.mwsu.edu/psychology/Laura.Spiller/Experimental/sample_apa_style_litreview.pdf

Chapter 3: Methodology

The **methodology** chapter gives a detailed explanation of the methods used to collect and analyze the data. It includes a description of the research environment, sampling design, procedures, and data analysis plan. The intent is to provide readers with enough detail to replicate the research.

Research environment

Providing a background of the research location can be an important initial subsection of the methodology chapter. It is used primarily as a means of describing the research environment. It is especially important to provide background information if it has direct relevance to the nature of the research. The following example clearly describes the background and setting:

This research was conducted at a Midwest county adult detention facility, which made the transition from a traditional linear facility to a podular, direct supervision one. In 1965 the county built a 100-bed traditional linear jail and hired a jail staff of 28. In 1974 jail inmates filed a class action lawsuit in federal court alleging Eighth Amendment violations. As a result, a 220-bed podular direct supervision jail opened in March 1988 with a staff complement of 50, which included transfer of all 28 staff from the traditional jail. New staff had a minimum of 6 months' experience in the traditional jail before the facility was closed and all inmates and staff were transferred.[10]

Design

This subsection specifies the type of study conducted and describes the instrumentation (i.e., experimental design, survey questionnaires, records, etc.) used in the data collection effort. The following excerpt describes a research design:

This exploratory study seeks to determine whether demographic characteristics explain variations in levels of occupational identification. Relationships between race, age, length of service, military experience, and educational attainment and occupational identification and levels of socialization among personnel in small or medium-sized departments are evaluated. The departmental characteristics, size, and population density were measured as to their impact on occupational identification and levels of socialization.

A self-administered questionnaire was distributed to four sessions of a regional police academy. The underlying assumption guiding the research suggests that over-identification with an occupational subculture may not be an occupational universal, but may be mediated by various background characteristics. Levels of identification will be determined from responses to attitudinal items on the survey.

The survey instrument is a modification of several empirically tested measures. The level of socialization measure is a modification of Chao, O'Leary-Kelly, Walz, Klein, and Gardner's (1994) organizational socializations scale. This scale evaluates items of organizational politics and organizational culture. For purposes of this study, factors that were task related were removed. This modification was necessary since original measures of task efficiency directed to specific tasks were not consistent or immediately identifiable to organizational members. Furthermore, in some instances, generic references were replaced by occupational-specific terminology.

The survey consists of 37 questions in three areas: socialization levels, feelings of isolation, and organizational solidarity. The demographic variables measured are age, race, gender, military experience, educational level, and past law enforcement experience. Two departmental variables, department size and community population, are included. A total of eight independent variables are measured. On the perceptual section of the questionnaire, responses were scaled on a Likert scale. In the demographic section of the questionnaire, individuals were given open-ended questions that after review were categorized by the researcher.[11]

Sampling

This subsection provides information about study subjects; for example, details about the number of cases sampled and how individuals were chosen. It also describes response rates and other factors that set the limits on generalizability of the sample data.

Procedures

This subsection, often combined with sampling information, summarizes the procedures followed during the research. The aim is to disclose all steps taken to gather data. The following excerpt combines descriptions of sampling and procedures:

The data for this study were collected in spring 1994 via a telephone survey of households in Knox County, Tennessee, which is home to the city of Knoxville and the University of Tennessee. The questionnaire was based on the instrument used in the 1990 FVS study (Boyle, 1992). The telephone interviews were conducted by experienced interviewers at the University of Tennessee's Social Science Research Institute using computer-assisted telephone interviewing software.

The samples were drawn using random digit dialing. Of the 835 persons contacted, 400 agreed to be interviewed for an overall response rate of 48%. Although the response rate is slightly lower than desired for a telephone survey, we have two reasons for believing that it did not adversely affect the validity of our findings. First, our results replicate similar studies by Titus et al. (1995) and Boyle (1992) in that we found nearly identical victimization rates and similar patterns of correlation with demographic variables. Second, our sample is representative of the population from which it was drawn.[12]

Data analysis

In the final subsection of the methodology chapter, the researcher explains processing of data after collection. Measures of qualitative data relate to the specific content analysis techniques used. When the data collected is quantitative, descriptive and inferential measures used are explained. The following is an example of a data analysis subsection:

> We conducted two separate analyses to assess the impact of gang membership on charging and sentencing decisions. First, we estimated logistic regression models to determine the net impact of gang membership on each of these decisions after controlling for other offender and offense attributes. Second, we estimated separate logistic models for gang and non-gang cases to evaluate whether offense and offender characteristics were considered equally important in both types of cases. We conducted formal tests of the interactive models' improvement of fit over a main effects model to assess whether estimating separate models for gang and non-gang cases was the more appropriate specification.[13]

Chapter 4: Findings or Results

After the methodology has been explained and the data analyzed, the **findings** may be disclosed. This chapter may also be called **results**; some researchers may prefer to combine the results and discussion sections within in one chapter.

Typically, the chapter on findings begins with descriptive statistics. Data are summarized in frequency distributions, measures of central tendency, measures of variability, and correlations. Tables and figures are used to present results visually. Often, most of the text explains what the visual presentations show. Next, the results of inferential statistical tests are presented. Again, narrative is used to explain visual displays such as correlations, matrices, diagrams, and other illustrations. The text shows how numerical values were derived and what they indicate. Listed below are suggestions for writing the findings chapter. These points apply when the findings are written as a unique chapter apart from the discussion chapter.

- This chapter is specific and dedicated to the presentation of the findings of the research. Do not add personal comments or value judgments, and do not interpret the results.

- Provide all results in this section. The aim of the text is to disclose what the data show.

- When applicable, the findings should be presented logically, based on the order of inquiry. Be consistent by organizing the data in a structured way that reflects the data collection effort.

- All visual presentations such as tables and figures should be of high quality and easy to understand.

- Always describe and explain the data in the tables and figures in the narrative text.

- Set up the discussion chapter by providing appropriate comments that lead to it.

Chapter 5: Discussion

The **discussion** chapter is of particular importance because that is where the findings are interpreted. The researcher's primary task is to explain the data results. Issues regarding the usefulness and limitations of the research should be addressed. Typically, the chapter begins with a general statement of the results. Often, this statement reflects the most significant findings. Next, it is common to comment on whether the results were anticipated or unexpected and why. Much of the text should contain a discussion of the relationship between the findings and the aim of the research and indicate whether the findings can be generalized. Also, comparisons should be drawn with the results of previous studies. Finally, a conclusion should address the practical implications of the study and make recommendations and suggestions for further research.

Reference Section

This section lists all documents used as source materials in the report. The main purpose of the **reference list** is to give credit where credit is due and draw a clear line between your work and that of other scholars. The list should provide the information necessary for a reader to identify and retrieve each source. The specific format for documenting source on a reference list varies, depending on the academic field and your academic supervisor's preference.

Every academic discipline has specific rules about citing sources and the rules must be followed precisely. Style manuals such as the *Publication Manual of the American Psychological Association* explain how to properly cite periodicals, books, technical reports, doctoral dissertations, electronic media, and all other types of source materials. In social science, the most common style manuals are the *Publication Manual of the American Psychological Association*,[14] Goehlert's *Political Science Research Guide*,[15] the Sociology Writing Group's *A Guide to Writing Sociology Papers*,[16] and Sternberg's *Writing the Sociology Paper*.[17]

Abstract

The final segment is the **abstract**. Although this section is presented before the introduction, it is written last. The reason is that its purpose is to provide a brief, comprehensive synopsis of the full report. It allows readers to quickly understand the research problem, the methodological approach used to collect the data, the findings, and the conclusions and implications. The length of the abstract varies according to style manuals; it is typically no longer than 300 words.

summary

- The writing task may be made easier if it is viewed as a process that begins with making notes about your research ideas. These notes provide an important foundation for what will be written in the formal document, especially pertaining to the research prospectus that encompasses the introduction, literature review, and methodology sections.

- The introduction sets up the rest of the report. It introduces readers to the study by explaining the research problem and why an investigation of the problem is important.

- The purpose of the literature review is to cite research that has been previously conducted in the area of study. In general, the review should include pertinent research published in journals, books, monographs, etc. It is important to stress that a review of the literature does not necessarily mean an exhaustive report of every study ever performed, but includes key studies that are directly related to the problem under investigation.

- The methodology chapter gives a clear and accurate explanation of the methods used to collect and analyze the data. Subheadings in the methods section include research environment, design, sample, procedures, and data analysis.

- The fourth section is the findings or results chapter that presents and describes the results of the data collection effort as they relate to the testing of the hypothesis. Tables and figures can be used to augment the narrative of results. Both descriptive and inferential statistical analysis test results are presented.

- The final chapter discusses the major findings. Comparisons may be drawn between the results of the study and the study findings from related research. Typically, a summary is provided that includes the researcher's recommendations for future research.

- A final component of the research report is the reference list that cites all documents used as source materials in the research report. The specific form for documenting a source on a reference list varies, depending on the academic field or the preference of the academic supervisor.

terminology

Research prospectus

Introduction

Statement of hypothesis

Literature review

Methodology

Findings or results

Discussion

Reference list

Abstract

discussion points

1. What is a research prospectus?

2. When should a researcher acquire a "model" research report? Why?

3. What are the important elements of the introductory chapter?

4. List and briefly explain each subsection found in the methodology chapter.

5. What is the purpose of the reference list?

endnotes

1. Adapted from P. E. Secret and J. B. Johnson. The effect of race on juvenile justice decision-making in Nebraska: detention, adjudication, and disposition, 1988–1993. *Justice Quarterly* 14: 445–478, 1997.

2. L. J. Moriarty. and J. E. Williams. Examining the relationship between routine activities theory and social disorganization: an analysis of property crime victimization. *American Journal of Criminal Justice* 21: 43–59, 1996.

3. Adapted from R. N. Haan and M. Morash. Gender, race, and strategies of coping with occupational stress in policing. *Justice Quarterly* 16: 303–336, 1999.

4. Adapted from S. T. Holmes, K. M. Reynolds, R. M. Holmes et al. Individual and situational determinants of police force: an examination of threat presentation. *American Journal of Criminal Justice* 23: 83–106, 1998.

5. L. Cao, S. Stack, and Y. Sun, Public attitudes toward the police: a comparative study between Japan and America. *Journal of Criminal Justice* 26: 279–289, 1998.

6. L. W. Sherman and D. P. Rogan. Effects of gun seizures on gun violence: hot spots patrol in Kansas City. *Justice Quarterly* 12: 679–693, 1995.

7. H. J. Brumm and D. O. Cloninger. Drug war and the homicide rate: a direct correlation? *Cato Journal* 14: 509–517, 1995.

8. D. A. Brent., J. A. Perper, C. J. Allman et al. Presence and accessibility of firearms in the homes of adolescent suicides: a case control study. *JAMA* 266: 2989–2995, 1991.

9. M. L. Birzer and D. E. Craig. Gender differences in police physical ability test performance. *American Journal of Police* 15: 93–108, 1993.

10. G. J. Bayens, J. J. Williams, and J. O. Smykla. Jail type makes a difference: evaluating the transition from a traditional to a podular, direct supervision jail across ten years. *American Jails* 11: 32–36, 1997.

11. Adapted from M. T. Britz. The police subculture and occupational socialization: exploring individual and demographic characteristics. *American Journal of Criminal Justice* 21: 127–146, 1997.

12. J. Van Wyk and M. L. Benson. Fraud victimization: risky business or just bad luck? *American Journal of Criminal Justice* 21: 163–179, 1997.

13. Adapted from T. D. Miethe and R. C. McCorkle. Gang membership and criminal processing: a test of the "master status" concept. *Justice Quarterly* 14: 407–427, 1997.

14. *Publication Manual of the American Psychological Association*, 6th ed. Washington: American Psychological Association, 2010.

15. R. U. Goehlert. *Political Science Research Guide*. Monticello, IL: Vance Bibliographies, 1982.

16. Sociology Writing Group. *A Guide to Writing Sociology Papers*. New York: St. Martin's Press, 1986.

17. R. J. Sternberg. *Writing the Psychology Paper*. Woodbury, NJ: Barron's, 1977.

program evaluation and policy research

introduction

In the 1960s, evaluation research came into prominence as millions of dollars were allocated for social programs. Today, legislation establishes the necessity of evaluating federally funded programs to ensure their accountability. On the local level, law enforcement and corrections administrators are routinely obligated to conduct evaluations of publicly supported programs. Such evaluations provide decision makers with information to determine how effectively criminal justice programs are achieving their intended goals and whether funding should continue. In short, they want to know what the programs accomplish, what they cost, and how they should be operated to achieve maximum cost effectiveness.

In this chapter we provide an overview of the basic principles of program evaluation and policy research. In the first section, we define evaluation research and discuss some of the common reasons for conducting a program evaluation. Next, we list the four broad categories of evaluation research and consider several preliminary matters that need to be carefully considered when choosing an evaluation project. This section concludes with a discussion of various available research designs and methodologies.

In the second section of this chapter, we tackle policy research. Although the type of research projects that policy researchers have implemented varies, we discuss their common characteristics. Next, we list several important activities to be considered during the planning process and explain why reporting the progress of a project is an integral component of a research project.

defining evaluation research

Evaluation research is a methodological approach used to examine the relationship between an activity and its outcome. In criminal justice, evaluation research most often involves a study of the worth of a program implemented by a law enforcement, corrections, or other relevant agency. In most instances, worth is determined by whether the program is accomplishing its intended goals. Because criminal justice agencies are publicly funded, value becomes an equally important concern of evaluation research. Value is typically determined by whether the program is operated with economic prudence. In addition to the two basic elements, of worth and value, evaluation research involves several other important qualities. Consider the following definition provided by Michael Q. Patton, a notable social sciences researcher and author of several books on evaluation research:

> The practice of evaluation involves the systematic collection of information about the activities, characteristics, and outcomes of programs, personnel, and products for use by specific people to reduce uncertainties, improve effectiveness, and make decisions with regard to what those programs, personnel, or products are doing and affecting.[1]

Note that an integral component of this definition is its focus on decisions, which gives some indication of the objective of evaluation research. Evaluation research is aimed at action rather than answering questions about phenomena in order to discover new knowledge and test theories and/or hypotheses.

purposes of program evaluation

The goal of most **program evaluations** is to provide useful information to a variety of decision makers who have vested interests in the program. The type or scope of the evaluation varies, depending on the issues to be addressed. Evaluation can be an important tool in improving the quality of a program. An evaluation helps to determine whether a program makes a difference, and can furnish the information personnel need to enhance service delivery. Some other common reasons for conducting a program evaluation include:

- Program improvement—determining how to improve a program
- Continuation—deciding whether to continue a program
- Distribution—making a decision whether to implement a program at another site
- Accountability—deciding whether to continue the level of funding of a program.
- Intervention—determining whether to intervene in program management
- Policy decisions—making decisions about the development and/or implementation of policies

Each of these reasons for conducting a program evaluation has at least in part the goal of determining the extent to which a program is effective. A fundamental activity in any evaluation is measuring how well a program accomplishes its intended goals. The Bureau of Justice Assistance suggests that a first step toward determining effectiveness of a criminal justice program is to develop criteria that define an effectively managed program. A handbook titled *Assessing the Effectiveness of Criminal Justice Programs* prepared by the Justice Research and Statistics Association notes that criminal justice system activities are diverse.[2] For criteria to apply across programs, they should not relate only to specific types or classes of programs, organizational arrangements, and management styles. Consequently, the criteria are described in terms of the program management and accountability processes. These two processes define, on a case-by-case basis for a program, what the program is and how its effectiveness is to be judged.

Four criteria define an effectively managed program. They set ideal conditions for program implementation and performance—conditions to be brought about through the management and accountability processes. Because the criteria describe the ideal, the relevant question is, to what extent does a program achieve the four criteria? The criteria and brief descriptions follow:

Acceptable description of goals and objectives—Goals, the end results that programs pursue, are realistic and clearly stated.

Program objectives (effects or results to be achieved by the program in pursuing its goals) are both measurable and achievable.

Linkage between program activities and objectives—The program has sufficient and appropriate activities in place to achieve the objective (results) expected by its managers. Sufficient and appropriate activities are defined as evidence that the existing pattern of program activities can produce the results expected. In other words, the causal linkage between program activities and objectives is plausible.

Performance Information—Performance measures are developed to signal whether and/or to what extent the program meets its objectives (achieves expected results). This information is obtained by measuring the actual results, then comparing them with the expected results.

Acceptable Performance—The program meets or exceeds the expectations (objectives) set for it, and its actual performance is acceptable to program managers and oversight officials. This criterion recognizes that at times a program may not fully achieve its objectives (due to unforeseen and uncontrollable events), but is nevertheless considered to be performing successfully.

categories of program evaluation research

The choice among several categories of program evaluations depends on the purpose of the assessment. Additionally, each category consists of various types of evaluations that can be distinguished by the activities undertaken during research. Table 12.1 lists several of the more common categories and types of program evaluation research.

choosing a program evaluation

Conducting a program evaluation is very appealing to students who are considering academic research projects. One reason is that many students, especially graduate students working in the field, are familiar with evaluations because they are increasingly popular activities in criminal justice agencies. Most newly implemented programs require evaluation certain stages or within specific time periods. Another reason is that evaluation research is the applied type, concerned with problems affecting people in real-life conditions. Program evaluation can be beneficial to a criminal justice agency when it

RESEARCH IN ACTION 8: GUIDE TO FRUGAL EVALUATION FOR CRIMINAL JUSTICE[3]

Evaluating new and innovative justice programs, along with applying evaluation methods to ongoing activities, can address several concerns. Evaluation makes programs and their agencies accountable. It can help distinguish what works from what doesn't, and in doing so steer limited resources to the most promising strategies for controlling crime and violence. At the same time, evaluation is built into the problem-solving approaches that are increasingly used by police and other justice agencies. Finally, evaluation can lend support to effective law enforcement, prevention, and other criminal justice programs. Showing that something works or does not work can overcome the natural tendency of officials to base decisions on arguments presented by simple advocacy.

The purpose of this publication is to show justice professionals how to use simple but potentially powerful evaluation methods. Because simple methods are often possible, evaluations need not be costly; hence the *frugal evaluation* label. The concept rests on three simple assumptions.

1. The most promising criminal justice policies and actions are flexible, purposive, and collaborative. Evaluation should also be flexible, purposive, and, in many cases, collaborative.
2. Justice professionals, ranging from those in operations to executive positions, are better able to do their jobs if they understand the basics of evaluation methods and appropriate applications of those methods.
3. In many circumstances, self-evaluation is possible; public agencies, community groups, and other organizations can conduct internal evaluations. In other circumstances, justice professionals should be active participants in evaluation partnerships.

Many approaches to evaluation are possible, depending on the type of activity or program to be evaluated and the purpose of the evaluation. Whatever approach is used, three elements are essential. Evaluations must be purposive, analytic, and empirical.

Purposive means that an evaluation must have a specific goal or objective—a reason for conducting the evaluation. At one level this may seem an obvious or trivial point. Just as many programs are launched without clear goals, evaluations are too often begun without a clear view of what is to be learned. For example, it is not uncommon for a busy public official or organization staffer to assume that academic experts will know what to do—that's why they're experts. An evaluation should cover both the purpose of the program or other activity and the purpose of the evaluation in clear language.

Analytic refers to the logic of a program and the logic evaluation. Justice programs are devised with goals in mind, and various resources and procedures are set in place to achieve them. However, some programs are not as carefully thought out as they might be or the implied logic breaks down. Analyzing whether key program elements and critical assumptions make sense is an important evaluation activity. In a more general sense, *analytic* means that all evaluation activities should be logically connected. Evaluation objectives are derived from program goals; program activities pursue those goals through a logic model or theory of program action; measures and data collection activities must conform to activities and goals; samples and other selection procedures should reflect intended targets; comparison strategies are based on a careful specification of what should and should not change as a result of program activities.

Empirical means that evaluation results are based on experience—on actual data. This is in contrast, for example, to expert judgments about whether a program works or does not work. Empirical data can come from agency records, structured interviews, open-ended interviews, or observations of program activities or conditions. *Empirical* is commonly equated with *quantitative*, but that oversimplification is misleading. Experience comes in many forms, some more readily quantified than others.

All evaluations should contain these three key elements. Every evaluation should be purposive, analytic, and empirical. Beyond that, evaluations can take a wide variety of forms. Traditional approaches emphasize control through formal evaluation designs, most notably random experiments. More flexible approaches recognize that the three evaluation elements can be applied in situations where traditional, formal designs are not possible. A more flexible approach also recognizes two key features of the evaluation environment faced by justice professionals. First, innovative justice policy is rarely implemented in the kind of stable environment assumed by traditional evaluation designs. Instead, officials often tinker with new interventions after they are implemented. Second, evaluations rooted in social science methods often strive for generalized understanding. Local officials are more interested in solving local problems.

TABLE 12.1: COMMON CATEGORIES OF PROGRAM EVALUATION RESEARCH

Category	Type
Front-end Evaluation: Analysis prior to initiation	• Needs assessment (determines who needs the program and how great the need is)
Formative Evaluation: Aimed at strengthening or improving program	• Process assessment (determines how program is implemented and operates)
Monitoring Evaluation: Ongoing data collection concerning program activities to determine compliance with policy	• Accreditation evaluation (determines whether program meets minimum standards) • Quality assurance (determines whether attributes of program are routinely and systematically provided)
Summative Evaluation: Addresses whether program has its intended impact and should continue	• Impact evaluation (determines overall net effects of a program); cost effectiveness analysis (determines relationship of program costs and outcomes)

contributes knowledge that helps generate solutions to immediate problems.

When you choose a program evaluation as a research project, several preliminary matters must be considered and decided. The Office of Juvenile Justice and Delinquency Prevention's publication titled *Evaluating Juvenile Justice Programs: A Design Monograph for State Planners* notes that:[4]

Having decided that you wish to conduct evaluation, and presuming that not all programs can or will be evaluated, the problem becomes that of deciding which program(s) to evaluate. There are practical and political considerations in this selection process as the following series of questions shows:

Which programs are accessible for evaluation? As the specialist or evaluator, you will find that not all of the programs are accessible for evaluation, for a variety of reasons. Some may be geographically distant, or cover multiple jurisdictions, and so prohibit evaluation because of travel costs and logistics. (In the case of a multisite program, one or a few sites may be selected for evaluation.) Some programs may even be mobile! Some program administrators may find evaluation threatening or distasteful and deny access or, if not denying access, make it difficult.

Which programs will, or do you hope will, stay in operation for some time into the future? Since evaluation takes time, and the impact of some programs takes time to be felt, seriously consider the length of time you expect a program candidate for evaluation to be in operation for more than a year or two.

How expensive are the programs? More expensive programs will usually justify, or warrant, evaluation, since the grantees and the taxpayers have a right to know how their money is being spent. Generally, there will be much more demand for information about an expensive program than for an inexpensive one. On the other hand, the more expensive programs tend to be expensive to evaluate, and sufficient funds may not be available for a thorough job. In almost every case, though, the demand for information overrides the danger of evaluating a program only halfway.

Which programs are controversial? Programs may be controversial in a positive or negative fashion. They may be new and generate excitement in the juvenile and criminal justice communities and, for this reason, receive attention in the field and from the media. They may receive bad press, due to politics or sensational cases. In some instances, these circumstances will necessitate evaluation, and in others they will work against it. In any case, controversy affects the evaluation decision. However, a program need not be controversial to be a good candidate for evaluation. Some programs may have been operating for years under the assumption that they are working, at least as intended.

Such assumptions should always be questioned and evaluated, if possible.

Which programs are identified as priorities either by your office or other significant officials? There are times when the demand for evaluation of a program does not fit into practical considerations but will be strong enough to win out. For example, evaluation may be mandated by law, executive order, memorandum of agreement, or some other official source. Similar programs in other states may have been evaluated with inconclusive results, and practitioners may turn to you for more data.

Program Evaluation Methodology

After a researcher has decided to conduct a program evaluation, he or she decides how the project will proceed. Most of the procedure decisions relate to developing strategies for collecting the necessary data to perform the evaluation. Several of the more important decisions to be made are discussed below.

Identifying consumers of evaluation—Identification of potential **consumers** (users) of an evaluation will help determine the most important issues and ultimately the focus of the evaluation. Likewise, it provides a first step toward identifying the sample population.

Identifying policy makers—Be keenly aware of the **policy makers** and their perspectives on the purpose of the evaluation. Some may regard research as an intrusion that can only delay, complicate, or even undercut a policy and its implementation. Others may have political agendas and fear that an evaluation would show that a program they (or their bosses) favor is ineffective. Still others may see an evaluation as a potential threat to funding sources, especially if continued funding is contingent on the success of the program. In short, evaluation is likely to cause policy makers to behave in ways that diverge from the interests and orientations of researchers.[5]

Choosing evaluation methodology—After the focus of the evaluation is established, the researcher should decide what data is needed, what analyses should be conducted, and how results will be disclosed to the consumers.

Outlining work plan—It is critical to create a step-by-step **work plan** to conduct data collection and analysis. An evaluation of a criminal justice agency will require that certain resource-intensive functions be performed:

Data collection: conducting interviews, administering questionnaires, observing program operations, reviewing or entering data from existing data sources.

Data coding: collating information gained through data collection, ensuring its accuracy, translating collected data into usable formats for analysis.

Data analysis: performing statistical analyses related to evaluation hypotheses, preparing summary statistics, charts, tables, and graphs.

There is no single research design or methodology for collecting and analyzing data when conducting evaluation research. Performing a program evaluation is still research and therefore employs research designs similar to those used in other types of research. Two of the more popular methods used to conduct program evaluations are the pre-experimental and quasi-experimental designs (see Chapter 5). A pre-experimental design is a one-shot case study involving a single group that participates in the program and then is measured. It is possibly the most popular design utilized by evaluators. When quasi-experimental methods are employed, the time series design (multiple measures of a single group before and after exposure to the program) is a common choice. A catalog of some of the analytic approaches used in evaluation studies has been compiled by the Bureau of Justice Assistance; it is titled *Evaluating Drug Control and System Improvement Projects: Guidelines for Projects Supported by the Bureau of Justice Assistance.*[6]

policy research

A discussion of program evaluation would not be complete without a brief introduction to **policy research**. It differs from program evaluation research in that it does not attempt to judge the utility of an existing social program. Rather, it is an example of applied research that aims to assist decision makers in formulating policies and implementing practices to alleviate some social problem. Policy research evolved during the twentieth century and is considered an integral part of public policy making. Although the types of research projects implemented vary, they share common characteristics.[7]

Policy research projects are finite. Unlike research programs that serve general ongoing goals such as controlling crime, research projects have specific information needs, such as testing whether a certain intervention reduces neighborhood burglaries. The research objectives of a project are accomplished within specified limits of time, funds, and other resources. They have a definite endpoint at which they are considered complete and their objectives are met.

Policy research projects are nonrepetitive. They address specific problems in a particular context. While they may be designed to contribute to the accumulation of general knowledge through a research program, they are one-time efforts for the particular researchers involved. This means that policy research projects are creative and focus on the unique requirements of a situation.

Policy research projects are complex. While projects may be limited in terms of time and staff participation, they are complex in the sense that their results are not obvious. They require problem structuring, identification of appropriate information needs, and skillful interpretation of results along with consideration of the policy's multiple perspectives and many **stakeholders**.

policy research planning

When a decision is made to conduct a policy research project, it is essential that a detailed plan be developed before the start of data collection, analysis, and reporting. While the substance of each plan is uniquely tailored to meet the informational needs of the project, several important activities must be considered during the planning process. They are described below.

Preparatory activities—The initial activity of a policy research project is to accumulate as much information as possible about the social problem. The researcher's objective is to gain knowledge about the magnitude and complexity of the problem. Written information about previous research efforts, important legislative initiatives, existing policies and procedures, organizational charts, and other pertinent documents should be collected. Likewise, it is important to interview stakeholders. In addition to gathering their perceptions of the social problem, an interview may indicate whether the stakeholders are committed to the study.

Developing appropriate methodology—After the research problem is identified, the next step is to design a methodological approach that establishes the data collection strategies and analysis. As with evaluation research, no special research design or methodology for the collection and analysis of data exists for policy research. Conducting a policy research project therefore employs research designs similar to other types of research.

Selecting personnel—The overall direction and supervision of a policy research project is the sole responsibility of the research director. However, other persons will serve as auxiliary personnel to ensure that certain tasks are accomplished throughout the work. For example, if the research is considered an "outside" project, the researcher must identify a contact person to serve as liaison to the agency. A liaison should be familiar with the operations of the facility, possess the proper authority to ensure that administrative tasks are accomplished, and be interested in the project. If research assistants, a project secretary, or other personnel are selected to take part in the research, matters of training and wages should be considered.

Identifying non-personnel resources and costs—It is important as early in the planning process as possible to identify a budget outlining the resources and related costs required to complete the research project. Non-personnel costs (telephone, travel, computer analysis, reproduction of documents, etc.) must be evaluated.

Scheduling project tasks—After a researcher is adequately familiar with the social problem, has developed an appropriate methodological approach, and identified key personnel and costs of the resources needed to carry out the project, the next activity is to devise a task schedule. One method for scheduling tasks is the **Gantt chart**, a graphic representation of project tasks in relation to each other and in relation to time. Each activity can be drawn so that the researcher can visualize all the components and schedule events to occur in a logical and economic fashion. Figure 12.1 provides a sample Gantt chart showing major tasks and timelines.

policy research reporting

After a project plan has been devised, it is time to implement it. An important task during implementation is reporting progress. How information is reported may influence user perceptions of the proficiency of the researcher and merits of the research project. Close communications between researcher and policymakers offer several additional benefits as well:

- Teaching policy makers to appreciate constraints and realities of research to reduce the skepticism with which research is viewed.

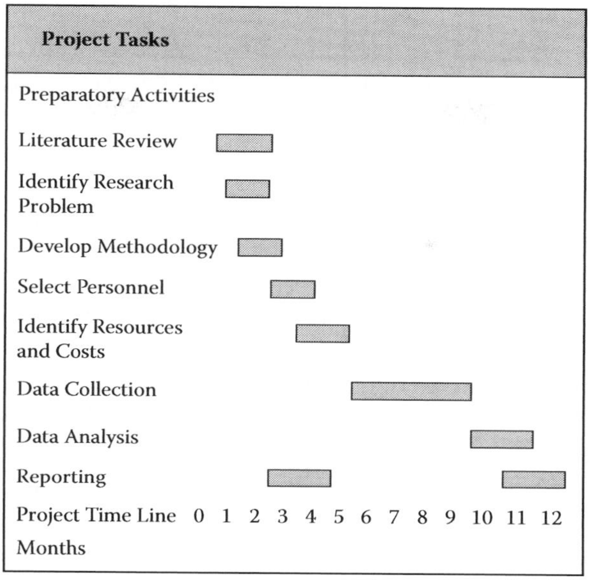

Figure 12.1 Gantt chart showing tasks and time lines.

- Teaching researchers about constraints and realities of the policy maker's world.

- Keeping policy makers knowledgeable about information that may become relevant later.

- Keeping policy researchers knowledgeable about changes in the policy arena that may affect a study.

Reporting should start at the inception of the policy research and continue throughout the project. Oral communication provides a quick means of presenting information about progress. Written reports provide a formal presentation of the research objectives, methods, findings, conclusions, and major caveats of a study. It is suggested that a minimum of two reports be generated for users: a progress report prepared at the midpoint and a final report completed at the conclusion of the project.

summary

In general, evaluation research is applied research that aims to measure the effects of a program already in operation. In criminal justice research, evaluation research most often involves studies of the values of programs implemented by police and corrections agencies. Program evaluations fall into several categories, depending on the purpose of the assessment. Additionally, each category includes various types of evaluations distinguishable by the activities undertaken during the research. The most common types of program evaluation research are front-end, formative, monitoring, and summative evaluations.

- When choosing a program evaluation as a research project, several preliminary matters must be considered. In addition to identifying the consumers and policy makers, it is critical to create a step-by-step work plan for conducting data collection and analysis.

- Policy research is an example of applied research that aims to assist decision makers in formulating policies and implementing practices to alleviate a specific social problem.

- When the decision has been made to conduct a policy research project, it is essential that a detailed plan of the activities be developed prior to starting data collection, analysis, and reporting.

terminology

Evaluation research

Progress evaluation

Consumer

Policy maker

Work plan

Policy research

Stakeholder

Gantt chart

discussion points

1. List five reasons for conducting a program evaluation.

2. Describe some of the more common characteristics found in policy research.

3. What is a Gantt chart? What is its purpose in a research project?

endnotes

1. M. Q. Patton. *Practical Evaluation.* Beverly Hills, CA: Sage, 1982.

2. R. A. Kirchner, R. K. Przybylski, and R. A. Cardella. *Assessing the Effectiveness of Criminal Justice Programs.* Prepared for U.S. Department of Justice. Washington: Justice Research and Statistics Association, 1994.

3. Adapted from M. G. Maxfield. *Guide to Frugal Evaluation for Criminal Justice.* Washington: U.S. Department of Justice, Bureau of Justice Assistance, Grant 95-IJ-CX-0029, 2001.

4. J. R. Coldren, T. Bynum, and J. Thome. *Evaluating Juvenile Justice Programs: A Design Monograph for State Planners.* Washington: U.S. Department of Justice, Office of Juvenile Justice and Delinquency, 1991.

5. R. P. Nathan. *Social Science in Government: Uses and Misuses.* New York: Basic Books, 1988.

6. National Institute of Justice. *Evaluating Drug Control and System Improvement Projects: Guidelines for Projects Supported by the Bureau of Justice Assistance.* Prepared for U.S. Department of Justice. Washington: National Institute of Justice/ABT Associates, 1992.

7. P. J. Burman. *Precedence Networks for Project Planning and Control.* London: McGraw-Hill, 1972.

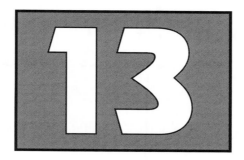

writing research and grant proposals

introduction

> Good writing and finding the right sponsor is no guarantee of funding.
>
> **Soraya M. Coley**[1]

Proposal writing is a learned art. The grant proposal is a persuasive presentation for the receipt of resources.[2] It is also a marketing tool. A good proposal presents what the researcher intends to do and provides an image to any prospective funder. This is a highly competitive process. Accordingly, the proposal writer must learn not to take rejection personally. Almost half the proposals for grants received by most funding agencies are resubmissions. If a proposal is rejected, rewrite and resubmit at a later evaluation period or to a different agency. If you believe that your project is worthwhile, be persistent.

Successful research requires the ability to think clearly. Accordingly, any research or grant proposal should demonstrate that the researcher has that ability. If a proposal is poorly organized, loaded with extraneous material and details, and unfocused, the proposal reviewers will naturally conclude that any research accomplished under the proposal will suffer the same faults. Too often inexperienced individuals assume that a research or grant proposal is a literary project. The proposal should be more like a blueprint for research. When you are developing a proposal, think like an architect working on a blueprint rather than a Hollywood writer working on a screenplay.

getting started

"Where shall I begin?" he asked.
"Begin at the beginning," the King said, "and stop when you get to the end."

Lewis Carroll, *Alice in Wonderland*

Proposals are written section by section. Many individuals, wanting to submit proposals for funding pet projects will take a request for proposal (RFP) from an agency, read it, and file it away as too difficult. The proper attitude to take when writing all but the most basic proposal is that a proposal is a series of small steps rather than one major step.

Often, when facing a task such as writing a major proposal, a researcher faces "writer's block" when he or she lacks a clear picture of the writing task. There are several techniques used to overcome writer's block, including taking the project piece by piece. Some tricks commonly used to overcome writer's block are listed below:

- Outline the sections before you start writing.
- Complete the easiest sections first.
- Brainstorm about the contents and topics needed in each section.
- Put words on paper. Edit later.
- Recognize that your first draft will not be the final draft. Only you and the waste paper basket see the first draft.
- Take regular breaks and think about what you are trying to do.
- Ask yourself what you want to say and then put your answer in writing. This could be your first draft.

building a blueprint

"If you don't know where you are going, any road will get you there."

Lewis Carroll, *Alice in Wonderland*

Coley and Scheinberg recommend a nine-step conceptualization process before starting the writing process.[3]

1. Understand the problem.
2. Brainstorm solutions.
3. Identify solutions.
4. Describe expected results and benefits.
5. Determine tasks to accomplish solutions.
6. Estimate resources needed.
7. Reassess viability of solutions.
8. Reassess expected benefits.
9. Identify measurement of outcomes.

You should first develop a clear sense of the need and/or problem you are addressing in the proposal by asking a number of questions. What is the problem? Why is it a problem? Who is experiencing the problem? After you clearly understand the problem, begin the process of brainstorming from an idealistic perspective. Robert Kennedy once stated, "Dream of what is possible, rather than accept what has happened." Ask yourself what could be done in an ideal situation to create change and achieve positive results? This is a time to think beyond the way the problem was addressed in the past.

The third step in conceptualization is identifying solutions. After you create a list of possible solutions by brainstorming, edit the list and select items you wish to focus on, then list the results and/or benefits that may be expected if the selected solutions are implemented. Determine what changes would occur and what will happen if the selected solutions are implemented. The fifth step is to determine what tasks must be completed to accomplish the proposed solution. Later, these tasks should be linked to a time line. At this point, step back and reassess your proposed solutions and expected benefits. Finally, identify measurements of outcome. Only after you complete the conceptualization process can you start writing the proposal.

overview of proposal process

A proposal should reflect the thoughtful planning of the researcher. If you are responding to a **request for a proposal (RFP)**, you should follow the format set forth in the RFP. If no specific format is requested or required, then follow a straightforward plan like the one below:

- **Cover letter or introduction** serves to introduced the subject and the researcher to the funding agency.
- **Statement of needs and/or problem** describes the issues to be addressed.
- **Project description** clearly explains the goals and objectives of the project and describes plans for delivery of results.
- **Evaluation plan** explains the measurement procedures to be used to determine whether the goals and objectives are met.
- **Budget** section contains an itemized list of expenditures and rationales justifying use of funds.
- **Qualifications and capability** section demonstrates the ability to accomplish the proposed results. It should include a description of the project structure, including information about policy-making boards, staff members, volunteers, and advisory boards.
- **Future funding plans** section covers plans for continuation of the project beyond the requested funding period.
- **Local and community support** section details the nature of the local community support for the project.

The Grantsmanship Center proposes the following format:[4]

- **Summary:** Concisely summarizes the proposal.
- **Introduction:** Includes the researcher's qualifications or credibility.
- **Problem statement or needs assessment:** Describe the needs to be met or problems to be solved by the proposal.
- **Objectives:** Describes the benefits of funding the research in measurable terms.
- **Methods:** Describes how the activities are to be employed to achieve the desired results; may require an entire section.
- **Evaluation:** Includes the plan for determining the degree to which objectives are met and methods are followed.
- **Future or additional funding:** Lists any plans for continuation beyond the proposed research or grant period and the availability of other resources to implement the research.

- **Budget:** Delineates the costs to be met by all funding sources and those to be provided by the researcher or other parties.

Paul Leedy suggests the following format:[5]

- **Problem and its setting:** Includes the statement of the problem and any subproblems, hypotheses, delimitations, and definition of terms.
- **Review of literature**
- **Treatment, handling, and interpretation of data:** Includes the research methodology and the criteria governing the admissibility of data.
- **Qualifications of researcher**
- **Outline of proposed study**
- **Selected bibliography**

Introduction Section

The introduction section should describe your qualifications or those of your agency as an applicant for funding. The introduction statement should not be short because your qualifications (or **credibility**) constitute a major influence on whether your proposal is funded. Often, instead of requesting an introduction, a request may instruct you to describe the background of the applicant—this is the same as an introduction. Official stationery and well prepared brochures can help establish your credibility. Listing the members of your advisory board or board of directors and their organizational affiliations may also enhance credibility. Make sure that your introduction is readable. Do not enmesh readers in the intricacies of your agency. Focus on credibility for funding. Some items to include in your introduction are:

- A statement of purpose, goals, and philosophy of your agency or organization
- When and how your agency or organization got started
- Prior accomplishments and their impacts
- Current activities
- Important publications
- Referring agencies

- Size and characteristics of your constituency or clientele
- Present and prior funding sources
- Results of internal and external evaluations
- Quotes, recommendations, support letters from clients, experts in the field, and other agencies

Statement of Needs or Problem

The needs/problem statement not only provides a rationale for the proposed problem intervention, but demonstrates to the funder the applicant's knowledge of the big picture.

Soraya M. Coley[6]

The problem statement should be a no-nonsense beginning to your proposal and should indicate that you know what a proposal should be. In any document, paragraph, chapter, etc., the most important position is the first sentence. Make good use of that position.

Although formats of grant and research proposals may differ, certain key sections are required in most proposals. The most important is the need or problem statement. A problem statement is generally used in research-related proposals. Needs statements are usually reserved for proposals seeking funding for programs or services. Generally, a proposal should start with a statement of the problem rather than an introduction. This is not the time or place to insert a prologue or statement of the reasons why you are interested in this subject. One cardinal rule is that the proposal should not be cluttered with extraneous material. It should begin with a straightforward statement of the problem to be researched. The statement of the problem should stand on its own merit without the need for explanatory material. Anyone reading the statement of the problem should be able to understand what the proposed research will be about and whether it is something that deserves further inquiry. If the statement contains irrelevant material, the reviewers will tend to conclude that you cannot separate essential and nonessential elements, and your stature as a researcher will be questioned. The statement of the problem should clearly delineate what you plan to do.

Coley and Scheinberg contend that the statement of needs or problems should accomplish three tasks:

1. Depict the needs and/or problems you seek to address.
2. Describe the causes of the problem and/or the circumstances creating the need.
3. Identify approaches or solutions to date.

Clearly, the statement examines what is happening that requires attention, attempts to explain why it happened, and discusses the past and current conclusions about the situation. Generally, this section is one of the first parts of a proposal to be written. One method of writing the statement of needs or problems is to start with task 1 and describe the needs or problems you seek to address. Next, discuss the causes of the problems. Finally, identify and describe the approaches or solutions applied to date. Taking this approach will ensure that the required elements are present in the statement.

A rational and objective need or problem statement requires supportive data. Use only reliable and current data sources. Scrutinize the data carefully to ensure that it states your case in the most favorable light. You must, however, use the data with integrity. The worst mistake a researcher can make is to manipulate or alter data. If the validity of certain data is questionable, omit the data or address the questions regarding its validity.

One major task requires condensing and editing the data to make a powerful statement in a limited number of pages. Too little or too much data will weaken your proposal. In writing the statement of needs and problems, keep in mind that the result should be a clear, comprehensive statement describing the situation, interweaving the data to support your rationale for funding. You want a statement that is comprehensive, but not overloaded with facts and data.

Project Description

The project description generally should include three major subdivisions: program objectives and goals, methods, and evaluation.

Program goals and objectives

A goal projects the ideal or hoped-for state. Goals are ambitious statements. Most projects cover only a few goals. When writing the goals for your project, look at the need or problem and state the major reasons for undertaking the project. They are the long-term results desired for your program.

The program objectives are the outcomes of your activities[7]— not the activities. Program objectives that are measurable become the criteria by which the effectiveness of your project is measured. Objectives are the ends of your project, not the means. Too often we talk about the means rather than the ends. Program objectives should accomplish the following:

- Tell who
- Is going to be doing what
- When
- How much
- And how we measure it

In writing about program objectives, the Grantsmanship Center recommends that you use words such as *increase, decrease,* and *reduce* rather than words such as *provide, establish,* and *create.* Use of the former words will more likely result in your writing about objectives, not methods. Objectives should state a timeframe for the service or study, the target group, the number of clients to be reached, the expected measurable results or benefits, and the geographical location or service locale.

Methods

The needs or problems have been described in your proposal along with your goals and objectives. The methods section describes the means by which you will achieve the goals and objectives. Terms such as *methodology, activities, procedures,* and *strategies* are often used instead of *methods.* The requirement is the same: describe how you intend to meet your goals and objectives. The methods section should flow naturally from the objectives. The main requirements are clarity and justification. The description of the proposed methods should be understandable and you should explain why you think the methods will work. In most cases, the methods section should discuss staff selection and training and the selection of participants. A good methods section clearly describes program activities, states reasons for selection of activities, describes the sequence of activities and staffing, and presents a reasonable scope of activities that can be accomplished.

Evaluation

The four basic steps to developing an evaluation plan are:

1. Formulating evaluation questions
2. Determining the types and sources of evidence needed for evaluation
3. Developing a data analysis plan
4. Identifying reporting procedures

First, study the RFP or application instructions to determine the types of evaluations required by the funding agency. Evaluation plans are generally simple because of financial constraints. For practical examples of evaluation processes, look at similar reported research and note the evaluation processes used. The two types are process evaluations and outcome evaluations. Process evaluations are used to assess the procedures for conducting the project. Outcome evaluations are used to assess whether goals and objectives are reached. When you evaluate a project, you are assessing the success of the objectives. If the objective was to reduce crime by 10%, frame your evaluation questions to determine whether you met that objective.

recommended steps for obtaining state and federal funding

This section will focus on the recommended steps to take when applying for funds from state and/or federal agencies to support a research endeavor.

Step 1: Review the requirements set forth in the RFP. Pay special attention to eligibility requirements and due dates. If you cannot meet the eligibility requirements, consider carefully before investing the time and effort to apply for grant money for which you do not qualify.

Step 2: Read the application package instructions from cover to cover to familiarize yourself with the application process and the required forms. Pay particular attention to all required components of the application package and to other format and content guidelines.

Step 3: Prepare the application package with all the required components, forms, budgets, assurances, certifications, and other disclosures. Include program and budget narratives that contain all major components. Also include time lines and resumes of key personnel who will be involved in the research.

Step 4: Review the application package to ensure that it is complete and that all required forms are completed and signed.

Step 5: Submit the original and required number of copies using a delivery service that will ensure arrival by the required date and time. Generally, the original application should be marked as such. Keep copies of all documents submitted.

bases for rejection

All applications submitted to a state or federal funding agency must be complete and contain all the requested information. Most RFPs also require the inclusion of certain forms, certifications, and disclosures in an application. Failure to submit any of the required items will normally result in return of the application with no action taken. Some of the most common reasons for denial of funding include:

- The requesting organization or researcher is not eligible to participate in the funding.
- The application is received after the specified receipt date.
- The application is incomplete
- All or portions of the application are illegible.
- The application exceeds the specified page limitations for the program narrative, biographical sketches, or job descriptions.
- The application is not submitted in the proper format.
- The proposal is not responsive to the program guidelines.
- The application contains insufficient material or data to permit an adequate review.

Project Narrative

In most cases, the RFP will require that the application contain a project narrative. Many organizations limit the number of pages in this section. The narrative should be written in a manner that is self-explanatory to reviewers unfamiliar with the applicant's prior related activities. It should be succinct and well organized, include section labels that match those cited in the table of contents, and contain all the information necessary for the reviewers to understand the proposed research. As a general rule, the project narrative should include these sections:

- Problems to be addressed
- Goals and objectives
- Research design
- Management and organizational capabilities
- Budget

Problems to Be Addressed

The problems to be addressed should be clearly stated. The importance and need of the research should also be addressed in this section. This section replaces the statement-of-the-problem section discussed earlier in this chapter. Note that the requirements discussed in that section also apply to this section.

Goals and Objectives

The goals and objectives of the proposed project should be clearly defined, measurable, and attainable. The objectives should relate to measurable action steps needed to achieve the goals.

Project Design

Applications should address how the major evaluation activities will be carried out and should present a detailed and clear design for accomplishing all the research goals and objectives.

Management and Organizational Capabilities

The project management and overall organization should demonstrate the researcher's ability to successfully operate and support the project. The appendix should include resumes of key personnel.

Budget

Budgeted costs should be reasonable, allowable, and cost-effective for the proposed activities. Most RFPs require detailed budget worksheets or narratives. Items required in a detailed budget include personnel costs, fringe benefits, travel, equipment, supplies, construction, consultants, and indirect costs. Normally these items should be listed separately with explanations included. Some of the generally allowable items of expenditures include:

- Salaries, wages, and fringe benefits of project professional and support staff.
- Travel directly related to carrying out activities of the approved project.
- Supplies, communications, and rental of equipment and space directly related to approved project activities.
- Contracts for performance of activities of the approved project.
- Other items necessary to support approved project activities as long as they are allowable under the applicable cost principles.

Table 13.1 and Table 13.2 tabulate costs of salaries and fringe benefits for inclusion in a proposal. Three researchers will be assigned exclusively to work on the project. A 2% cost-of-living adjustment is scheduled for all full-time personnel 6 months prior to the end of the project. The half-time secretary will prepare reports and perform other clerical duties. The graduate interns will be involved in data collection. Compensation for employees engaged in research activities will be paid consistent with compensation paid for similar work within the

TABLE 13.1: LIST OF PROJECT PARTICIPANTS AND COSTS

Name and Position	Computation	Cost ($)
John Jones, researcher	($50,000 × 100%)	50,000
Assistant researchers (2)	($50,000 × 100% × 2)	100,000
Part-time secretary	($30,000 × 50%)	15,000
Cost-of-living increases[a]	($165,000 × 2% × 0.5 year)	1,650
Graduate interns (2)	($11.25/hr × 500 hrs × 2)	11,250
	Total	**177,900**

[a] $50,000 × 3 researchers = $150,000 + $15,000 (part-time secretary) = $165,000 basis for cost-of-living increases.

TABLE 13.2: FRINGE BENEFIT COSTS FOR PROJECT PARTICIPANTS

Fringe Benefit	Computation	Costs ($)
Employer's FICA	($177,900 × 7.65%)	13,609
Retirement	($166,650 × 6%)	9,999
Health insurance	($166,650 × 12%)	19,998
Workers' compensation	($177,900 × 1%)	1,779
Unemployment compensation	($177,900 × 1%)	1,779
	Total	**47,164**
Total personnel cost ($177,900) plus fringe benefits		**225,064**

TABLE 13.3: BUDGET SUMMARY EXAMPLE

Budget Category	Amount
A. Personnel	_____
B. Fringe Benefits	_____
C. Travel	_____
D. Equipment	_____
E. Supplies	_____
F. Construction	_____
G. Consultants/Contracts	_____
H. Other	_____
Total Direct Costs	_____
I. Indirect Costs	
Total Project Costs	_____
Federal Request	_____
Non-Federal Amount	_____

department. Most applications require budget summary. Table 13.3 is a typical budget summary format used for most federal grants.

Appendixes

Appendixes should not be used to extend or replace any of the required sections of the narrative statement. You may include in the appendixes a time line of major milestones and resumes of all personnel. Appendixes should be clearly labeled; page numbers should continue in sequence from the last page of the program narrative.

Single Point of Contact

Most RFPs require that a single point of contact (SPOC) be designated for each proposal submitted. In some cases, the federal government requires appointment of one SPOC for each state. If this applies, each SPOC must receive a complete copy of the proposal.

selection criteria

Agencies generally follow established review criteria. A recent joint RFP from the U.S. Department of Justice and Department of Education involving the Safe Schools/Healthy Students Initiative contained the following review criteria:[8]

Understanding the problem (20 points)—An applicant must demonstrate a clear understanding of comprehensive community-wide strategies to create safe and drug-free schools and promote healthy childhood development. Applicants should discuss how to apply state-of- the-art evaluation methods and models, including collection of surveillance data and economic analyses, to achieve evaluation objectives.

Goals and objectives (10 points)—Applicants must specify goals and measurable objectives for coordinating and implementing a project consistent with the initiative's goals and objectives. These should be guided by the requirements in this solicitation and should be clearly defined and attainable. The extent to which the proposed evaluation strategy will meet the established goals and objectives must be addressed.

Project design (35 points)—An applicant must present a detailed and clear design for accomplishing all project goals and objectives. He or she must include a timetable or work plan and detailed budget for accomplishing the goals and objectives and delivering the required products. Applicants must describe how they will carry out the major evaluation activities—surveillance, process evaluation, and intensive outcome, including economic evaluation—and outline the research questions to be answered through each activity. More specifical, an applicant must present a plan for the collection of a core set of surveillance data from all sites, including an indication of what this core set may include and a draft protocol for data collection across all sites.

Management and organizational capabilities (25 points)—The application must include a discussion of how the applicant will coordinate and manage this evaluation to achieve goals and objectives. The applicant must identify responsible individuals and key consultants, their primary areas of expertise, their time commitment, and major tasks. The range of expertise represented by key staff and consultants should include significant experience in all major evaluation areas.

Budget (10 points)—An applicant must provide a proposed budget that is complete, detailed, reasonable, allowable, and cost effective in relation to the activities to be undertaken during year 1. The budget must be comprehensive and should include costs such as support to local evaluators for collection of common cross-site surveillance and process data, any data collection by local evaluators as part of the intensive outcome analyses, and costs for collateral activities, e.g., the periodic convening of an advisory panel.

peer review

In most situations, state and federal applications for funding are subjected to a peer review process. For example, many federal agencies use interagency peer review panels that represent the agencies collaborating in the funding initiative. The peer review recommendations are advisory and do not bind an agency to make recommended selections, but agencies normally give full consideration to peer review recommendations in selecting projects to fund.

- Generally, a minimum of three peers review each application. Peer reviewers are selected from a pool of qualified consultants. Any individual with the requisite expertise may be selected from the pool. The peer reviewers are subcontractors of the agency. Consultant experts are selected for the pool to maintain a wide range of experience and background including ethnic, gender, and geographic representations. The peer reviewers should make their recommendations based on these factors:
    - Is the problem to be addressed clearly stated?
    - Are the objectives of the project clearly defined and the outcomes measurable?
    - Is the project design sound, and does it contain program elements directly linked to the achievement capacity to successfully operate and support the project?
    - Does the project management and overall organizational capability demonstrate the applicant's capacity to successfully operate and support the project?
    - Are budgeted costs reasonable, allowable, and cost-effective for the proposed activities?

project termination

Governmental agencies may suspend, in whole or part, terminate funding for or impose other sanctions on a grantee for many reasons. The most common include:

- Failure to substantially comply with the requirements or statutory objectives of the program guidelines or other provisions of federal law

- Failure to make satisfactory progress toward the goals or strategies set forth in the application
- Failure to adhere to grant agreement requirements or special conditions
- Failure to submit required reports
- Filing of a false certification in applications, reports, or other documents
- Proposal of substantial plan changes to the extent that, if originally submitted, would have resulted in the application not being selected for funding
- Other good cause shown

Prior to any cancellation or imposition of sanctions, agencies will normally provide reasonable notice to a grantee of their intent to impose sanctions and attempt to resolve the problem.

summary

- Proposal writing is a learned art. The proposal is a persuasive presentation for the receipt of resources and also a marketing tool. A good proposal presents what a researcher intends to do and provides an image to a prospective funder.
- If a proposal is poorly organized, loaded with extraneous material and details, and unfocused, the reviewers will naturally conclude that any research accomplished under the proposal will suffer the same faults.
- The proper attitude to take when writing all but the most basic proposal is that a proposal is a series of small steps rather than one major step.
- A nine-step conceptualization process is recommended before starting the writing.
- The introduction describes your qualifications or those of your agency as an applicant for funding. The introduction statement should not be short because your qualifications and/or credibility exert a major influence on being funded.
- The needs and problems statement is the most important section of your proposal. The problem statement is generally used in research-related proposals and the needs statement

is usually reserved for proposals seeking funding for programs or services.

- Goals are ambitious statements that project the ideal or hoped-for state. Most projects include only a few goals. Objectives are the actions taken to obtain the goals.
- The methods section should flow naturally from the objectives. The main requirements are clarity and justification. Thus, the methods should be understandable and an explanation given as to why you think they will work.
- The four basic steps to developing an evaluation plan are formulating the evaluation questions, determining the types and sources of evidence needed for evaluation, developing a data analysis plan, and identifying the reporting procedures.

terminology

Request for proposal (RFP)
Credibility

discussion points

1. Explain the difference between goals and objectives in a funding proposal.
2. What is the purpose of the statement of needs or problems?
3. What are the steps involved in developing an evaluation plan?
4. Why should you use a conceptualization process before you start writing a proposal?
5. What steps can you take to overcome writer's block?
6. What are some of the reasons that proposals are rejected by state and federal funding agencies?

endnotes

1. S. M. Coley and C. A. Scheinberg. *Proposal Writing*. Thousand Oaks, CA: Sage, 1990, p. 13.
2. Ibid.

3. Ibid., p. 18.

4. *Program Planning and Proposal Writing.* Los Angeles: Grantsmanship Center.

5. P. D. Leedy. *Practical Research: Planning and Design,* 5th ed. New York: Macmillan, 1993.

6. Coley and Scheinberg, p. 14.

7. Ibid., p. 40.

8. Ibid., p. 20.

index